IN COLD WAR SKIES

MICHAEL NAPIER

IN COLD WAR SKIES

NATO AND SOVIET AIR POWER, 1949–89

CONTENTS

INTRODUCTION		8
CHAPTER 1	**A Peace That Is No Peace, 1949–59** Formation of alliances, the development of nuclear weapons and jet aircraft	10
CHAPTER 2	**We Will Bury You! 1960–69** International crises, supersonic aircraft and the switch to low-level	76
CHAPTER 3	**Freezing Frontiers, 1970–79** Detente and a consolidation of capability	128
CHAPTER 4	**Tear Down This Wall! 1980–89** The time of *Glasnost* and *Perestroika*, agile aircraft and all-weather capability	178
	In Neutral Skies Sweden, Finland, Austria, Switzerland, Yugoslavia, Albania and Spain	232
	AFTERWORD	278
	APPENDIX – Air Orders of Battle	280
	INDEX	312
	GLOSSARY	316
	ACKNOWLEDGEMENTS	318

OSPREY PUBLISHING
Bloomsbury Publishing Plc

Kemp House, Chawley Park, Cumnor Hill, Oxford OX2 9PH, UK
29 Earlsfort Terrace, Dublin 2, Ireland
1385 Broadway, 5th Floor, New York, NY 10018, USA
Email: info@ospreypublishing.com
www.ospreypublishing.com

OSPREY is a trademark of Osprey Publishing Ltd

First published in Great Britain in 2020

© Michael Napier, 2020

Michael Napier has asserted his right under the Copyright, Designs and Patents Act, 1988, to be identified as Author of this work.

For legal purposes the Acknowledgements on page 319 constitute an extension of this copyright page.

All rights reserved. No part of this publication may be reproduced or transmitted in any form or by any means, electronic or mechanical, including photocopying, recording, or any information storage or retrieval system, without prior permission in writing from the publishers.

Every attempt has been made by the publishers to secure the appropriate permissions for material reproduced in this book. If there has been any oversight we will be happy to rectify the situation and written submissions should be made to the publishers.

A catalogue record for this book is available from the British Library.

ISBN: HB 9781472836885; eBook 9781472836892; ePDF 9781472836861; XML 9781472836878

22 23 24 25 26   10 9 8 7 6 5 4 3 2

Conceived and Edited by Jasper Spencer-Smith
Cover Design and Art Direction: Stewart Larking
Layout by Isobel Fiske
Index by Michael Napier
Produced for Bloomsbury Publishing Plc by Editworks Limited, Bournemouth BH1 4RT, UK
Printed and bound in India by Replika Press Private Ltd.

Front cover:
An English Electric Lightning F6 climbs almost vertically away from its base at RAF Binbrook, Lincolnshire in the late 1970s. The aircraft is armed with two Hawker Siddeley Red Top air-to-air missiles (AAM). (Richard Cooke)

Front flap:
A MiG-21bis of the Ilmavoimat (Finnish Air Force) taking off from a highway strip during an exercise in 1978. (Laukkanen)

Back cover:
A regiment of Soviet MiG-23 fighters [NATO reporting name Flogger] taxy out for a sortie during an air exercise in the Ukraine SSR in 1977. (Sputnik)

Back flap (top):
The author in front of a Tornado GR1 during an operational deployment to Saudi Arabia. (Napier)

Back flap (bottom):
A North American F-86A Sabre of the California ANG in the early 1950s. (USAF)

Title pages:
The Boeing B-47B Stratojet medium bomber formed the front-line of the US Strategic Air Command (SAC) in the mid-1950s. (USAF)

Contents pages:
A Tupolev Tu-95RT maritime reconnaissance aircraft [NATO reporting name Bear-D] of the Soviet Naval Aviation seen over the shoulder of a USAF interceptor crew. (Getty)

Imprint pages:
A McDonnell Douglas F-4 Phantom of the US Air Force closes with a Soviet Tupolev Tu-95 Bear. (US National Archives)

Osprey Publishing supports the Woodland Trust, the UK's leading woodland conservation charity.

To find out more about our authors and books visit www.ospreypublishing.com. Here you will find extracts, author interviews, details of forthcoming events and the option to sign up for our newsletter.

INTRODUCTION

"It is an unfortunate fact that we can secure peace only by preparing for war."
John F Kennedy, 1960

Looking back from the comfort of the 21st Century, it seems inconceivable that just over 30 years ago the world was never more than a few minutes away from nuclear Armageddon. Also it is difficult to believe that Europe was divided by an 'Iron Curtain' and that on either side of it, bomber aircraft loaded with nuclear weapons, stood ready to launch at a few moments' notice. It seems incredible to think that that fighter aircraft based in Europe, in North America and in the Soviet Union were frequently scrambled from Quick Reaction Alert (QRA) to intercept potentially hostile intruders and it seems unimaginable that reconnaissance aircraft regularly probed the defences of the other side and that those aircraft were occasionally attacked and were sometimes even shot down.

Yet all of the above are true, and it is perhaps a paradox that the world enjoyed an unprecedented period of peace at the very time that it seemed, on many occasions, to be teetering on the very brink of nuclear war. During the 40 years between the formation of NATO and the fall of the Berlin Wall, the world was polarized between two super-powers each of which sought to defend its homeland and the sovereignty of its allies. The Cold War, which touched the lives of everyone during that time, was a very real phenomenon. It is a crucial part of world history and one in which air power played a vital role, so it is important that it is not forgotten or discarded.

Having served as a front-line strike/attack pilot during the Cold War, I am well qualified to understand and record that history. In this book I have charted the evolution of the air forces of NATO, the Warsaw Pact and the non-aligned nations (see page 230) of Europe. Also I have described the development of military aircraft at a time when improvements in performance and capability were fast-moving and defence funding seemed almost unlimited – in short, a 'golden age' of military flying. In covering such a large topic, this volume is necessarily limited in scope, dealing only with land-based combat aircraft. The transport fleets, though an important arm of the air forces, are not described in detail, while naval and maritime aircraft should be the subject of a separate volume.

MICHAEL NAPIER
OXFORDSHIRE, APRIL 2020

The author in the cockpit of a BAe Hawk T1 during his tour as an instructor at No.2 Tactical Weapons Unit (2TWU), RAF Chivenor. (Napier)

CHAPTER 1
A PEACE THAT IS NO PEACE
1949–59

"The atomic bomb… is a rare and costly object as difficult to produce as a battleship, it is likelier to put an end to large-scale wars at the cost of prolonging indefinitely a peace that is no peace." George Orwell, 1945

As World War II reached its final stages, the spirit of co-operation between the Soviet Union (USSR) and the western Allies was replaced by an air of suspicion and mistrust. This change was partly driven by the ideological gulf between Stalinist communism on one hand and capitalist democracy on the other and partly because of the mutual suspicion that each party had aggressive designs on the other. Soviet paranoia was also provoked by the fact that United States of America (USA) was armed with nuclear weapons whereas the USSR possessed no such arsenal. The Soviet Union had lost more than 25,000,000 people killed during the Great Patriotic War and its leadership was determined to secure its borders to ensure that such a disaster could never happen again. By the end of World War II, the borders of the USSR had been restored to those of pre-World War I Russia and the occupation of central European countries had established a buffer zone between the West and Soviet territory. The Soviet regime also seized this opportunity to further its ideological beliefs by establishing Communist government in those satellite states.

To western eyes, Soviet moves marked an aggressive expansion into Europe, a view reflected in the words of Sir Winston Churchill in 1946 that 'from Stettin in the Baltic to Trieste in the Adriatic, an iron curtain has descended across the continent.' Although the West and the Soviets disarmed in the aftermath of World War II, both sides also kept a wary eye on each other and political and military tension built up steadily during the late 1940s. That tension became a crisis on 1 June 1948 when the Western Allies announced their intention to form a new state in western Germany: on 23 June, the Soviets responded by closing land access to West Berlin, in the hope of discouraging the formation of the new state and perhaps to rid themselves of that western outpost deep within eastern Germany. However, the Soviets had miscalculated the resolve of western governments and a massive airlift of essential supplies began – 26 June 1948 to 12 May 1949 – breaking the blockade of railway, road and waterway traffic. This action also spawned the formation of the North Atlantic Treaty Organization (NATO) on 4 April 1949. The document was signed in Washington, DC by Belgium, Netherlands, Luxemburg, France and the United Kingdom (UK) – original signatories of the 1948 Brussels Treaty – also the USA, Canada, Portugal, Italy, Norway, Denmark and Iceland. The organization

The three-man crew of a Boeing B-47E Stratojet walk out to their aircraft. The type entered service with the USAF Strategic Air Command (SAC) in 1951 and became the pre-eminent component of the US strategic nuclear deterrent. (USAF)

was formed as a defensive alliance primarily to protect member countries from Soviet expansion into Western Europe; it also covered the overseas interests of member states from the North Pole to the Tropic of Cancer.

But NATO was not simply an alliance of like-minded nations: it quickly developed into an integrated military structure linking the armed forces of its constituent nations. In its European command, led by the Supreme Allied Commander Europe (SACEUR), NATO forces were divided into three regions: the northern region covering Norway and the Arctic Ocean, the central region covering the area from the Baltic to the Alps and the southern region covering Italy and the Adriatic Sea. The same constraints of geography also meant that these three regions closely matched the Soviet concept of north-western, western and south-western *Teatr Voennykh Deystviy* (TVD – theatre of military operation), From the Soviet perspective, the north-western TVD and south-western TVD were relatively secure: in the north Finland, though nominally neutral, could be controlled through diplomatic and economic pressure, Sweden remained non-aligned and northern Norway, some 1,600km from Oslo, did not have the infrastructure to support an offensive force. In the south-west, Communist states controlled the territory all the way to the Black Sea and the eastern Adriatic Sea and Communists enjoyed popular support in the neighbouring countries of Greece and Italy. For NATO, however, the short border between Norway and northern Russia was vulnerable and although the Soviet Navy was, for the time being, just a coastal force, its access from their main base at Murmansk to the Atlantic Ocean would be through the Norwegian Sea. For both sides, the critical area was the North European Plain, stretching from the North Sea to the Urals and intersected by the Inner German Border (IGB). This was ideal 'tank country' which, from the Soviet perspective gave NATO the means to mount an invasion of the western USSR and from the NATO standpoint offered Soviet forces ideal terrain to launch a strike through Germany and the Low Countries to the North Sea. Thus, the central region/north-western TVD became the focal point of the Cold War in Europe. At the end of World War II, both Germany and Austria had been

A Yakovlev Yak-9U fighter of the Bulgarian Air Force. The national markings were changed early in the Cold War to a red star incorporating a red/green/white roundel. (Jarrett)

A PEACE THAT IS NO PEACE, 1949-59

Above:
The Petlayakov Pe-2 [Buck] was the standard light bomber in the Polish Air Force serving with 7 Pulk Bombowego (PLB – bomber regiment) at Poznan. Over 11,000 examples of this fast and manoeuvrable aircraft were built. (Jarrett)

Left:
After the Communists took control of the country in 1948, all British-supplied aircraft were destroyed. Subsequently, the Czechoslovak Air Force operated only Soviet types including the B-33, a Czech-built version of the Russian designed Ilyushin Il-10 [Beast]. (Jarrett)

Among the World War II types that remained in front-line service in the early years of the Cold War was the Hawker Hurricane, which equipped the Portuguese Army Aviation fighter flight at Tancos air base. (Jarrett)

divided and administered on a quadripartite basis by the US, the USSR, the UK and France and each nation had an army of occupation stationed in Germany. The *Gruppa Sovetskikh Voysk v Germanii* (GSVG – group of Soviet forces in Germany), occupied eastern Germany, the British Army of the Rhine (BAOR) was based in the northwest of the country and the United States Forces European Theater (USFET) occupied the south; a smaller French contingent occupied areas along the Franco-German border.

MILITARY AVIATION IN THE LATE 1940s

The late 1940s were a period of fundamental change in two areas of aircraft design: the development of the jet fighter and the production of long-range aircraft capable of delivering a nuclear weapon. During World War II, the Germans had led the way with jet engine technology, but in the immediate post-war years the British had become pre-eminent. Both the Gloster Meteor and de Havilland Vampire were in service with the Royal Air Force (RAF) and the Vampire also equipped the air forces of Canada, France, Italy and Norway as well as the non-aligned Sweden and Finland. In the US, the Lockheed F-80 Shooting Star and the Republic F-84 Thunderjet were both in front-line service and the Soviet air-defence forces were flying the Mikoyan-Gurevich MiG-9 [NATO reporting name: Fargo] and the Yakovlev Yak-15 [Feather] and Yak-23 [Flora]. However, all of these types were straight-winged aircraft and had a similar performance to late-generation propeller-driven fighters. The only advantage of the jet engine in these early types was that it was less complex and lighter than a high-powered piston engine. Furthermore, the straight-winged jets were badly affected by the effects of compressibility as the aircraft reached high sub-sonic speeds. The Soviets led the field in understanding the aerodynamics of transonic flight; in particular the advantages of the swept wing, but Soviet-designed jet engines could not produce sufficient power for an aeroplane to reach such speeds. A solution to this problem was provided in 1946 by the ill-considered sale, approved by the British government, of a small number of Rolls-Royce Nene engines, which in turn were 'reverse engineered' and then improved by the Soviets to produce the Klimov VK-1. The result was the Mikoyan-Gurevich MiG-15 [Fagot], a high-performance swept-wing day fighter. At around the same time in the US, North American Aviation produced a swept-wing fighter, the F-86 Sabre which was broadly similar in performance to the MiG-15.

The reason for the Soviet urgency to produce a high-performance fighter was to counter the threat posed by the US bomber force. From 1945 the USA was the only country to have a nuclear capability, leaving the USSR at a strategic disadvantage until 1949, when the Soviets detonated their first nuclear weapon. For both countries the major problem, having produced an atomic bomb was how it would be delivered. The US already had the Boeing B-29 Superfortress, but unlike the US and British, the Soviets had not prosecuted a strategic bombing campaign against Germany and therefore its air force had no heavy bombers. Once again, the solution was provided unwittingly by the opposition: a number of B-29s had landed in Soviet Outer Manchuria following raids against targets in Japan during the war. Russian engineers were tasked with producing an exact replica of the type: the Tupolev Tu-4 [Bull]. Meanwhile, the USAF had taken delivery of the improved Boeing B-50 Superfortress and also had accepted the six (later ten)-engine Convair B-36 Peacemaker – the first truly inter-continental bomber – into service.

Although the US had an initial monopoly of nuclear weapons, the numbers involved were not large. In 1949, the US had a stock of some 50 weapons and 121 aircraft modified to capable of dropping a nuclear bomb; more limiting, however, was the number of weapon assembly teams – just seven. The US nuclear stockpile and the numbers of aircraft, crews and weapon assembly teams increased dramatically after 1950, but even so, it was probably not until the mid-1950s that either side had a truly credible nuclear war-fighting capability.

THE SOVIET AIR FORCE, 1949 – 50

The air arms of Soviet forces underwent a major re-organization in 1949, when the air-defence arm was hived-off to become an independent force. The new

Some 2,400 Bell P-63 Kingcobra [Fred] fighters were supplied to the USSR during World War II, and many remained in service into the 1950s. The aircraft was fitted with a 37mm cannon – which fired through the propeller hub – and was used in the fighter, rather than a ground-attack role. (Getty)

In the early 1950s, two Supermarine Spitfire PR XI photo-reconnaissance aircraft were based at Sola, Norway, where they were operated by 331 Skvadron (Skv – squadron) of the Royal Norwegian Air Force – RNoAF. (Luftfartsmuseum)

force was charged with the air defence of the Soviet Union and was designated as *Proti-Vovozdushnaya Oborona Strany* (PVO-Strany – air defence of the homeland); it controlled all the anti-aircraft artillery and radar systems, as well as fighter aircraft. The latter were grouped in the *Istrebitel'naya Aviatsiya* (IA-PVO – fighter aviation of the PVO). This arrangement left the *Voyenno-Vozdushnye Sily* (VVS – Soviet Air Force) to concentrate on the functions of the *Dal'naya Aviatsiya* (DA – long-range [strategic] aviation) and also the *Frontonaya Aviatsiya* (FA – frontal [ground-attack] tactical aviation). Within the USSR, the FA and the IA-PVO were organized into 16 *Voyennyy Okrug* (VO – military districts) and the FA was also deployed to support Soviet forces in their satellite states in Central Europe.

Both the IA-PVO and VVS were divided into *Vozdushnaya Armiya* (VA – air armies), each of which was formed as two or four *Aviatsiya Korpus* (AK – aviation corps). An AK would be typically divided into two *Aviatsionnyy Diviziya* (AD – aviation divisions) each consisting of three *Aviatsionnyy Polk* (AP – aviation regiments). In turn, an AP would be made up from up to three *Aviatsionnaya Eskadril'ya* (AE – squadrons), each of which, depending on aircraft type, would have between ten and 15 aircraft. The role of units was indicated by an initial letter: *Istrebitel'naya* (I – fighter), *Bombardirovochnaya* (B – bomber) or *Tyazhelaya Bombardirovochnaya* (TB – heavy bomber), *Shturmovoy* (Sh – assault [ground-attack]) and *Razvedyvatel'nyy* (R – reconnaissance).

The main strength of the IA-PVO was concentrated around Moscow and the *Moskovsky Okrug PVO* (Moscow air-defence region), with four IAK, the 33rd, 31st, 37th and 32nd, which were based respectively to the north-west, north-east, south-east and south-west of Moscow. Each IAK contained two IAD, each with three IAP equipped with MiG-15 fighters. Additionally, the 151st *Gvardeyskiy* (Gv – Guards), IAD and two independent reconnaissance squadrons were also allocated to the Moscow air-defence region. The south of the country was defended by the *Bakinsky Okrug PVO*, (Baku air-defence region), which included three IAK. Other PVO-*Strany* commands included the 25th *PVO Armiya* (air-defence army), which defended Leningrad with just two fighter divisions. In 1949 these

A PEACE THAT IS NO PEACE, 1949–59 17

Above:
A Republic F-47N Thunderbolt fighter of the 198th FS, Puerto Rico Air National Guard (ANG). This aircraft had previously been in service with the Pennsylvania ANG. (Jarret)

Left:
In 1949, 615 (County of Surrey) Squadron, Royal Auxiliary Air Force (RAuxAF) was operational at RAF Biggin Hill and equipped with the Supermarine Spitfire F22. The RAuxAF fighter units supplemented the air defence of the UK until they were all disbanded in 1957. (Crown Copyright)

two divisions were equipped with an amalgamation of Yakovlev Yak-9, Yak-17, Lavochkin La-11 [Fang] and Supermarine Spitfire IX, but by 1950 all obsolescent propeller-driven types had been replaced by the MiG-15.

The bulk of the DA bomber force was deployed in the west of the country: the 43rd VA in the Ukrainian SSR and the 50th VA in the Byelorussian SSR. The remaining air army, the 65th VA, was based in the far east of Russia. Most of these units still operated piston-engine aircraft; the Ilyushin Il-4 [Bob], Tupolev Tu-2 or the US-supplied North American B-25 Mitchell. However, the entire long-range bomber force was in the process of being re-equipped with the four-engine Tupolev Tu-4, to give the VVS for the first time a genuine intercontinental capability, as well as a means of delivering the Soviet atomic weapon.

All the FA armies were based in each VO and equipped with an amalgam of Ilyushin Il-10 [Beast] and Bell P-63 Kingcobra. The fact that the Il-10 would remain in front-line service long into the 1950s showed that priority had been given to the development of jet fighters and long-range bombers at the expense of tactical ground-attack aircraft. Three further VA were based in Soviet-occupied Germany, Poland, Austria and Hungary. Throughout the Cold War, the VA

supporting the GSVG was the best equipped and most powerful tactical air force within the VVS, since it would be in the critical frontline. In 1949 this was the 24th VA, which included the 80th BAK which had two divisions equipped with the Petlyakov Pe-2 [Buck], 75th ShAK consisting of two divisions of Il-10, and the 61st GvIAK and 71st GvIAK, both of which contained three divisions of MiG-15. Tactical reconnaissance for the GSVG was provided by 886th *Otdel'nyy* (independent) RAP, equipped with the Pe-2R and the 931st RAP with the Yak-23. In Poland, the 37th VA supported the *Severnaya Gruppa Voysk* (SGV – northern group of forces), while the *Central'naya Gruppa Voysk* (CGV – central group of forces) was supported by the 59th VA. This latter was deployed over two countries with two divisions (the 164th and 177th GvBAD) equipped with the Pe-2 in Austria, one division (195th GvIAD) with the MiG-15 in Hungary; a further division (237th GvIAD) equipped with the P-63 Kingcobra was also deployed in Austria.

THE UNITED STATES AIR FORCE, 1949 – 50

The National Security Act of 1947 separated the United States Army Air Force (USAAF) from the army, creating the independent United States Air Force (USAF). In

The 194th Fighter Squadron, California ANG was equipped with the North American F-51D until 1954 when the unit was received the North American F-86 Sabre. (USAFM)

20 IN COLD WAR SKIES

Right:
Once the largest heavy bomber in World War II, the Boeing B-29 Superfortress was re-classified as a medium bomber in the late 1940s. It was replaced in the early 1950s, but the reconnaissance variant continued in service until 1960. (USAFM)

Below:
Although unorthodox in shape, the North American F-82 Twin Mustang was highly effective when operating as an escort or night fighter. (Jarrett)

the early years of its existence, the USAF underwent numerous organizational changes: headquarters were established, disbanded and re-formed in short timescales and operational units moved frequently both geographically and between command structures. However, in general and despite having a complex command and control structure, the USAF was organized along similar lines to the Soviet Air Force: a Strategic Air Command (SAC), a Tactical Air Command (TAC) and an Air Defense Command (ADC). In addition, there were two more regional commands, the Far East Air Force (FEAF), which covered the Pacific region and the Alaskan Air Command (AAC). These commands were broken down into numbered air forces, which were analogous to the Soviet VA, but with a less rigid structure. Some air forces were sub-divided into air divisions, while others administered their units directly. The main combat and administrative unit in the USAF was the wing, a self-sufficient organization which included an Operations Group comprising, typically three flying squadrons, as well as a maintenance group, a supply group, an airdrome [airfield] support group, and a medical group. Like the Soviet system, the unit title included its role, for example bombardment wing (BW), fighter interceptor wing (FIW), fighter-bomber wing (FBW) or strategic reconnaissance wing (SRW). The size of the squadrons depended on the aircraft type, but would usually be some 20 aircraft.

In addition to the regular USAF, there was also a smaller parallel force, the Air National Guard (ANG). Each state had its own independent ANG unit which was under the direct control of the state governor,

The Boeing B-50D Superfortress was an ungraded – more powerful engines and a taller tailfin – post-war variant of the B-29. A number of the type were modified to serve as air-to-air refuelling (AAR) tankers and remained in service into the 1960s. (USAFM)

although the President had the authority to 'federalize' the ANG and mobilize individual units for operational service with the USAF. In some states the ANG unit was a wing and in others it was a single squadron, the equipment varied considerably and included the Republic F-47 Thunderbolt, North American F-51 Mustang, Lockheed F-80, Republic F-84 and Boeing B-29. As a result of the Korean War and the deteriorating diplomatic relations between east and west, units of the ANG were federalized between late 1950 and early 1951. Some replaced regular units which had been deployed to the Far East, while others were used to train reinforcements for Korea. Two FBWs equipped with the F-84 were deployed to Korea for operations: the 116th FBW, consisting of the 158th FS (Georgia), the 159th FS (Florida) and the 196th FS (California) and also the 136th FBW, comprising the 111th FS (Texas) and 154th FS (Arkansas). Four more wings deployed to Europe. The Douglas A-26 Invader-equipped 126th BW (with elements from Illinois and Texas) was deployed to Bordeaux, while two F-84-equipped wings, the 123rd FBW (North Carolina, Kentucky and West Virginia) deployed to RAF Manston and the 137th FBW (Oklahoma, Kansas and Georgia) to Chaumont, France. The reconnaissance assets of the 117th TRW operated from airfields in Germany: RB-26 of 112th TRS (Ohio) from Wiesbaden, near Frankfurt, the RF-80 of 157th FBS (South Carolina) from Fürstenfeldbruck, near Munich and the RF-80 of the 160th TRS (Alabama) from Neubiburg in the same area. The ANG was eventually stood down in late 1952, once they could be relieved by regular units.

In the regular USAF, the 2nd, 8th and 15th Air Forces were assigned to SAC. The 2nd AF comprised the 305th, 306th and 307th BWs, which was based in Florida and equipped with a mix of B-29s and B-50s and the 31st Fighter Escort wing (FEW) in Georgia, which flew the Republic F-84 Thunderjet. Unlike the Soviet DA, SAC included strategic reconnaissance aircraft. These were mainly the RB-29, but the 2nd AF also included the 91st SRW which operated the North American RB-45 Tornado; these latter aircraft were frequently detached for operations in Europe and the Far East. Another role unique to the USAF was air-to-air refuelling and the SAC wings included KB-29 or Boeing KC-97 tankers in order to give their

A Republic F-84 Thunderjet refuels from a Boeing KB-29 tanker. This refuelling arrangement, a probe on the wingtip of the receiving aircraft proved unsatisfactory and was replaced by the flying boom type. (USAFM)

The massive Convair B-36 Peacemaker intercontinental bomber had a wingspan of 230ft and was powered six 3,500hp Pratt & Whitney Wasp Major radial engines driving 'pusher' propellers. Later models also had four J-47 jet engines mounted on underwing pylons to improve take-off performance. (USAFM)

bombers the range needed to reach targets in Russia. The 15th AF was equipped in a similar way to the 2nd AF, with a mix of B-29/B-50 and RB-29 wings with KB-29 tanker support. The first B-36 units were the 7th and 11th BW at Carswell Air Force Base (AFB), Texas and the 28th Strategic Reconnaissance wing (SRW) at Ellsworth AFB, South Dakota, all of which were under the command of the 8th AF which also included four wings of B-29/B-50 and the F-84-equipped 27th FEW for fighter escort duties.

On the western rim of the Pacific Ocean, the 5th AF, 13th AF and 20th AF were assigned to the FEAF, and between them they accounted for a B-29-equipped wing, another with the Douglas A-26 Invader and four FIW equipped with the F-80 day fighter and the North American F-82 Twin Mustang night-fighter. In Alaska, 57th Fighter Group (FG) was responsible for the air defence of the southern sector with three squadrons equipped with the F-80 and the 449th Fighter All-Weather Squadron (FAWS) was responsible for the northerly sector with the F-82. In 1950, the 57th FG re-equipped with the Lockheed F-94 Starfire, but the F-82 remained in service with the 449th Squadron until 1953.

While the 1st AF, 4th AF and 10th AF had originally been assigned to ADC, a re-organization in 1949 had replaced the AFs with two geographically-based air-defence forces. Eastern Air Defense Force (EADF) assumed responsibility for the air defence of the eastern half of the continental USA, east of longitude 102°W. Initially it comprised the 33rd FIW with F-84 based at Otis AFB, Massachusetts, the 52nd FIW with F-82 based at McGuire AFB, New Jersey and the 56th FIW flying the F-80 from Selfridge AFB, Michigan. Additionally, it incorporated five ANG wings, the 101st (Maine – F-80), 103rd (Connecticut – F-47), 122nd (Indiana – F-51), 128th (Wisconsin – F-51) and 133rd (Minnesota – F-51). The western half of the country was protected by the Western Air Defense Force (WADF), which included the 1st FIW in California and the 81st FIW in New Mexico flying the F-86, the 78th FIW in California with the F-51 and F-84 and of the 325th FIW in Washington with the F-82 and F-94.

Left:
The Mikoyan Gurevch MiG-9 [Fargo] was quickly superseded by the more capable Mikoyan-Gurevich MiG-15 [Fagot] in the early 1950s. (Jarrett)

Below:
The Yakovlev Yak-17 [Feather] was based on the Yak-15, and was a conversion from the piston-engined Yak-3. Some 430 of the type were built and most were used to train jet pilots. (Jarrett)

These units were augmented by Oregon ANG equipped with the F-51.

During 1949 and 1950, both TAC and ADC were overseen by Continental Air Command (ConAC) which also administered the ANG and USAF Reserve. Since the priority of the day was the defence of the US, most of the tactical assets were assigned to ADC, leaving most of the tactical aircraft, which included F-47, F-51, F-80, F-84 and B-26, and most of the airlift capability under the command of TAC. The command also controlled two formations in Germany, the 36th FBW equipped with F-84 at Fürstenfeldbruck and the 86th FW at Neubiberg which was in the process of converting from the F-47 to the F-84.

NATO AIR FORCES, 1949 – 50

In the immediate post-war period, the Royal Canadian Air Force (RCAF) was a small reconnaissance and transport force with no combat units. However, by 1950 the RCAF had been expanded to include six Vampire squadrons, four F-51 squadrons and two B-25 squadrons. North-West Air Command at Edmonton controlled air operations the western part of the country and 1 Air Defence Group at Quebec was responsible for the air defence of the eastern part. There was also a tactical group and in 1950, 1 Air Division was formed for operations in continental Europe. The initial deployment was in 1950 when 410 Sqn, now equipped with the F-86 Sabre, flew to RAF North Luffenham.

The second largest air force in the NATO alliance was that of the UK. The RAF was divided into four operational home commands (Fighter, Bomber, Coastal and Transport Commands) two overseas air forces (Middle East Air Force [MEAF] and the Far East Air Force [FEAF]) the British Air Forces of Occupation (BAFO) in Germany. These commands and air forces were analogous to the USAF air forces, while a group (Gp) was similar to a USAF division. The basic unit of the RAF, as for most western European air forces, was the squadron (Sqn) of between 10 and 20 aircraft, although in the late 1940s each squadron may have had considerably fewer aircraft. The operational squadrons on each base would form a wing (Wg), which was somewhat similar to a USAF group. By 1950, Bomber Command comprised 24 squadrons equipped with the Avro Lincoln, while Coastal Command contained 120 Sqn, 203 Sqn, 210 Sqn and 224 Sqn all equipped with

On 21 September 1953 a defecting North Korean pilot, Lt No Kum-Sok, landed a complete MiG-15 at Kimpo air base, near Seoul, South Korea. The aircraft was subsequently flown for evaluation by a number of USAF test pilots, including Chuck Yeager. (NARA)

Left:
The Douglas B-26 Invader was the standard light bomber in the ANG during the early 1950s. The 126th Bomb Wing (Light) of the Illinois ANG deployed to France in 1951 when the ANG was federalized. (Jarrett)

Below:
A Republic F-84E Thunderjet of the 525th TFS on a snow-covered dispersal at Neubiburg, Germany in the winter of 1951. The F-84 was the most widely used tactical aircraft in NATO during the 1950s. (USAFM)

Two RAF Gloster Meteor F4 fighters overfly a Lockheed F-80 Shooting Star of the 22nd FS, based at Fürstenfeldbruck, Germany. In 1950, the squadron was re-equipped with the Republic F-84 Thunderjet. (RAeS/Mary Evans)

A PEACE THAT IS NO PEACE, 1949-59

the Avro Lancaster. The most modern aircraft were 13 squadrons of Gloster Meteor F4 and three squadrons of de Havilland Vampire F3 day fighters of Fighter Command, which were augmented by a further nine Vampire-equipped squadrons, five Meteor-equipped squadrons and six squadrons of Spitfires flown by the Royal Auxiliary Air Force (RAuxAF). Night-time air defence was provided by 23 Sqn, 25 Sqn, 29 Sqn, 151 Sqn, 219 Sqn and 264 Sqn equipped with the Mosquito night fighter. The UK fighter force operated within an integrated air-defence system which included a chain of air-defence radar stations. In 1949, the strength of BAFO was seven squadrons: 3 Sqn, 16 Sqn and 26 Sqn were based at RAF Gütersloh flying the Vampire, while RAF Wahn (Cologne) was home to 2 Sqn equipped with the photo-reconnaissance Spitfire and 11 Sqn, 14 Sqn and 98 Sqn with the Mosquito bomber.

Like most of the western European nations in the post-war years, the *Kongelige Norsk Luftforsvaret* (Royal Norwegian Air Force – RNoAF), was a very small force in 1950 and was largely equipped with cast-offs from the RAF. Two *Skvadroner* (squadron – Skv), operated the Supermarine Spitfire: 331 Skv flew from Vaernes (Trondheim) and 332 Skv was based at Bardufoss. Another unit, 334 Skv equipped with the de Havilland (DH) Mosquito, operated from Sola (Stavanger). In addition, 336 Skv and 337 Skv equipped with the DH Vampire were based at Gardemoen to the north of Oslo. A Consolidated Catalina-equipped unit, 333 Skv, operated from at Fornebu.

The *Kongelige Dansk Flyvevåbnet* (Royal Danish Air Force – RDAF), was formed in 1950 by merging the air arms of the Danish navy and army. In the following year, the order of battle of *Flyverkommando* (air command), contained a single *Eskadrille* (Esk – squadron) 722 equipped with the Spitfire, and two units, Esk 723 flying the Meteor F4 and Esk 724, operating the Meteor F8 at Aalborg. The *Koninklijke Luchtmacht* (Royal Netherlands Air Force – RNLAF), was larger and better equipped than its Scandinavian partners. One unit, 322 Sqn, still operated the Spitfire at Twenthe, but the bulk of the *Commando Lucht*

A Gloster Meteor F4 in service with the fighter school of the Belgian Air Force based at Koksijde, West Flanders. The type also equipped the 1st Wing at Beauvechain in the early 1950s. (Jarrett)

Based at Aalborg, 724 *Eskadrille* (squadron) of the Royal Danish Air Force flew the Gloster Meteor F8 between 1952 and 1956. The type was replaced by the Hawker Hunter. (Jarrett)

Verdediging (air-defence command) was formed of six squadrons equipped with the Meteor; 323 Sqn, 324 Sqn and 326 Sqn at Leeuwarden, 327 Sqn and 328 Sqn at Volkel and 325 Sqn at Twenthe.

Despite being required to defend a small country, the *Belgische Luchtmacht/Force Aérienne Belge* (Belgian Air Force), was formed as four fighter wings. The 1st Wing at Beauvechain comprised 349 Sqn and 350 Sqn, equipped with the Meteor F4: 10 Sqn and 11 Sqn flew the Mosquito night fighter. The 2nd Wing at Florennes (1 Sqn, 2 Sqn and 3 Sqn) and the 10th Wing at Chièvres (23 Sqn, 27 Sqn and 31 Sqn) were equipped with the Spitfire; the 7th Wing (7 Sqn and 8 Sqn), also at Chièvres, was equipped with the Meteor.

The *Armée de l'Air Française* (French Air Force), was in the process of being rebuilt after World War II, but like the armed forces of Britain, those of France were heavily committed to fighting insurgencies in their colonies. French aircraft were involved in conflicts in North Africa and Indochina, but the air defence of the country was vested upon *Défense Aèrienne du Territoire* (DAT) with three *Escadres de Chasse* (EC – Fighter Wings), equipped with the Vampire. These were EC2, with three *Escadron* (Ec – squadron), at Dijon, EC3 with two Escadron at Reims and EC4 with four half-squadrons at Freidrichshaven, Germany.

The Paris peace treaty of 1947 placed limitations on the size of the Italian armed forces, but even so by 1951 the *Aeronautica Militare Italiana* (AMI – Italian Air Force), had five combat *Stormo* (wing), each made up of two *Gruppo* (group). Each group contained some 18 aircraft; a similar size to a squadron. The 2° *Stormo*, 3° *Stormo* and 6° *Stormo* all operated the F-51 at Vicenza, Villafranca and Ghedi respectively, while the 5° *Stormo* flew the F-47 from Villafranca. The 4° *Stormo*, based at Capodochino was the first to operate the DH Vampire, being followed by 2° *Stormo* and 6° *Stormo*.

The Portuguese army and navy both had their own arms until 1952. The *Aeronáutica Militar* (Army Air Service), the, mainly consisted of transport and liaison aircraft, but in 1950 it also included one combat unit, the *Grupo Independente de Aviação de Caça* (GIAC – independent fighter aviation group), based at Espinho airfield (near Porto), which operated the Hawker Hurricane.

A Republic F-84G Thunderjet of *Escadron de Chasse* (fighter squadron) 1/1 'Corse' based at St Dizier in the mid-1950s. Aircraft of Ec 2/1 had yellow tip tanks and Ec 3/1 had green. (Bannwarth)

Opposite:
During the 1950s, 115th FIS, California ANG was responsible for the air defence of Los Angeles and was equipped with the North American F-86A Sabre. (USAFM)

EASTERN BLOC AIR FORCES, 1949 – 50

In 1949, the *Wojska Lotnicze* (Polish Air Force), was formed as seven combat regiments and one transport regiment. The 1.*Dywiczja Lotnictwa Myśliwskiego* (DLM – Fighter Division), which was commanded by a Soviet officer, comprised three regiments of Yak-9. The 1st *Pulk Lotnictwa Mysliwskiego* (PLM – fighter regiment), was based north of Warsaw at Modlin, the 2.PLM was at Krakow and 3.PLM at Gdynia. The 1.*Dywiczja Lotnictwa Szturmowego* (DLS – Attack Division), also commanded by a Soviet officer, comprised 4th *Pulk Lotnictwa Szturmowego* (PLSz – ground-attack regiment), at Bydgoszcz, 5.PLSz at Lodz and 6.PLSz at Wroclaw, all of which operated the Il-10. The 7th *Pulk Lotnictwa Bombowego* (PLB – bomber regiment), was equipped with the Pe-2 and based at Poznan. The Polish Air Force began to receive Yakovlev Yak-23 jet fighters in 1951.

At the end of World War II, during which it had fought on the German side, the *Magyar Királyi Honvéd Légierő* (MKHL – Royal Hungarian Air Force), destroyed all of its remaining aircraft, so that the Soviets found no serviceable aircraft in the country. Building a new *Magyar Légierő* (ML – Hungarian Air Force), started in 1948 and by late 1950, the fledgling air force comprised two *Vadasz Ezred* (VE – fighter regiments), of Yak-9 (*Vércse* [Kestrel]) and two *Csatarepüle Ezred* (CE – assault regiments), of Il-10 (*Párduc* [Panther]). One fighter and one assault regiment were based at Veszprém and the other two regiments were at Tököl. However, most of the pilots had received jet training in Russia and delivery of the MiG-15 (*Jaguár* [Jaguar]) to the air force started in 1951.

In 1950, the *Forțele Aeriene Române* (FAR – Romanian Air Force) consisted of a fighter division, a bomber division and three independent regiments for liaison, transport and reconnaissance. The *Divizia 1 Vanatoare* (D1V – 1st Fighter Division), comprised *Regimentul de Aviatie 1 Vanatoare* (R1AvV – fighter regiment) at Popesti, R2AvV at Gratova and R3AvV at Ploestii. These units were equipped with La-9 fighters. Divizia 2 Bombardment included an assault, assault, regiment, a bomber regiment and a fighter regiment: R4AvAs at Galati with Il-10, R6AvB at Brasov and R7AvV also at Brasov. The bomber unit, R6AvB was equipped with Pe-2 and also a small number of Heinkel 111. The 10th and 11th *Regimente de Aviatie Reactoare* (RAvR – jet fighter regiment), were formed at Lanca in eastern Romania with Yak-23 in 1951.

The *Balgarski Voenno Vŭzdushni Sili* (BVVS – Bulgarian Air Force), was nominally made up of three divisions in 1949, but they were very lightly equipped, so the real strength was nearer to just one division.

Right:
The French Air Force also operated the SNCASE SE-532 *Mistral*, a licence-built version of the de Havilland Vampire. (Jarrett)

Below:
In 1951, No 421 Squadron, RCAF was temporarily based at RAF Odiham, England and was equipped with 18 de Havilland Vampire FB5 aircraft loaned from the RAF. (Jarrett)

A PEACE THAT IS NO PEACE, 1949–59

Left:
In the early 1950s, the strength of the RNoAF included two squadrons equipped with the de Havilland Vampire FB5 and one squadron with the de Havilland Mosquito FB VI. (Luftfartsmuseum)

Below:
The first RAF squadron to be equipped with the de Havilland Vampire F1 was 247 Squadron. The unit operated the type from 1946 until 1949. (Jarrett)

Below:
A North American B-45C Tornado bomber; the majority of those built were the RB-45C reconnaissance variant, a type that was used in 1952 and 1954 by the RAF for clandestine flights over the USSR. (USAFM)

Two North American F-86A Sabres of the 116th FIS take off from RAF Shepherds Grove, Suffolk. The unit was based here during 1951. (Getty)

The 6th *Iztrebitel Aviatsionnen Diviziya* (IAD – fighter division), comprised 16th Iztrebitel Aviatsionnen Polk (IAP – fighter regiment), at Sofia and 26th IAP at Karlovo, both of which consisted of two squadrons each of seven Yak-9. The ground-attack capability was provided by the 12th and 22nd Polk (based at Plovdiv and Gorna Orehovitsa respectively) each of which comprised two squadrons of eight Il-2. Finally, the 5th *Bombardirovuchen Aviatsionnen Diviziya* (BAD – bomber division), contained the 15th *Bombardirovuchen Aviatsionnen Polk*, (BAP – bomber regiment, with two squadrons each with eight Pe-2 at Graf Ignatiev and the 25th *Torpeden Aviatsionnen Polk*, (TAP – torpedo regiment), with 12 Tupolev Tu-2 based at Balcik. In 1950, the Bulgarian Air Force received the Yak-23, their first jet-powered aircraft. After the Communist coup d'etat in Czechoslovakia in 1948, the *Československé Letectvo*, (Czechoslovak Air Force), was purged and all British-supplied Spitfire and Mosquito aircraft were destroyed. By the end of 1949, the *Československé Letectvo* had only 12 combat squadrons. One *Stíhací Letecký Pluk* (SLPl – fighter regiment), was based at Pilsen with three squadrons equipped with Czech-built Avia S-199 aircraft, a variant of the Messerschmidt Bf-109. A *Bitveny Letecký Pluk* (BiLPl – ground-attack regiment), equipped with 18 Pe-2 shared Kbely airfield near Prague with a jet training unit equipped with Avia S-92, a Czech-built version of the Messerschmidt Me-262. Two squadrons of Aero C-3 (Czech-built Siebel S-204D) reconnaissance aircraft made up the regiment at Malovice and two SLPl equipped with S-199 and Lavochkin La-5 were based at Brno. In 1950, a number of Yak-23 jet fighters (known as the S-101) were supplied by the Soviet Union, but at the beginning of 1951 a total of 40 MiG-15 (known as S-102) were delivered to Czechoslovakia.

THE ARMS RACE BEGINS, 1951–55

Although the fault line of the Cold War ran through Germany, the flashpoint for the first conflict

38 IN COLD WAR SKIES

Right:
The swept-wing Republic F-84F Thunderstreak, which was entered service in 1954, was a very different aircraft to the straight-winged F-84 Thunderjet. It was much faster and could carry a heavier weapons load. (USAFM)

Below:
The tactical reconnaissance Republic RF-84F Thunderflash is identifiable by having wing root engine intakes. This allowed camera equipment to be housed in the nose section rather than carried externally. (USAFM)

A line of Soviet Air Force Mikoyan-Gurevich MiG-17 [Fresco] fighters. The type proved very successful: over 10,000 were built, including the Polish Lim-5 ground attack variant, and it remained in service into the 1970s. (Sputnik)

between its protagonists was far away in Korea. The invasion by North Korea into its southern neighbour in the summer of 1950 was halted by a mainly US-led United Nations (UN) force, but the rapid advance northwards by UN forces was, in turn, stopped by Chinese intervention. By the time an intractable stalemate was resolved by an armistice three years later, Soviet and US jet aircraft had engaged in combat in the skies above Korea and many lessons had been learnt. The air war over Korea had vindicated the Soviet concept of the MiG-15 as a bomber-destroyer: attacks by regiment-sized formations directed by Ground Control Intercept (GCI) radar had wrought havoc amongst the B-29 force during daylight raids, forcing the bombers to be operated exclusively at night. The corollary, of course, was that the Tu-4, being an exact copy of the B-29, suffered from the same vulnerabilities. In any case, the Tu-4 lacked the range for intercontinental operations, except on a one-way mission, so the case for a longer-range replacement became urgent. For the western European nations, the poor performance of the Gloster Meteor, which was flown by the Royal Australian Air Force (RAAF), in combat against the MiG-15 emphasized the need to replace their front-line fighters with high performance swept-wing types.

The success of the GCI/MiG-15 combination in a small area of Korea could not be completely replicated in the USSR because of the scale of distances involved, so PVO strategy was to concentrate the air-defence forces around Moscow and other critical areas of the USSR. However, this approach inevitably led to large gaps in the defences which USAF and RAF reconnaissance aircraft were able to exploit. The closed borders and secretive society in the USSR and its satellites made it difficult to judge Soviet intentions and capabilities, which meant that strategic aerial reconnaissance took on a new importance. A new generation of NATO jet-powered aircraft, including the Boeing RB-47 Stratojet and the English Electric Canberra PR3, entered service in the early 1950s; these types had sufficient performance to out-run the MiG-15. Both British and USAF electronic intelligence (ELINT) aircraft had probed the Soviet defences from the start of the Cold War, but the first overflight of the western USSR was Operation *Jiu Jitsu* carried out by RAF crews flying USAF North American RB-45C Tornado reconnaissance aircraft from RAF Sculthorpe on 17 April 1952. Meanwhile the US military was also interested in eastern Siberia, where airfields might give bombers the range to strike the US mainland; on 15 October 1952, a B-47B took off from Eielson AFB in Alaska and flew to Ambarchik in north-eastern Siberia before turning east to overfly and photograph military installations in the region. In early 1953, another overflight of the Soviet missile testing facility at Kasputin Yar near Stalingrad was carried out by an RAF Canberra PR7 and a further Operation *Jiu Jitsu* mission was flown on 28 April 1954. Although the IA-PVO was powerless to stop these overflights, the Soviet and Eastern Bloc air defences became more aggressive in defending their airspace and a number of less agile intelligence-gathering aircraft were attacked on the periphery of the USSR and its neighbours. On 10 March 1953, two USAF Republic F-84G Thunderjet fighter-bombers from the 36th Fighter-Bomber Group (FBG) based at Fürstenfeldbruck strayed into Czechoslovak territory and were intercepted over the village of Merklìn by two S-102 (MiG-15) fighters from the 2nd squadron of 5.SLPl. In the subsequent engagement Lt J. Sramek shot down the aircraft flown by Lt W.G. Brown, who ejected safely. Two days later the crew of an RAF Avro Lincoln B2 ELINT aircraft from 192 Squadron perished when it was shot down close to the IGB by a Soviet MiG-15.

The introduction of the Mikoyan-Gurevich MiG-17 [Fresco] into service from 1953 also meant that NATO jet-powered reconnaissance aircraft were no longer immune to Soviet air defences: on 8 May 1954, an RB-47 from the 91st TRW, flown by Capt H.R. Austin took off from RAF Fairford on a mission to photograph nine Soviet airfields near Murmansk. After photographing the second airfield from 40,000ft, it was intercepted near Arkhangelsk by three MiG-17s of 1619th IAP.

The prototype Boeing XB-52 parked in front of the Convair B-36 that it would eventually replace. Note the XB-52 was originally fitted with a B-47-style tandem canopy; also the jet engines on the B-36. (USAFM)

RB-47 OVER MURMANSK

8 MAY 1954
Capt H.R. AUSTIN 91ST TRW

We had been over Soviet territory an hour and were at 40,000 feet. We had been briefed by Intel that the MiG-15 would not be able to do any damage to us at 40,000ft with our true air speed on the order of 440kts. Well, you can imagine what we called those Intelligence weenies as the first Soviet MiG-17, not a MiG-15, made a firing pass at us from the left rear and we saw cannon tracer shells going both above and below our aircraft. And, the MiG was still moving out rather smartly as he passed under us in front. So enough of this 40,000ft stuff, I pushed the RB-47 over, descending a couple thousand feet picking up about 20kts indicated airspeed in the process. The second MiG-17 made his firing pass and I don't care who knows, it was scary watching tracers go over and under our aircraft. The co-pilot turned around backward to operate our tail guns after the first MiG shot at us. It was typical for the two remotely controlled 20mm cannons not to fire... Fortunately, when the third MiG started his pursuit pass, our guns burped for a couple of seconds. General LeMay did not believe in tracers for our guns but the Soviet pilots must have seen something because the third guy broke off his pass and the flight of six, and the next flight which joined us later, stayed out about 30 to 40 degrees to the side, out of the effective envelope of our guns. Of course, the MiGs didn't know that our guns would not fire again even though the co-pilot pleaded, and I believe he did, at least, kick the panel trying to get them to work. The fourth MiG of this flight made a firing pass and made a lucky hit through the top of our left wing, about 8ft from the fuselage through the wing flap. It exploded into the fuselage in the area of the number one main tank and knocked out our intercom... By now we had covered our last photo target and had turned due west toward Finland to get the hell out of there... Real soon another three MiGs showed up. Two MiGs of this flight made individual firing passes but our added speed obviously made it a bit tougher... After those two made passes, one of the MiGs came up on our right side, close enough to shake hands and sat there for two or three minutes. Two more MiGs tried

To speed up production, the Boeing B-47E Stratojet was manufactured by three companies: Boeing built 691 airframes, Lockheed produced 386 and Douglas 264. The RB-47E reconnaissance variant remained in service until the mid-1960s. (USAFM)

firing passes, but without hitting us, by this time we were well out of Soviet territory. Our excitement for this mission was not over... We really weren't sure how the damage to our left wing and fuselage would affect fuel consumption. Initially it didn't look that bad... As we coasted-out off Norway, it was obvious we had fallen behind the fuel curve. We climbed to 43,000ft and throttled back to max-range cruise. It did appear however, that we could get to a base in England and we knew there was a strip alert tanker at Brize Norton awaiting our call.

After refuelling from a KC-97 Stratofrieghter, at a perilously low fuel state, the damaged RB-47 was able to recover to Fairford.

The formation of NATO, the Soviet nuclear tests in 1949 and the start of the Korean War the following year had initiated an arms race which, in turn, saw massive re-armament and re-equipment in the US, the USSR and in Europe. At the same time, diplomatic relations between the two sides deteriorated steadily during the early 1950s. In response to the conflict in Korea and the looming political crisis in Europe, US President Harry S. Truman federalized the Air National Guard (ANG) in 1951 and authorized the Mutual Defence Assistance Programme (MDAP) to provide equipment – specifically some 2,000 Republic F-84E/G fighter-bombers – to European nations. In the early 1950s, NATO air forces carried out a series of mass exercises over Western Europe: Exercise *Ombrelle*, in the summer of 1951, involved 500 aircraft from six nations and Exercise *Cirrus*, in the following autumn, involved over 1,000 aircraft from eight participating nations. These exercises enable NATO to resolve the difficulties of working together within an integrated command structure. A similar-sized Exercise *Coronet* took place two years later. The Soviet and Eastern-Bloc air forces also expanded rapidly in the next few years, but only carried out more modest bi-lateral exercises. However, these exercises were extremely realistic and

The Boeing B-47 Stratojet required AAR in order to reach targets in the USSR, so the Boeing KC-97 Stratofreighter was a vitally important element of the SAC nuclear force. In the mid-1950s, the KC-97 was replaced in SAC by the jet-powered Boeing KC-135. (USAFM)

A PEACE THAT IS NO PEACE, 1949–59   43

Above:
Each large wingtip pod on the Northrop F-89D Scorpion was a combined 380-gallon fuel tank (rear two-thirds) and a rocket launcher (front third) containing 52 Mighty Mouse rockets. The aircraft is in service with the 321st FIS, based at Paine AFB, Washington. (USAFM)

Left:
The Lockheed F-94B Starfire all-weather fighter was based on the T-33 airframe and equipped with a Hughes E-1 fire control system incorporating an AN/APG-33 radar. The type equipped 26 squadrons in Air Defense Command (ADC). (USAFM)

The Lockheed F-94C Starfire all-weather interceptor was powered by a Pratt & Whitney J48-P-5 engine, a licence-built version of the Rolls-Royce Tay and fitted with an afterburner. Each of the pods mounted midway on the wings housed [12] 2.75-inch Mighty Mouse free flight anti-aircraft rockets. (USAFM)

A PEACE THAT IS NO PEACE, 1949-59

Originally designated the F-95 and intended as an insurance in case the Northrop F-89 Scorpion was delayed into service, the North American F-86D 'Sabre Dog' was fitted with an afterburner and equipped with AN/APG-37 radar. (USAFM)

an army division-sized exercise at Totskoye in the Orenburg Oblast of central Russia in September 1954 involved the dropping of a live nuclear airburst weapon being dropped from a Tu-4. This was similar to the Exercise *Desert Rock* series held on the Nevada Proving Grounds between 1951 and 1955 in which battalion-sized ground forces exercised in an area following a nuclear detonation.

NORTH AMERICA: STRATEGIC FORCES, 1951–55

For the USAF, the issue of the vulnerability of the B-29/B-50 Superfortress bomber was resolved with the introduction of the Boeing B-47 Stratojet which entered service with the 306th BW at McDill AFB, Florida in 1951. The new aircraft represented a quantum leap in performance over the B-29, but the range of the B-47 was very similar, so it still required air-to-air refuelling to reach a target. Another solution to the range problem was to deploy aircraft forward to bases in Europe and North Africa: Operation *Reflex* saw all B-47 Bomber wings rotating on 90-day deployments to RAF Fairford in the UK or to Nouasseur, near Casablanca, Morocco, where they would be held at 15-minute readiness. Over the next four years B-29 and B-50 units re-equipped with the B-47 and a number of new units were formed; by 1955 SAC had 27 BW and four SRW equipped with the new type.

Build-up of the longer-range Convair B-36 Peacemaker continued and reached maximum strength in 1954, the force comprised eight BWs and two SRWs, the 5th and 99th SRWs. However, the days of the B-36 and the B-47 were numbered after the first flight of the Boeing B-52 Stratofortress in 1952. In 1955, the 93rd BW at Castle AFB, California was the first operational unit to receive the type, replacing the B-47.

At this time, SAC also included four Strategic Fighter Wings (SFW) equipped with the swept-wing Republic F-84F Thunderstreak in the fighter escort role. These were the 12th and 27th SFW at Bergstrom AFB, Texas, the 31st SFW at Turner AFB, Georgia and the

407th SFW at Great Falls, Montana. The 71st SRW at Larson, Washington operated the Republic RF-84F Thunderflash reconnaissance variant.

The expansion of SAC was mirrored in ADC, with new units being formed and those already established being re-equipped. The ADC expanded with insertion of another air-defence region, the Central Air Defense Force (CADF) which took over responsibility for the southern and south-eastern states. By 1955, some 20 FIW in the continental US were equipped with the radar-equipped North American F-86D 'Sabre Dog' all-weather fighter, which had entered front-line service in March 1951 with the 317th FIS at McChord AFB, Washington. In the northerly regions, the Lockheed F-94 Starfire was replaced by the Northrop F-89 Scorpion and by 1955, there were squadrons equipped with the type based at Thule, Greenland (74th FIS); Keflavik, Iceland (57th FIS) and Ernest Harmon AFB, Newfoundland (61st FIS). In the Alaskan Air Command, the 18th FIS, 433rd FIS and 449th FIS based at Ladd AFB and the 64th FIS, 65th FIS and 66th FIS at Elmendorf AFB were all equipped with the F-89.

The US ADC worked closely with the Canadian Air Defence Command, which had also been expanded and re-equipped. By 1955, there were eight squadrons of Avro CF-100 Canuck all-weather fighters in Canada: 409 Sqn at Comox (Vancouver), 419 Sqn with 423 Sqn at St Hubert (Montreal), 428 Sqn and 445 Sqn at Uplands, Ontario, 432 Sqn and 440 Sqn at Bagotville and 433 Sqn at North Bay. Additionally, a line of early warning radars, known as the 'Pine Tree Line', had been built along the 50° North Parallel to detect aircraft approaching the main cities of Canada or the US from the north.

The inventory of Tactical Air Command (TAC) was also progressively modernized, first with the F-84E/G or F-86 and then from 1953, the F-84F. Most TAC units were based in the Far East or in Europe, but two fighter-bomber wings, the 366th FBW at Alexandria AFB, Louisiana and the 405th FBW at Langley AFB, Virginia, flew the F-84F in the US. In April 1955, the 479th wing, at Foster AFB, Texas, converted from the F-86 to the North American F-100 Super Sabre, the first of the new 'Century Series' fighters.

USSR: STRATEGIC FORCES, 1951 – 55

Incursions into Soviet airspace by USAF RB-45 and RB-47 reconnaissance aircraft forced military planners

The North American F-86K Sabre was the NATO version of the F-86D and was armed with four 20mm M24A1 cannons, an MG-4 fire-control system and APG-37 radar. North American produced 120 of the type and FIAT Aviazione assembled 221 from supplied components. Here an F-86K of the Italian Air Force is parked next to the prototype of its successor; the FIAT G-91. (Jarrett)

The Canadair CF-100 Canuck was the mainstay of the RCAF air-defence force through the 1950s. In the latter part of the decade the type was used to equip four squadrons in the 1st Air Division Europe. (Jet Heritage)

to realize that the MiG-15 and the more powerfully-engined MiG-15-bis were largely ineffective against the new generation of US-built jet bombers. The introduction of the MiG-17, which had improved performance and handling characteristics, into the IA-PVO went some way to restoring the balance and by 1955, most fighter units in the IA-PVO had been equipped with the MiG-17 or the MiG-17F (F – *Forsazh* [reheat]). In the 22nd VA, which included IA-PVO aircraft responsible for the defence of the Karelia/Murmansk region, 518th IAP at Vaskovo (Arkhangelsk) flew the MiG-17P (*Perekhvatchik* – interceptor), a radar-equipped variant with a limited all-weather capability. A more efficient all-weather capability was introduced when the two-seat, two-engined Yakovlev Yak-25 [Flashlight], entered service with the 611th IAP-PVO at Dorokhovo in 1954. From the introduction of this type into service, the all-weather fighter divisions tended to operate with a mix of Yak-25 and MiG-17P, using the former for longer-range interceptions.

In the early 1950s, the VVS still lacked a long-range bombing capability, but this changed when the Tupolev Tu-16 [Badger] entered service in early 1954. The first units to receive the new aircraft were 203rd TBAP at Baranovichi and 402nd TBAP at Balbasovo, both being part of the 45th TBAD, 50th VA in Byelorussia. They were followed by the 13th TBAD in Ukraine, comprising 185th TBAP, 202nd TBAP and 226th TBAP. An electronic intelligence (ELINT) version of the aircraft, the Tu-16P was operated by 477th *Radiotekhnicheskaya Razvedka* AP (RRAP – radio intelligence regiment). However, the remaining 17 regiments, representing the vast majority of in the 43rd VA and 50th VA, the DA bomber forces in Ukraine and Byelorussia, were still equipped with the Tu-4.

In the early 1950s, the obsolete Pe-2 light bombers in service with the FA were replaced by the Ilyushin Il-28 [Beagle], but the ageing Il-10 remained in service with the assault regiments. The Il-28, which had a better range than the Pe-2, could reach far into

A PEACE THAT IS NO PEACE, 1949–59

Belgium procured 53 Canadair CF-100 Mk5 and was the only overseas country to acquire the type. The aircraft, which entered service in 1957 were operated by 11 Sqn, 349 Sqn and 350 Sqn at Beauvechain until 1964. (Jarrett)

Western Europe and also had the capability to deliver tactical nuclear weapons: bomber units based in the western USSR military districts were the first to receive the aircraft. In time of war their nuclear task would be a high–low profile attack; a high-level transit as far as Polish airspace, then letting down to low-level to penetrate the NATO defences in Germany. After a rapid climb to around 3,000ft, the weapon would be released and the aircraft return to low-level for an egress to a refuelling base in either East Germany or Poland.

NORTHERN AND CENTRAL REGIONS, 1951–55

By 1955 the NATO command structure in Europe was firmly established. Allied Air Forces Northern Europe (AAFNE) was made up of the air forces of Norway and Denmark, while Allied Air Forces Central Europe (AAFCE) was further divided into the 2nd Allied Tactical Air Force (2ATAF) covering the northern half of the region and composed of the air forces of the Netherlands and Belgium plus the RAF units based in continental Europe, and 4ATAF in the southern half controlling the US, Canadian and French forces in the region.

In the early 1950s, perhaps the most important development in the northern and central regions, from the NATO perspective, was the transfer of some 2,000 F-84E/G Thunderjets from the USAF to European air forces under the MDAP scheme. In most countries this influx of large numbers of modern aircraft was accommodated by forming new combat units within the air forces. In Norway, the existing squadrons flying the Spitfire and Mosquito were re-equipped with the F-84E/G in 1952 and three more squadrons were established, to give a total of six F-84 units stationed at Gardemoen, Sola and Ørlund. In Denmark, newly equipped F-84 squadrons formed two wings at Karup and Skrydstrup, and in the Netherlands, 311 Sqn which formed at Volkel in 1951, was the first of seven new squadrons to be equipped with the F-84E/G.

The Yakovlev Yak-25 [Flashlight-A] patrol interceptor was equipped with an RP-6 Sokol radar which gave the type a good all-weather capability but the aircraft lacked the performance to intercept a high-flying USAF B-47. The Yak-25 entered service in 1955. (Jarrett)

The pattern continued in Belgium, where F-84 fighter-bomber wings were formed at Florennes, Kleine-Brogel and at Bierset. Also the Mosquito night fighter was replaced with the Armstrong Whitworth (AW) Meteor NF11.

The air defence capability in the Central Region was greatly enhanced by the deployment to Europe of 1 Air Division RCAF in 1952. The division was made up of four fighter wings equipped with the Canadiar-built CL-13 version of the F-86 Sabre. The USAF in Europe (USAFE) was also strengthened, and by 1955, six wings of F-86 were based in continental Europe. A further F-86 wing, 406th FIW was based at RAF Manston. In 1952, the 20th FBW based at Langley AFB, Virginia had pioneered the use of tactical nuclear weapons using the F-84G armed with the Mk 7 nuclear bomb. The aircraft were fitted with the Low Altitude Bombing System (LABS) which enabled the weapon to be released during a pull-up, lobbing it towards the target while the aircraft carried out an escape manoeuvre in the opposite direction. Later that year the wing deployed to the UK, with the 55th FBS and 77th FBS were deployed to RAF Wethersfield and the 79th FBS to RAF Bentwaters.

They were transferred to USAFE control and became the first NATO tactical aircraft to maintain nuclear-armed Quick Reaction Alert (QRA); also known in the USAF as Victor Alert (VA). By 1955, USAFE controlled two nuclear-capable F-84F wings in the UK, the 20th FBW at Wethersfield and the 81st FBW at Bentwaters. Other tactical nuclear forces in the theatre included the 38th BW at Laon-Couvron, equipped with the Martin-built B-57 Canberra and the 47th BW, equipped with the B-45, based at RAF Sculthorpe. This base also received frequent detachments by the 19th TRS to fly reconnaissance missions with the RB-45. The RAF had a dedicated reconnaissance wing at RAF Wyton, which was home to 58 Sqn, 82 Sqn, 540 Sqn and 542 Sqn, all of which flew photo-reconnaissance versions of the English Electric Canberra. The bomber version of the Canberra had entered service with 101 Sqn at RAF Binbrook in 1951, replacing the Lincoln. By 1955 Bomber Command had a front-line strength of 22 Canberra squadrons. The first of the four-engined 'V-bombers' had also entered squadron service by then: 138 Squadron at Gaydon received the Vickers Valiant strategic bomber earlier in the year. Fighter Command

was also in the process of being modernized. In 1954 two squadrons, 66 Sqn and 92 Sqn at RAF Linton-on-Ouse, had re-equipped with the Canadair-built Sabre as a temporary expedient until the Hawker Hunter or Supermarine Swift became available in sufficient numbers. In the same year, 43 Sqn at RAF Leuchars was re-equipped with the Hunter and was followed by 222 Sqn at Leuchars, 54 Sqn at RAF Odiham and 257 Sqn and 263 Sqn at RAF Wattisham. The Swift F1 also entered squadron service that year with 56 Sqn, but the type proved to be unsuitable for the day-fighter role and was soon withdrawn. The night-fighter force was also modernized with jet-powered aircraft in the shape of the de Havilland Venom NF2 and Armstrong Whitworth Meteor NF11.

In Germany the BAFO had been re-named the 2nd Tactical Air Force (2TAF) and been substantially reinforced. Like Fighter Command, it had received the Canadair Sabre to bridge the gap between the Vampire and delivery of the Hunter day-fighter. The air-defence force comprised four wings of Sabre day-fighters and two wings of Meteor NF11 night fighters, while the ground-attack role was carried out by three wings of de Havilland Venom FB1 fighter bombers. Tactical reconnaissance was provided by Canberra PR3 or PR7 and Meteor PR10-equipped squadrons. Additionally, 551 wing equipped with Canberra bombers was based at RAF Gutersloh, where it had been rusticated while the infrastructure of UK bases was upgraded to receive V-bombers; the wing was nominally part of 2TAF, but in practice it remained under the direct control of Bomber Command.

VENOM

1954
Flt Lt R.N. BROAD
14 SQUADRON (2ATAF)

We were a day-fighter/ground-attack squadron equipped with 16 Venoms and one or two Vampire T11s. There were around 20 pilots and they would be expected to fly 240hr a year each which equated to a 400hr monthly flying target for the squadron. However, sortie lengths were not very

By the mid-1950s, the tactical bomber squadrons of the Soviet and Warsaw Pact air forces were equipped Ilyushin Il-28 [Beagle] light attack bomber. The normal bomb load was only 1,000kg, but the aircraft could be armed with a nuclear weapon. (Jarrett)

The Canadair CL-13 Sabre was a Canadian-built version of the North American F-86E. The type was powered by a Canadian-built Orenda 14 engine which delivered 7,275-lb thrust, and gave the CL-13 the best performance of all Sabre variants. (USAFM)

long, averaging under an hour so get the 20hr each day which was the target would require some 30 sorties. RAF Fassberg ran a 5½ day working week with normal working hours from around 08:00hrs to 17:30hrs. The pilot's day started at 08:30hrs with a Wing Met [weather] briefing at which any items of note might be brought up and then pilots dispersed to their squadrons to get on with the days flying. What flying actually was done depended upon the weather and possibly the availability of the range. There was a training schedule which set out exactly what each pilot should do each month – so many gunnery sorties, so much tactical flying, so much navigation and low flying but not a great deal of notice was taken of this; flight commanders tried to balance aircraft availability and pilot requirements.

The Venom was a simple aircraft with the same primitive electronics of the Vampire; what the Venom did have was a good rate of climb and one could get to 50,000ft easily. It also had, with its two tip tanks, a useful amount of fuel (just under 500 gallons). In level flight one could achieve about .82M, but if .86M was exceeded (which was actually not all that easy and required a dive from height) then all control was be lost and the Venom whirled round the sky until you hit thicker air and slowed. It was easy to fly and to land and all in all should have been a robust inexpensive ground-attack fighter. The aircraft's main weakness was poor serviceability. The problem was, I think, quality control at the manufacturers. Our Venoms were not well made and we had terrible maintenance problems – quite apart from wing failures and engine fires.

The French Air Force also continued to station forces in Germany. 1ier *Commandement Aérien Tactique* (CATac – Tactical Air Command), was assigned to 4ATAF and comprised five squadrons equipped with F-84E/G fighter-bombers, of which the 9ème EC was based at Lahr-Hugsweier; in addition, 4ème EC, one of the two air-defence squadrons allocated to 1ier CATac, flew the Dassault MD450 *Ouragan* (Hurricane) from Bremgarten. Of the four *Escadres* allocated to DAT, one flew the De Havilland (DH) Vampire, one the SNCASE SE535 *Mistral*, a French-built version of the DH Vampire FB5, another the *Ouragan* and one the AW Meteor NF11.

NORTH-WESTERN TVD AND WESTERN TVD, 1951–55

Undoubtedly the most significant political event east of the Iron Curtain was the signing of the Warsaw Pact in 1955. However, in practice it made little military difference since Soviet forces were based in many of the countries and most of the national air forces had already adopted the Soviet organizational structure and operated Soviet equipment. Unlike NATO, the Warsaw Pact had no integrated command structure, with the exception of the air-defence forces which were controlled by the Soviet PVO headquarters. Non-Soviet Warsaw Pact (NSWP) forces were closely supervised by Soviet general officers and joint operations between Soviet and NSWP forces were governed by bilateral arrangements within each country.

The Czech Air Force expanded rapidly in the early 1950s and many of the Soviet-designed aircraft that it operated were manufactured under license by Avia at their factory in Prague: Czech-manufactured MiG-15 and MiG-15bis were designated S-102 and S-103, the Il-10 was known as the B-33 and the Il-28 as the B-228. In 1955 the air force was composed of five *Stíhací Letecký Divise* (fighter air division), one *Bombardovací Letecká Divize* (bomber aviation division) and one *Bitevní Letecka Divize* (assault air division) plus two independent reconnaissance regiments. Each division comprised between two and four *Pluk* (Pl – regiment), which in turn consisted of three or four *Letka* (squadrons). Between them, the SLDs accounted for 14 *Pluk* which operated the S102/103 and a further regiment, 7.SLPl based at Košice, which had re-equipped with the MiG-

The West German Luftwaffe ordered 226 Canadair Sabre Mk 6s, which equipped *Jagdgeschwaden* 71, 72 and 73 from 1959. The aircraft in the foreground crashed at Decimomannu, Sardinia, in 1965. (USAFM)

17. Three BoLPl flew the B-228, although 24.BoLPl still operated the Aero C-3 from Hradčany while it waited for its B-228s to arrive. The BiLPl at Brno, Piešťany and Trenčín soldiered on with the obsolescent B-33. The reconnaissance regiments, 45.*Letecky Delostrelecky Pluk* (artillery aviation regiment) at Plzeň and 47.*Průzkumný Letecký Pluk* (reconnaissance air regiment) at Mlada were both equipped with the MiG-15R.

Like Czechoslavakia, Poland had greatly enlarged its air force in the early 1950s. By 1955 the fighter force of the Polish Air Force had expanded to six *Dywizja Lotnictwa Myśliwskiego* (DLM – fighter aviation division), all of which were equipped with the MiG-15, Mig-15bis or the Polish-built versions, the PZL-Mielec Lim-1 and 2 (*Licencyjny myśliwiec* – 'licence fighter'). There were also two *Dywizja Lotnictwa Szturmowego* (DLSz – attack aviation division) operating the Il-10 (or the Czech-built B-33) from airfields at Bydgoszcz, Pila and Mirosławiec and a *Dywizja Lotnictwa Bombowego* (DLB – bomber aviation division) based at Modlin, equipped with the Il-28. The 21.*Pułk Lotnictwa Rozpoznawczego*, (PLR – reconnaissance aviation regiment), operated the Il-28R from Sochaczew Bielice and a further Lim-1 or 2-equipped fighter regiment, 34.PLM, flew from Gdynia-Babie Doły in support of naval operations.

Although there were no Soviet air units permanently deployed in Czechoslovakia, the 37th VA supporting the SGV was based in Poland. In 1955, the fighter divisions in Poland, 149th and 239th IADs benefitted from an influx of operational experience from Soviet regiments which had recently fought in the Korean War; they were also in the process of converting from the MiG-15 to the MiG-17. The tactical bombing role was fulfilled by the Il-28 from the 183rd BAD with three regiments based at Brzheg. Close support of troops was provided by three Il-10-equipped regiments from 172nd ShAD.

By 1954, the long-serving Il-10 had been replaced in some of the assault regiments of the Soviet 24th VA and 75th ShAK in East Germany. The 635 and 725 GvShAP at Finsterwalde and 664 GvShAP at Falkenburg had all been re-equipped with the MiG-15 for the ground-attack role, but 710 GvShAP at Stendal and 823 and

A North American F-86F Sabre of 336 Skv based at Rygge, one of seven F-86 units in the RNoAF which were operational in the late 1950s. (Luftfartsmuseum)

830 GvShAP at Brandenburg were still flying the Il-10. The fighter regiments of 24th VA were still equipped with the MiG-15 and the bombing regiments of the 63rd and 132nd BAD both operated the Il-28, while 11 and 197 ORAP flew the Il-28R reconnaissance variant from Altenburg and Stendal respectively. In 1954, US intelligence sources reported that the fighter regiments in Germany regularly carried out night air-to-air firing: a sleeve target would be towed by an aircraft flying at 5,000ft and on a signal the sleeve would be illuminated by searchlights while fighter aircraft made gunnery passes on the target. The same sources also recorded MiG-15 units practising ground-strafing and bombing, usually in pairs using a steep dive attack profile.

There was, as yet no East German air force, but preparations for establishing one were well underway. Members of the *Volkspolizei Luft* (VPL – People's Air Police), operating under the cover of the *Verwaltung des Aeroclubs* (VdA – administration of the aero club), had established three aero clubs at Cottbus, Drewitz and Bautzen. Each of these so-called 'clubs' closely matched the organization of a Soviet air regiment and personnel received training from Soviet instructors. In 1953, the MiG-15 arrived at Cottbus and German pilots were trained on the type.

SOUTHERN REGION & SOUTH-WESTERN TVD, 1951–55

When Soviet forces withdrew from Austria in 1955, the 59th VA was disbanded and the units that had been based in Austria returned to the USSR. However, the elements which were based in Hungary remained in the country. Thus, the Il-28s of the 177th BAD stayed at Debrecen and Kunmadaras, as did the MiG-17 regiments of the 11th GvIAD at Szentkirályszabadja, Tököl and Papa.

In Hungary the air force grew quickly in its first few years and received its first jet fighters in the early 1950s. By late 1955, the air force boasted a front-line fighter force of two Vadászrepülő-Hadosztály (VadHo – fighter divisions), each of which controlled three *Vadászrepülő-Ezred* (VadE – fighter regiments), flying

In 1951, 101 Squadron became the first jet bomber unit in the RAF when it was equipped with the English Electric Canberra B2 replacing the Avro Lincoln B2 [top]. During the 1950s, the Canberra equipped 25 squadrons in Bomber Command and a further five in 2nd Tactical Air Force in Germany. (Getty)

MiG-15bis, (known as the '*Sas*' [Eagle]), and a small number of MiG-17s. The obsolescent 'Párducs' of the 28.*Csatarepülő-Hadosztály* (CsHo – assault division), were operated by 23.*Csatarepülő-Ezred* (CsE – assault regiment) at Tapolca, 30.CsE at Székesfehérvár and 59.CsE at Börgönd. The 82.Bombo-Hadosztály (BombHo – bomber division), had formed with Tu-2 bombers in 1952, but it was disbanded two years later because of a lack of funding. Some of the aircraft, as well as four Il-28 were passed to the 37.*Önálló Felderítő Repülő Ezredhez* (ÖFE – independent reconnaissance aviation regiment), which shared the airfield at Kiskunlacháza with 47.VadE.

In the early 1950s, the *Forțele Aeriene Române* (Romania Air Force) had also evolved in size and organization. By 1955 the three *Divizia Vanatoare de Aviatie Reacti* (DAvVtR – jet fighter divisions), were equipped with the Mig-15 or MiG-17. In common with other Warsaw Pact air forces, the close air support role was filled by the Il-10, which equipped the three *regimentuls* (regiments) of D68AvAs flying from Brașov, Sibiu and Turda. There were also two bomber units, R239AvBom at Bucharest-Otopeni and R282AvBom at Titu-Boteni which operated a mix of Tu-2 and Il-28 bombers.

Like its Romanian counterpart, the *Balgarski Voenno Vuzdushni Sili* (Bulgarian Air Force) had also grown to a combat strength of three *Iztrebitelen Aviatsionen Diviziya* (IAD – fighter division), which were equipped with a mixed force of MiG-15 and MiG-17. The 5th *Shturmova Aviatsionen Diviziya* (ShAD – assault division), comprised three ShAP equipped with the Il-10 and the two *Bombardirovuchen Aviatsionen Diviziya* (BAD – bomber division), operated elderly Tu-2 and Pe-2 types. A reconnaissance capability was delivered by 26th RAP flying Tu-2 and Il-28 from Gorna Oryahovitsa.

Further to the south and west, the *Forcës Ajrore* (Albanian Air Force) was formed in 1951, but it

During the early 1950s, 12 night fighter squadrons in Fighter Command were equipped with the Armstrong Whitworth-built Meteor NF11. Another four NF11-equipped squadrons were based in Germany. (Pitchfork)

Above: The ultimate variant of the Meteor night fighter was the NF14, which was designed and built by Armstrong Whitworth. This type was fitted with a clear vision 'bubble' canopy, but no ejection seats for the crew. The long nose section housed the air interception (AI) Mk21, AN/APS-57 radar. (Pitchfork)

Left: The de Havilland Venom NF3 was equipped with the same radar as the Meteor NF14 and had a better performance, but the single-engined aircraft was not suited to the night-fighter role. (Pitchfork)

Between 1953 and 1956, the RAF operated 430 Canadair-built Sabres as an expedient between the retirement of the de Havilland Vampire and delivery of the Hawker Hunter. The aircraft were operated by ten squadrons in the 2nd Tactical Air Force, Germany. Another two operated in Fighter Command. (Jarrett)

Left: Supermarine Swift fighters of 56 Squadron RAF. The type entered service in 1954, but was withdrawn after only a year because of its poor handling qualities. (Jarrett)

Below: With the arrival of the Hawker Hunter, the RAF had a swept-wing fighter with sufficient performance to take on the latest generation of Soviet-built fighters. In the second half of the 1950s, the type became the front-line day fighter in RAF service. (Jarrett)

Dassault MD450 *Ouragan* (hurricane) fighter-bomber of EC 3/4 'Flandre' based at Bremgarten, Germany. The type entered service in 1952, but began to be replaced by the Dassault Mystère in late 1955. (Getty)

was not until 1955 that its first combat unit, the *Regjimentit* 23 të Aviacionit Gjuajtës (23rd Fighter Aviation Regiment) based at Kuçovë, received the MiG-15. Eventually the air force would expand to three regiments, each comprising three *Skuadrilje* (squadrons) of some 12 aircraft.

In the NATO Southern Region, 6ATAF was the AAFCE command responsible to controlling the air components of Portugal, Italy, Greece and Turkey. The *Força Aérea Portuguesa* (FAP – Portuguese Air Force), acquired the F-47 Thunderbolt when it was formed by the amalgamation of the air arm of the army and that of the navy in 1952. The aircraft were used by two units, *Esquadra* (Esq – squadron) 10 and 11 at Ota. After the arrival of F-84 Thunderjet at the base the following year, all F-47 were concentrated in Esq 10, which moved to Tancos. The F-84s were issued to Esq 20 and Esq 21 for the air-defence fighter role.

In 1953, Italy also was supplied with some 250 F-84G Thunderjets. The introduction of these aircraft caused a major re-organization of the air force structure and the original *Stormi* (St) became *Aerobrigati* (AB – air brigade), comprising three, instead of two *Gruppi* (groups). The 56th Tactical Air Force was established to command the three F-84 fighter-bomber air brigades in the north of the country. In 1954, the 3° St moved to Villafranca to convert to the RF-84F Thunderflash for the tactical reconnaissance role. Meanwhile, the 2° and 4° *Stormo Caccia* (StC – fighter wing), at Vicenza and Capodochino continued to operate the Vampire, while awaiting the delivery of the F-86 Sabre.

In 1952, the *Ellinikí Vasilikí Aeroporía* (EVA – Royal Hellenic Air Force), was a small force which had until recently been completely focused on the civil war in the country. Its front-line units comprised two *Moira* (squadron), one equipped with the Spitfire and the other with the Curtiss SB2C Helldiver. The delivery of some 340 F-84E/G began in 1952; by 1955, an F-84-equipped fighter-bomber wing had been established at Larissa along with a second at Nea Aghios. Also there was an F-86 fighter wing based at Elefsis.

When Turkey joined NATO, the country already had a large well-established Türk Hava Kuvvetleri (THK – Turkish Air Force), which was in the process of converting from World War II-built British and US types to modern jet aircraft. The organization of the THK loosely followed the USAF structure, with a numbered, *Hava Kuvveti* (HV – air force), commanding a number of subordinate wings, each of which was tied to an individual *Hava Üssü* (HU – air base). The first units to re-equip with the F-84 in 1952 were 191 *Filo* (squadron), 192 *Filo* and 193 *Filo*, at Balikesir. In the same year, F-84 wings were formed at Bandirma, Diyabarkir and Eskisehir bringing the total number of jet fighter-bomber units to 12 squadrons. Three air-defence fighter squadrons equipped with the F-86 had also been formed at Eskişehir and Merzifon.

SECURING THE FRONT LINES, 1956 – 59

After winning the power struggle that followed the death of Josef Stalin, Nikita Khrushchev eventually became the First Secretary of the Communist Party of the USSR in 1955. Khrushchev advocated a less adversarial policy of 'peaceful co-existence' between east and west, but where Stalin would have sacrificed the *Deutsche Demokratische Republik* (DDR – German Democratic Republic [East Germany]) in favour of a unified Germany outside NATO, Khruschev fully supported the regime of hard-line Communist Walter Ulbrecht. Thus, political tension both between the US and the USSR and within the NSWP countries remained high during the second half of the decade. A general strike in the DDR had been crushed by the Soviet Army in 1953, but popular resentment of Communist ideology (and its resulting lower standards of living) lingered in the following years. In early 1956, rioting broke out in Poland and this was also halted by military force. During the same year a popular anti-Communist uprising in Hungary brought a new government, which announced that it intended to leave the Warsaw Pact and become a neutral country. On 24 October 1956, Soviet forces moved into Budapest and fighting in the streets between Soviet troops and Hungarian rebels continued for the next few days. At Kecskemét, aircraft from 62.VadE carried out reconnaissance and leaflet dropping sorties. In response to a report from Tiszakécske that a mob had assembled to lynch the local Communist Party secretary, a MiG-17F flown by *Főhadnagy* (Lieutenant) G. Takács was sent with

A Flight of PZL Mielec-built Lim-5 [Fresco] fighters of the Polish Air Force. The Lim-5 was a Polish-built variant of the Mikoyan-Gurevich MiG-17. A dedicated ground-attack version, the Lim-6bis was developed, but did not enter service until the 1960s. (Jarrett)

Like most Warsaw Pact air forces, the standard light attack bomber in Polish Air Force service was the Ilyushin Il-28 [Beagle]. From the mid-1950s into the 1970s, Poland operated the Soviet built Il-28 and also the B-228, a Czechoslovakian-built version. (Jarrett)

instructions to disperse the crowd. Takács reported that the crowd seemed peaceful, but he was ordered to open fire, which he did killing 17 people and wounding a further 110. On 30 October, the air force joined the uprising and declared it was ready to attack any Soviet forces that had not left the country within 48 hours. The following day, a Hungarian reconnaissance aircraft was shot down over Debrecen, but the USSR agreed to withdraw its forces from Hungary.

These events unfolded at the same time that the UK and France were preparing for military intervention in the Suez Canal Zone. The Suez conflict began on 31 October with large-scale night attacks by RAF Canberra and Valiant bombers operating from Malta and Cyprus. The onslaught was continued for the following four days, with British and French naval aircraft operating from aircraft carriers, as well as RAF Venom and French F-84F Thunderstreak fighter-bombers based respectively in Cyprus and Israel, during the daylight hours.

Five days later, on the same day as Anglo-French assault landings took place in Egypt an overwhelming Soviet force invaded Hungary and re-instated a Soviet-approved government. The Hungarian Air Force was confined to its airfields and rendered non-operational by Soviet forces in the early hours of 4 November. The Soviet invasion was supported by tactical aircraft and the town of Dunapentele was heavily bombed on 7 November, but the next day a Soviet Il-28R, of 880th GvBAP, was shot down by Hungarian rebels. The uprising was finally crushed on 10 November.

Unable to condone one invasion and condemn another, the US was faced with little option but to voice disapproval of both. Furthermore, President Dwight D. Eisenhower was angered that the British, French and Israeli governments had acted without informing the US military of their intentions and had also provoked hostility towards the west amongst the Arab nations. The British and French were therefore forced to withdraw from the Canal Zone. While the Soviet regime continued its business as usual and went on to win a strategic victory with the launch of *Sputnik* the first artificial satellite, in the following year. Neither the UK nor France ever quite recovered from the loss of prestige. In France, the fallout from the Suez Crisis fuelled disillusionment about NATO and the election

The Avro Vulcan B2 was fitted with an improved wing and more powerful Bristol Siddeley Olympus engines. In 1960, the Vulcan B2 entered service with 83 Squadron and all were painted anti-flash gloss white. (Crown Copyright)

of General Charles de Gaulle as President in 1958 marked the beginning of a French withdrawal from the NATO military structure. France declined to join the NATO integrated air defence plan in 1958 and the following year the French government ordered that all US nuclear weapons be removed from its territory.

EUROPEAN AIR FORCES, 1956 – 59

A further blow for the British armed forces fell with the governmental defence review the year after Suez, which reduced defence spending by, inter alia, halving the size of 2ATAF, which by then was largely equipped with the Hunter F6 day fighter and Canberra B(I)8 interdictor. However, the re-equipment of the RAF strategic bomber and all-weather fighter squadrons continued, albeit with a reduced scope. The Avro Vulcan entered service at RAF Waddington with 83 Sqn in 1957 and the Handley Page Victor joined 10 Sqn at RAF Cottesmore the following year. By 1960, the Bomber Command 'V-Force' of strategic bombers comprised eight squadrons of Valiant, four of Victor and three of Vulcan, all armed with the British-built Yellow Sun nuclear weapon. The command also retained a large number of Canberra medium bombers, which were also nuclear-capable. The aircraft were

complimented by 20 squadrons of Douglas SM-75 Thor IRBM (intermediate range ballistic missiles). The night and all-weather combat capability of Fighter Command was dramatically improved with the introduction of the Gloster Javelin in 1956. The first unit to re-equip with the Javelin was 46 Sqn at RAF Odiham, the first of nine Javelin squadrons that would be based in the UK (plus a further three squadrons in Germany). From 1958 the Bristol Bloodhound SAM (surface-to-air missiles) was also introduced into the UK air-defence system to provide close-in defence of the V-Bomber bases and nuclear installations.

The French Air Force underwent another major re-equipment programme in the late 1950s. It improved its night/all-weather capability when *Escadre de Chasse de Tout Temps* 13 (ECTT – all-weather fighter wing), equipped with the F-86K Sabre formed at Lahr in 1956. The following year, ECTT30 based at Creil and Tours replaced the Meteor NF11 with the SNCASO SO4050 *Vautour* IIN (Vulture). From 1958, the bomber variant of this aircraft, the Vautour IIB, equipped the newly-formed 92e *Escadre de Bombardment* (EB – bomber wing), at Cognac providing France with a strategic bombing capability. From 1956, the Dassault MD452 *Mystère* (Mystery) became the standard

A Handley Page Victor B1 in formation with a Vickers Valiant B(PR)K1. Although both types were successful bomber aircraft, both the Valiant and the Victor went on to play important roles as AAR tankers. (Crown Copyright)

day-fighter, replacing other types in five air-defence squadrons, while the fighter-bomber squadrons re-equipped with the F-84F.

The replacement of the F-84E/G with the more capable F-84F was also repeated in Norway, Denmark, the Netherlands, Belgium, Italy, Greece and Turkey. The F-84F also formed the core of the new Luftwaffe (West German Air Force): four *Jagdbombergeschwader* (JaBoG – fighter-bomber wing), formed at Nörvenich, Lechfeld, Büchel and Fassberg between 1958 and 1959. The RF-84F was used to equip an *Aufklärungsgeschwader* 51 (AG – reconnaissance wing), at Erding. Although the air defence of the *Bundesrepublik Deutschesland* (BRD – Federal Republic of Germany [West Germany]) was still nominally provided by the UK and US, three *Jagdgeschwader* (JG – fighter wings), equipped with the Canadair Sabre were formed at Ahlhorn, Leck and Oldenburg in 1959.

To the east of the Iron Curtain, an East German air force, the *Luftstreitkräfte/Luftverteidigung der Nationalen Volksarmee* (LSK/LV – air force/air defence of the national people's army), had also formed. In 1959, the LSK/LV comprised six *Fliegergeschwader* (FG – air wings), based at Cottbus, Preschen, Drewitz and Rothenburg and predominantly equipped with the MiG-17F: From 1959, the MiG-17PF. The various other NSWP air forces also consolidated their strength in the late 1950s. The MiG-17 and MiG-17PF supplanted the MiG-15 in the air-defence role, while the MiG-15 replaced the Il-10 in many ground-attack units. Most of the East European air forces were also re-modelled in the Soviet fashion by establishing a separate air-defence arm, which included early warning, GCI and SAM units. The Polish Air Force was re-named to became the *Wojska Lotnicze i Obrony Przeciwlotniczej Obszaru Kraju* (WLiOPL OK – air and country defence forces). The *Magyar Légierő* had been disarmed within hours of the Soviet invasion in 1956, leaving the Hungarians to rebuild their air force for a second time. By 1958, the *Országos Légierő és*

The supersonic Mikoyan Gurevich MiG-19 [Farmer] was powered by two Turmanksy RD-9B engines with afterburners. The type entered operational service in the USSR in 1955 and over 2,000 were built. It was an effective fighter, but it was hampered by a very short range. (Sputnik)

A Tupolev Tu-16Z [Badger A] tanker and Tu-16K [Badger-B] carrying out AAR. The unique wingtip-to-wingtip transfer method was developed in the late 1950s: the port wingtip of the receiver had to make contact with a 40m hose streamed from the starboard wingtip of the tanker. (Sputnik)

Légvédelmi Parancsnokságot (OLLEP – national air force and air-defence command), was functional in Hungary again, although the majority of officers were Soviet, the remaining Hungarian personnel had been 'screened' and the combat strength of the air force had been reduced to just three regiments of MiG-15/MiG-17PF air-defence fighters based at Kalocsa, Kecskemét and Kiskunlacháza.

SOVIET AIR FORCES, 1956 – 59

Throughout the late 1950s, the Tu-16 continued to replace the Tu-4 in DA regiments and 13 TBAD maintained a number of armed bombers at readiness on ground alert. All Tu-16 units also started practising their unique wingtip-to-wingtip AAR technique with Tu-16Z (*Zapravshchik* – refueller) tanker aircraft, which increased the range of the bomber aircraft. The reach of the bombers could also be extended under the auspices of the *Operativnuyu Gruppu v Arktike*, (OGA – operational group in the Arctic), by using newly-built forward airfields such as Nagurskoye on Franz-Josef Land, Mys Shmidta, Tiksi and Amderma. These airfields opened up the possibility of attacking Canada and the US via a trans-polar route. In addition, the DA investigated the practicalities of operating from Arctic pack ice: In May 1958, a Tu-16 of 52nd TBAP successfully landed on the ice at the Soviet NP-6 Arctic research drift station. However, the aircraft was subsequently damaged as it manoeuvred on the ground and could not take-off for the return flight, so the concept was not taken any further. The VVS received its first truly intercontinental bombers in the mid-1950s. The four-engine Myasishchev M-4 [Bison] strategic bomber made a spectacular debut fly past during the 1954 May Day Parade: the type was to enter service with the newly-formed 201st TBAD at Engels, near Saratov. A redesigned version, the 3M superseded the M-4 at Engels in 1957 and also equipped the 73rd TBAD in the Far East. Although the main role of the 3M was that of strategic strike, the aircraft also proved useful for strategic reconnaissance and the M-4 found a new role as an AAR tanker. A second intercontinental bomber, the turbo-prop powered Tupolev Tu-95 [Bear] became operational in 1956 with the newly-formed 409th TBAP, part of the 106th TBAD at Uzyn, near Kiev. The most successful and longest-serving of the Soviet heavy bomber force, the Tu-95 was also issued to the 1006th TBAP at Uzyn and in the following year to 1023rd TBAP and 1226th TBAP at Semipalatinsk-

When the Myasishchev M-4 [Bison-A] bomber was seen in public for the first time at the 1954 May Day parade in Moscow, escorted by Mikoyan Gurevich MiG-17 [Fresco] fighters, there was much speculation in the West about the capability of the new bomber. (Jarrett)

Dolon, Kazakhstan. That year also saw the introduction of a new variant, the Tu-95K which was capable of carrying the Kh-20 air-launched cruise missile.

The first truly supersonic Soviet fighter, the MiG-19 [Farmer], entered service in 1954 as a day fighter, followed by a radar-equipped all-weather version, the MiG-19P/PF. Meanwhile, the MiG-17PF was upgraded in the IA-PVO to the MiG-17PFU (*Upravlyayemyy* – guided) variant which was armed with RS-1U semi-active radar homing air-to-air missiles (AAM) instead of cannons. In 1957 these aircraft were joined in PVO service by MiG-19PM (*Modifitsirovannyy* – modified), which also carried the RS-1U missile. During the late 1950s, the PVO-Strany also found a solution to defending a large country with short-range fighters by complementing the aircraft of the IA-PVO with SAM systems. The S-25 system [SA-1 Guild] was deployed around Moscow in 1956 and two years later, the first of the S-75 systems [SA-2 Guideline] became operational. While the S-25 was only used in the Moscow military district, the S-75 was widely deployed to cover cities, industrial complexes, military installations as well as the approach routes to them that might be used by US bombers or reconnaissance aircraft.

The Il-10 was finally withdrawn from service in 1956, when the entire assault aviation arm of the VVS was disbanded. Some of the ground-attack aviation regiments (ShAP) were re-equipped with the MiG-15, but most were simply disbanded.

US AIR FORCES, 1956–59

In 1957, ADC was transferred from ConAC to the newly-formed Continental Air Defense Command

Initial deployment of the Lockheed EC-121 Warning Star took place in 1954. Equipped with a ventrally-mounted AN/APS-20 search radar and a dorsal-mounted AN/APS-45 height finder radar. The aircraft were used to fly barrier patrols some 480km offshore. (USAFM)

(CONAD), which controlled the air defence assets of all four services in the USA. In turn, CONAD formed the US part of North American Air Defense Command (NORAD), which also incorporated the RCAF Air Defense Command, so that from 1958 the air defence of the whole of continental North America came under a single command. The 'Pine Tree Line' had largely been superseded by 90 Doppler detection sites of the 'Mid-Canada Line' and also, by the end of 1959, the Distant Early Warning (DEW) line which comprised 57 radar sites approximately along the 69th North Parallel running from Cape Lisburne, Alaska to Cape Dyer, Baffin Island. The ground-based radars were augmented by radar picket ships and also two wings of Lockheed EC-121 Warning Star (AEW&C – airborne early warning and command) aircraft. These were operated by the 551st AEWC wing, which was assigned to EADF (Eastern Air Defense Force) and the 552nd AEWC wing assigned to the WADF (Western Air Defense Force). All the radar feeds were connected to the Semi-Autonomous Ground Environment (SAGE) computer system that was intended to be at the heart of the NORAD command and control network.

Like the PVO-Strany, NORAD also incorporated SAM systems in its air defences. In the early 1950s, the Nike-Ajax system had entered service with the US Army and by the end of the decade a total of 258 Nike launch sites, including 84 of the improved (and nuclear-capable) Nike-Hercules system, had been established across the US. The first SAM system to be deployed by the USAF was the Boeing-Michigan Aerospace Research Center (BOMARC) CIM-10 missile, which entered service in 1959 with the 46th Air Defense Missile Squadron (ADMS), New Jersey. The fighter

By the time the Boeing KC-135 Stratotanker entered service in 1957, the flying boom had become the standard method for AAR in the USAF. Here a Boeing B-52 Stratofortress takes on fuel from a KC-135. (USAFM)

units of the USAF were also upgraded. By the end of the decade, ten squadrons flew the F-89J Scorpion and six the F-86L Sabre, both of which were variants of established types that had been modified to carry the Hughes GAR-1 (radar-guided) and GAR-2 (infra-red guided) Falcon AAM. Both types had been also equipped to fire the Douglas MB-1 Genie unguided AAM, which carried a nuclear warhead. However, the majority of NORAD squadrons had been re-equipped with, or were in the process of converting to, high-performance 'Century series' fighters. In addition to the nine RCAF squadrons equipped with CF-100, ten USAF squadrons were equipped with the McDonnell F-101B Voodoo and a further 22 flew the Convair F-102 Delta Dagger. Five more squadrons (the 27th FIS, 95th FIS, 456th FIS, 498th and 539th FIS) were converting to the newer Convair F-106 Delta Dart, which could be controlled directly via data-link through the SAGE system. There were also four squadrons (the 83rd FIS, 56th FIS, 337th FIS and 538th FIS) equipped with the Mach 2+ capable Lockheed F-104 Starfighter, which for short time was deployed as an air-defence fighter. In the mid-1950s, all ADC Wings had to maintain two aircraft on Interceptor Alert (IA), fully armed at 5min readiness, 24-hours a day; however, recognizing that this was not an efficient use of aircraft, the requirement was relaxed in 1957 so that only those units within a short distance of the Air Defence Identification Zone (ADIZ) were required to maintain interceptor alert.

Strategic Air Command (SAC) also underwent fundamental changes in its organization during the second half of the 1950s. From 1955 the three air forces that made up SAC were rationalized geographically: the 2nd Air Force controlled units in the south-east of the US, the 8th Air Force covered the north-east and the 15th Air Force the south and western US. The Boeing B-52 continued to replace the B-36 and the B-47 in SAC. On 16 January 1957, Operation

A PEACE THAT IS NO PEACE, 1949-59

Above:
An RF-84F Thunderflash tactical reconnaissance aircraft of 3° *Stormo* of the Italian Air Force, based at Villafranca. The type was replaced by the F-104G Starfighter in the mid-1960s. (USAFM)

At the end of the 1950s, development trials of the Republic F-105D Thunderchief had been completed and the type was ready to enter front-line service with the USAF. This particular F-105D was shot down over Hanoi in August 1966. (USAFM)

Power Flite involved three B-52s from the 93rd BW which took off from Castle AFB and, with support from Boeing KC-97 tankers, circumnavigated the world non-stop in two days. It was thought that the flight could have been completed more quickly if the bombers had been able to use the new Boeing KC-135 Stratotanker, which had recently entered service with the 93rd Air Refuelling Squadron (ARS) at Castle AFB. In 1958, the 'One Third Ground Alert' programme was instituted, requiring one third of the total SAC bomber force to be held at readiness on the ground, while an airborne alert programme, known initially as Operation *Head Start* and later Operation *Chrome Dome*, was also instituted. This involved keeping a strike force of ten nuclear-armed aircraft constantly in the air; bombers were either flying across the Atlantic to carry out AAR near Italy, or flying a rectangular route around the periphery of Canadian airspace. Both routes took 24 hours to complete and as one bomber landed the next aircraft would take off. Each day two aircraft were rotated to monitor the Ballistic Missile Early Warning System (BMEWS) station at Thule as a precaution against loss of communications with the site. In 1959, the last B-36 was retired from the 95 BW at Briggs AFB, Texas, and by the end of the decade the forces available to SAC comprised 12 Heavy Bomber Wings and ten Strategic Reconnaissance Wings all equipped with the B-52, 27 Medium Bomber Wings and three SRWs with the B-47 and RB-47, 20 AAR squadrons with KC-135 and 33 AAR squadrons with the KC-97. SAC also deployed the Northrop SM-62 Snark ground-launched cruise missile, which was operated by the 702nd Strategic Missile Wing at Presque Isle, Maine.

Another strategically significant event was the delivery of the Lockheed U-2 high-altitude reconnaissance aircraft in 1956. Under *Project Aquatone*, a joint CIA and USAF operation, U-2 overflights of the Warsaw Pact countries and the USSR commenced on 20 June 1956. The aircraft were flown from Wiesbaden in the BRD by a unit known as 'Detachment A' and over a three-week period it had carried out eight overflights of Warsaw Pact territory, including five flights over the USSR. US sources believed that Soviet radar systems (which were known to be based on equipment originally supplied by the

US during World War II) would be unable to find targets above 65,000ft, but in the event the Soviets were able to track the U-2 successfully at its cruising altitude of around 72,000ft; however, they were as yet powerless to prevent the U-2 sorties from overflying the USSR and its satellites at will. After a Soviet protest, the U-2 overflights were stopped, but recommenced in November 1956 in the wake of the Soviet invasion of Hungary. Another USAF reconnaissance operation in 1956 was Project *Homerun*, in which pairs of aircraft – an RB-47E of the 10th SRW and a B-47H ELINT aircraft of the 343rd SRW operating from Thule – flew a polar route over the Arctic Ocean to carry out a mapping and electronic survey of northern Russia. Over 140 of these sorties were completed.

In TAC, the North American F-100 Super Sabre progressively replaced the F-84F in the fighter-bomber role, eventually equipping ten Tactical Fighter Wings (TFW). The prime role of these aircraft was tactical nuclear strike and wings under USAFE command were included in the Central Europe Atomic Strike Plan. However, the French government banned US nuclear weapons from French soil, so the three USAFE wings based in the country had to be hastily redeployed to the UK or Germany. In 1959, the 49th FBW moved from Étain-Rouvres to Spangdahlem and the 50th FBW moved from Toul to Hahn; the following year

the final unit, the 48th FBW, moved from Chaumont to RAF Lakenheath.

THE FIRST DECADE

From a position of extreme disadvantage in 1949, ten years later Soviet air forces had largely closed the gap with the US forces. They had introduced nuclear-capable long-range bombers and had formed an effective integrated air-defence system. Thanks to their successful rocket/space programme, the PVO-Strany defences also incorporated effective SAM systems. In the last months of the decade, the VVS and IA-PVO were further strengthened with the arrival of high-performance types: The Mikoyan Gurevich MiG-21 [Fishbed], Sukhoi Su-7 [Fitter-A] and Su-9 [Fitter-B] fighters. However, the US had maintained its strategic lead and also prepared to enter the 1960s with high-performance aircraft either in service or, like the Republic F-105 Thunderchief, about to join front-line units. Both the US and the USSR had also ensured that their respective European allies had air forces that were equally well-equipped for war, should conflict arise. But the massive re-equipment and expansion projects on both sides of the Iron Curtain had been made at great cost and as the decade drew to a close, it was obvious that economic reality would restrict the defence budgets of all countries in the 1960s.

A North American F-100D Super Sabre, the first of the 'Century Series' fighters that entered service in the late 1950s. This aircraft is from the 20th TFW based at Wethersfield, England. (USAFM)

CHAPTER 2
WE WILL BURY YOU! 1960-69

"It doesn't depend on you whether or not we exist. If you don't like us, don't accept our invitations, and don't invite us to come to see you. Whether you like it or not, history is on our side. We will bury you!" Nikita Khrushchev, 1956

The 'Swinging Sixties' will doubtless be remembered as the genesis of popular music, avant-garde fashion and youth culture, but it was also a decade lived in the shadow of the nuclear bomb. At the start of the new decade, both the US and the USSR pursued a strategy of massive nuclear response in the event of hostilities. The balance of force remained heavily in favour of the US, but the USSR had acquired enough nuclear weapons to be more confident in its dealings with its main adversary. As a result, political tensions remained high and nuclear war seemed to be a real possibility. After a decade of expansion and almost continuous re-equipment, the air forces of NATO, the Warsaw Pact and the non-aligned nations had reached their peak strengths and most combat units were now equipped with high performance jet-powered aircraft. On either side of the Iron Curtain, nuclear-armed strike aircraft were maintained at high states of readiness and sophisticated air defence systems controlled all-weather interceptors.

Rocket technology had advanced rapidly in the late 1950s and the ballistic missile was fast becoming the preferred means of delivery for strategic weapons. The same technology had also produced effective SAM as well as AAM and these developments would dramatically change the face of military flying. In particular, long-range SAM were able to close off the high- and medium-level airspace to bomber aircraft, limiting operations to low altitudes in an attempt to fly under the radar coverage. From being the only practical nuclear delivery system in the previous decade, the strategic bomber aircraft became just one element of the 'nuclear triad' of Inter-Continental Ballistic Missiles (ICBM), Submarine-Launched Ballistic Missiles (SLBM) and manned bombers.

Although East–West tensions might have driven alliance partners closer together, cracks were appearing in both the NATO and the Warsaw Pact alliances. In NATO, France was becoming more suspicious of US and British motives and began to withdraw from the integrated military structure; also there was no sign of an end to the hostility between Greece and Turkey. In the Warsaw Pact, differing interpretations of Marxism-Leninism fostered ideological schisms, particularly in Albania, Romania and eventually Czechoslovakia. The early years of the 1960s were marked by three international crises, each of which seemed to bring the threat of nuclear war even closer.

In 1960, the Convair F-102A Delta Dagger equipped 22 interceptor squadrons in the US Air Defense Command. After the F-102 had been superseded in service by the F-106 Delta Dart, the type continued to equip a similar number of ANG units into the next decade. The F-102 could carry up to six Hughes AIM-4 Falcon AAM in a ventral weapons bay. (USAF)

THE U-2 CRISIS, 1960

By 1960, the PVO-Strany had begun the modernization of its interceptor force and also the upgrade of surface anti-aircraft capability. The IA-PVO interceptor force had begun to re-equip with the Sukhoi Su-9 all-weather interceptor, which had a considerably improved performance over its predecessors, but in 1960, the MiG-19 still formed the backbone of the IA-PVO fighter strength. Reflecting the threat posed by high-flying aircraft like the U-2, most PVO MiG-19 sqadrons also now included two MiG-19SV (*Spetsial'nyj Vysotnyy* – special high-altitude), which boasted more powerful engines and a lighter airframe than the standard aircraft. High-level interceptions were practised against the Yak-25RV (*Razvedchick Vysotnyy* – high-altitude reconnaissance) [Mandrake] strategic reconnaissance aircraft, which could climb to 65,00ft; however, even this was significantly below the operating altitude of a U-2 and to reach it the fighter had to follow a parabolic trajectory and hope for a firing solution as it reached the apogee. A more practical counter to a high-flying target was the S-75 SAM system [Sa-2 Guideline], which was deployed around the main urban and industrial centres of the USSR as well as the approach routes. Interestingly, US intelligence was totally unaware that the S-75 could reach a target flying at 80,000ft; a U-2 cruised at 75,000ft.

In the late 1950s, Detachment 'B' had commenced U-2 operations from Adana in Turkey and also from Peshawar in Pakistan. Overflights of the USSR had been halted in respect of Soviet protests; however in late 1959, President Eisenhower authorized a limited resumption in order to gather intelligence regarding the Soviet ICBM programme. In particular the Central Intelligence Agency (CIA) was eager to have more information on the activity at Tyuratam, the missile testing facility in Kazakhstan. Single missions to overfly Tyuratam were flown in July 1959, February 1960 and April 1960. A further overflight, named Operation *Grand Slam*, was planned to be the most ambitious mission to date, and involved a flight from the south of the USSR, over Tyuratam to Sverdlovsk and then past Kirov and onward to Arkhangelsk and Murmansk before landing at Bodø in Norway. The pilot selected for this operation was Francis Gary Powers, a very experienced U-2 pilot who had already completed 27 operational missions. The operation was planned for late April, but after a number of delays, Powers took off from Peshawar on 1 May 1960 and headed north over Tyuratam towards Sverdlovsk at 75,000ft. His aircraft was tracked by Soviet air defence radars and during the initial leg of his mission, 13 fighters were launched in an attempt to intercept his aircraft. None could reach the U-2, but as he reached Sverdlovsk, Powers entered the engagement zone of a S-75 battery. The battery fired a salvo of missiles, one of which detonated close enough to the U-2 to damage the aircraft fatally – another missile struck and destroyed a pursuing MiG-19. Powers was able to eject from his aircraft, but the wreckage provided enough evidence of the nature of his mission to cause a major international crisis. Once again overflights by the U-2 were halted and USAF had to reconsider how it might penetrate Soviet airspace in the event of war.

The crisis was further fuelled two months later, on 1 July 1960, when an RB-47H of the 38th Strategic Reconnaissance Squadron (SRS), 55th SRW, from Forbes AFB, Kansas was shot down off Cape Svyatoy Nos on the Kola peninsula. The aircraft and six-man crew: Maj W.G. Palm (pilot), Capt F.B. Olmstead (co-pilot) and Capt J.R. McKone (navigator) assisted by Maj E.E. Posa, Capt O.L. Goforth and Capt D.B. Phillips (air electronics operators), had deployed forward to RAF Brize Norton to fly an ELINT sortie off the coast of northern Russia. The aircraft took off at 10:00hrs and five hours later, after skirting the Norwegian coast, keeping some 50 miles offshore, it rounded the North Cape to follow the coastline of the Kola Peninsula. The RB-47H was soon identified by Soviet air defence radar which continued to track the aircraft as it approached USSR territory. At the Soviet PVO base of Kilpyavr near Murmansk, two pilots on 174 IAP were on QRA duty: *Kapitán* (Capt) V. Polyakov was at immediate readiness in a MiG-19 and *Stárshiy Leytenánt* (Senior Lt) A. Kotlyarov was at ten-minute readiness to fly a Su-9. As the US aircraft passed abeam Murmansk, both fighters were scrambled to make an interception.

The pilot, co-pilot and navigator ejected from the stricken aircraft, but Maj Palm subsequently died

The Lockheed U-2, strategic reconnaissance aircraft, had high aspect ratio wings which the enabled the type to fly at altitudes above 70,000ft. During the 1950s such an altitude gave immunity from the Soviet air defences. By 1960, the S-75 [SA-2 Guideline] SAM system had entered service and could reach the U-2. (USAF)

Although it had largely been supplanted by the Boeing B-52 Stratofortress, the Boeing B-47 Stratojet continued in service as a strategic bomber until 1965. Reconnaissance variants of the aircraft played an important intelligence gathering role throughout the 1960s. (USAF)

of hypothermia in his dinghy; unfortunately, the three remaining crew members did not escape from the aircraft and were killed.

RB-47 SHOOTDOWN

1 JULY 1960
Capt V. POLYAKOV

The scramble command was given to two crews: to me in the MiG-19 and to [Kotlyarov] in the Su-9. It was easier for me to take off first in the MiG than for my comrade starting from cold. It would take him ten minutes to don his helmet and overalls. In those days the Americans were insolent: they enjoyed all the advantages of speed and height and they trespassed freely into our airspace... When I was launched to intercept the intruder, I did not yet know that it was a B-47. After vectoring me onto the target, the controller gave the command "arm your weapons." In addition to the cannon, the MiG was armed with Neupravlyayemyy Reaktivnyy Snaryad (NURS) [S-5 unguided rockets]. I reported "I am visual with the target - request instructions." The response was

"Close in and identify". I approached the right wing of the reconnaissance aircraft to about 30 metres and I gave him the international "follow me" signal. But instead of complying with the instruction, the RB-47 turned away... As soon as the instruction to destroy the target came, I prepared for the attack. At first, I thought of using the rockets, but the target was too close. I fired a burst of cannon, at which the RB-47 shuddered and started to descend. I immediately pulled up sharply, in case the bomber fired back. At the top of my zoom climb, I saw bright pulsating points of light coming from the aircraft... The RB-47 started to smoke and then a tongue of flame appeared.

BERLIN CRISIS, 1961

Berlin became a growing problem for the DDR in the late 1950s and early 1960s, because it provided a channel for tens of thousands of East Germans to escape the Communist regime and resettle in the west of the country. In the USSR, First Secretary Khrushchev advocated a solution to the Berlin problem, and to the question of a divided Germany, which involved the termination of the Four Powers Agreement over Berlin, the establishment of a unified neutral Germany and the withdrawal of US military forces from Europe. Such a move was, however, unacceptable to western European nations which saw the presence of US troops as the guarantors of their freedom and sovereignty. The US presidential election on 9 November 1960 resulted in John Fitzgerald Kennedy being elected. On 4 June 1961, the President met the First Secretary in Vienna; during their opening exchanges Khrushchev sensed that Kennedy's position had been somewhat weakened by the U-2 crisis and the disastrous Bay of Pigs 'invasion' on 19 April 1961 – an attempt by US-backed Cuban exiles to overthrow Fidel Castro. Khrushchev seized the opportunity to announce that the USSR would unilaterally terminate the Four Powers Agreement and cede Berlin to the government of the DDR in the following year: The DDR closed the Berlin border on 13 August 1961, an act that precipitated the Berlin Crisis.

Even before the Kennedy/Khruschev meeting Soviet fighter aircraft had already begun to harass aircraft using the air corridors into Berlin and the pressure was increased by an announcement in July that the Soviet defence budget would be increased by 30 percent. In the same month several new types of military aircraft were displayed in public for the first time at the 1961 Aviation Day at Tushino; these included the Tu-128 long-range interceptor [Fiddler], the Tu-22 tactical bomber [Blinder], the Yak-28 fighter-bomber [Brewer], the Sukhoi T-5 interceptor – a development that would lead to the Su-15 [Flagon] – and the prototype Myasishchev M-50 supersonic strategic bomber [Bounder]. Meanwhile tensions steadily rose on the ground, culminating on 13 August in the barricading of all routes into and out of West Berlin and beginning the construction of the Berlin Wall.

During the summer, the US and NATO had begun to reinforce the Central Region. Eight F-100D squadrons and two F-104 squadrons, a total of 144 aircraft, were deployed to Europe from the US and the 36th TFW at Bitburg was re-equipped with the Republic F-105 Thunderchief. The *Armée de l'Aire* also deployed two F-100D units into Germany in June: EC 3 moved to Lahr and EC 11 replaced the F-84F-equipped EC 4 at Bremgarten. During August, the RAF Germany alert commitment increased and the one remaining day fighter unit in Germany, 14 Sqn at Gütersloh, held alert from dawn to dusk each day with two Hawker Hunter F6 at two-minute readiness, two more at five-minute readiness and a further pair at 30-minute readiness. The Hunters were augmented by Gloster Javelin FAW8 all-weather interceptors of 41 Sqn, which were armed with the de Havilland Firestreak AAM and were normally based at RAF Wattisham. Another Wattisham-based unit, 56 Sqn newly-equipped with the English Electric Lightning F1A interceptor, also deployed to Brüggen.

September saw NATO Exercise *Checkmate*, an intensive three-day exercise involving all AAFCE units in the Central region. During the exercise two Luftwaffe F-84F Thunderstreaks from JaBoG32 at Lechfeld became lost and strayed into East Germany. Soviet fighters launched to intercept them and the only means of recovering the aircraft safely was for them to make a dash for West Berlin, where they landed safely at Tegel airport in the French sector. Unfortunately, in doing so

82 IN COLD WAR SKIES

A Republic F-105D Thunderchief firing a pod of 2.75-inch Mighty Mouse rockets. A total of 610 of the all-weather strike aircraft were built, but over half were lost during the Vietnam War. (Getty)

they had breached the Four Powers Agreement, which inflamed the crisis still further. As the crisis escalated, a number of ANG units were mobilized and during Operation *Stair Step* the following month, 78 F-86H and 104 F-84F were flown to Europe via Newfoundland, Greenland, Iceland and Scotland. A further three squadrons of F-104A were transported to Europe in Douglas C-124 Globemaster transport aircraft; the 151st (Tennessee) and 197th (Arizona) TFS went to Ramstein and the 157th (South Carolina) TFS to Moron, Spain. Air bases in France were also reactivated to house the F-84F reinforcements. Chaumont became home to the 141st TFS from New Jersey, Étain hosted the 166th TFS from Ohio, Chambley housed the 163rd TFS from Indiana and Toul accommodated the 110th TFS from Missouri. The only complete ANG wing to deploy was the 102nd TFW from Massachusetts, which moved its three squadrons of F-86H to Phalsbourg.

Both the USA and USSR had also resumed nuclear testing during September 1961 and on 30 October the Soviets staged an impressive show of force by dropping the largest ever thermonuclear bomb over Cape Sukhoy Nos, on the island of Novaya Zemlaya in the Arctic Ocean. The 50-megaton RDS-220 device, codenamed *Vanya*, was carried in a specially modified Tu-95V, captained by *Podpolkovnik* (Lt Colonel) A.E. Durnovtsev. The aircraft was accompanied by a Tu-16A airborne laboratory 'chase aircraft' captained by *Mayor* (Major) V.F. Martynenko. Durnostev dropped the weapon from an altitude of 35,000ft and had managed to escape to a distance of 25 miles before the device detonated at an altitude of 13,000ft. The Tu-95 was subjected to extreme heat and four powerful shockwaves, which caused all four engines to flame out. It was not until the aircraft had glided to 22,000ft that one of the engines restarted and two more engines were relit at 16,000ft; the aircraft landed at Olenya airfield on three engines.

Over the next few months, both sides backed down from further confrontation. The ANG units returned to the USA in early 1962, but their aircraft remained in Europe and were used to form the 366th TFW, comprising four F-84F squadrons, based at Chaumont, Chambley, Étain and Phalsbourg. Although the USSR

The supersonic Convair F-102 Delta Dagger was the first gun-less US interceptor and carried its armament of six Hughes AIM-4 Falcon AAMs (typically a mix of three semi-active radar and six infra-red homing missiles) in a ventral weapons bay. (USAFM)

Above: The 317th FIS operated the Convair F-102A Delta Dagger at Elmendorf AFB with responsibility for the air defence of Alaska throughout the 1960s. (USAF)

A formation of three Tupolev Tu-128 [Fiddler] long-range interceptors. The type was armed with four Bisnoyat R-4 [AA-5 Ash] missiles, and was the largest interceptor ever built. (Sputnik)

had misjudged the US resolve over Berlin, the city remained divided and the Berlin Wall had become a symbol of the Cold War.

On 15 and 16 September 1962, two DA Tu-16 regiments carried out two *Letno-Takticheskogo Ucheniya* (LTU – flight tactical exercises), involving live drops of nuclear weapons in a regimental combat formation of 24 aircraft. The units involved were, the 132 TBAP from Tartu and 185 TBAP from Poltava, both of which deployed to Olenya for the exercises. *Generál-Leytenánt* (Lieutenant-General) V. V. Reshetnikov, commander of the 2nd *Otdel'nyy Tyazhelyy Bombardirovshchik Aviatsionnyy Korpus* (OTBAK – independent heavy bomber corps), flew as a member of one crew and eloquently described the experience:

LIVE NUCLEAR DROP

16 SEPTEMBER 1962
Gen Lt V. V. RESHETNIKOV,
2ND OTBAK

Suddenly, the brightest glow burst into the heavens, gilding the clouds. It illuminated all the space around us with intense light, which penetrated into the cockpit, scattering the shadows and illuminating the instruments. It lasted a second. The light had a kick like a mule, for a few moments after it appeared we were shaken again and again, as if we were crossing a railway at high speed along a broken

road. Dull blows shook the entire airframe, rattling our spines. The wings rocked, the nose twitched. On the instrument dials, the needles spun. We stroked the controls, comforting the aircraft, and once again she sailed obediently through the air. To the left of the smooth surface of the clouds, a huge white dome suddenly began to heave and grow rapidly. As soon as it formed into a hemisphere, it rose through the cloud layer, dragging behind it a wide smoke column, climbing rapidly to a huge height, already well above our own. And the top of it, a colossal turban of the gentlest tones of all the colours of the rainbow bathed in shimmering sunlight, hovering at an altitude of 20–30km. The entire regiment cruised around that turban as if in a circle of honour... I was happy with the successful delivery of the bomb, its successful detonation, the return of the regiment in without loss.

Unlike the USSR, which kept exclusive control of its nuclear arsenal and did not share the technology with its allies, the US deployed its weapons in the European theatre under NATO control and supplied them to selected allies. The UK, in particular, benefitted from this arrangement: US-supplied Mk 43 weapons were carried by Valiant and Canberra bombers under direct UK command (although the 'dual key' system meant that US authorization was required to arm the weapons).

After a disastrous and short service as a fighter during the mid-1950s, the Supermarine Swift FR5 proved to be an effective tactical reconnaissance platform This aircraft is from 79 Sqn based at RAF Gütersloh, Germany. (Pitchfork)

88 IN COLD WAR SKIES

A formation of Republic F-84F Thunderstreaks from 2 Wing of the Belgian Air Force based at Florennes. The US Mutual Defense Assistance Programme (MDAP) provided 1,300 of the type to NATO air forces. (Jarrett)

In addition, the UK was able to develop its own independent nuclear force equipped with the Vulcan and Victor, which were armed with the British Yellow Sun free-fall weapon and the Avro Blue Steel stand-off missile. Until 1962, the US Army, US Navy and USAF each had their own nuclear plan, independent of the other services; this resulted in a lack of co-ordination and duplication of both effort and targeting, so a Single Integrated Operation Plan (SIOP) was introduced which included all US nuclear weapons. From late 1963, the three RAF Bomber Command Valiant squadrons and the four RAF Germany Canberra strike squadrons were also integrated into the SIOP via the SACEUR atomic plan.

The deployment of US nuclear weapons to Europe was not limited to free-fall bombs: delivery of the Thor IRBM system to the RAF had commenced in 1959 and by late 1962 the RAF had 60 operational missiles. In first months of 1960 a total of 30 Chrysler PGM-19 Jupiter IRBM were delivered to Italy, where they were operated by the 36ª *Aerobrigata Interdizione Strategica*, (strategic interdiction wing), based at Gioia del Colle.

Two years later, a further a further 15 of the missiles were delivered to the Turkish Air Force at Cigli Air Base, near Izmir.

CUBAN MISSILE CRISIS, 1962

Unfortunately, the consequence deploying missiles in Italy and Turkey was an agreement between the USSR and Cuba to base R-12 Medium Range Ballistic Missiles (MRBM) [SS-4 Sandal] and R-14 [SS-5 Skean] IRBM, as well as nuclear capable FKR-1 cruise missiles and Il-28 aircraft on the island. The deployment of these weapon systems, Operation *Anadyr*, was carried out in complete secrecy in early September 1962. Air defence forces were also dispatched to Cuba; two S-75 SAM divisions and 32 GvIAP, equipped with the MiG-21F13, which had begun flying from Santa Clara airfield in September 1962. The island of Cuba had been under USAF surveillance since March that year, although there were no direct overflights, so the US remained unaware of the Soviet deployment. Initially ELINT sorties known as Operation *Quick Fox* were

A Hawker Hunter FR10 tactical reconnaissance aircraft of 4 Sqn based at RAF Gütersloh, Germany. The type served with RAF Germany (RAFG) through the 1960s. (Pitchfork)

Right:
The Lockheed F-104A Starfighter served as a short-range day fighter, but did not meet the requirements of Air Defense Command (ADC) which resulted in most of the aircraft being transferred to the ANG in 1960. (USAF)

Below:
It was standard practice to airlift the F-104 for overseas deployments. Here a dismantled F-104 is being loaded into a Douglas C-124 Globemaster of the USAF Military Air Transportation Service (MATS). (USAF)

flown by Lockheed GC-130A drone launchers, but these were superseded in June by Operation *Common Cause* involving weekly RB-47H sorties over the Gulf of Mexico flown by the 55th SRW from Forbes AFB. It was not until October that clearance was given for the 4080th SRW to carry out overflights using the U-2F. Three flights over Cuba on 14 and 15 October by Maj R.S. Heyser and Maj R. Anderson brought back imagery of a number of MRBM launch sites near San Cristobel, initiating another international crisis. The number of reconnaissance sorties was dramatically increased: Operation *Common Cause* missions were stepped up to two a day and on 17 October there were six U-2 overflights which identified more missile sites as well as 42 crated Il-28 bombers being assembled at San Julien airfield.

On 19 October 1962, SAC units began to withdraw from Florida to put them out of range of Soviet missiles. Meanwhile, the US tri-service Continental Air Defense Command, CONAD, reinforced Florida with 60 F-102 and F-106 interceptors and the McDonnell F-4B Phantom-equipped VF-41 of the US Navy. On 22 October, President Kennedy announced that the US would enforce a naval blockade of Cuba, starting at 14:00hrs GMT on 24 October. CONAD raised its readiness state from DEFCOM 5 (Defense Condition 5, the normal peacetime state of readiness) to DEFCON 3 at 23:00hrs GMT on 22 October. In the Montgomery sector, Combat Air Patrols (CAP) were mounted continuously over strategic points and fighter aircraft were kept at high states of readiness throughout each day; this ranged from engines-running ground alert at dawn to five minutes' readiness at other times of the day. SAC was also ordered to DEFCON 3 on 22 October, which precipitated dispersal of the B-47 force to wartime bases and an increase of the Operation *Chrome Dome* airborne alert from 12 to 66 aircraft. Of these, 28 would fly the southern route, 36 the northern route and two would cover the Thule monitor. Each B-52 was armed with either four Mk

RAF armourers prepare to load an Avro Blue Steel stand-off missile into an Avro Vulcan B2. The weapon, which could be carried by both the Vulcan and the Handley Page Victor B2RS, formed the British independent nuclear deterrent from 1963 until 1968. (Crown Copyright)

28 weapons or two Mk 15/39 weapons. There was also a commensurate increase in the number of AAR assets required to support Operation *Chrome Dome*: the number of KC-135 tankers in Spain (at Torrejon and Moron) was increased from six to 38 and at Loring AFB, Maine, from six to 13. On 24 October, the alert status was raised still further in SAC to DEFCON 2. At the beginning of the crisis, six Convair B-58 Hustler supersonic bombers were kept on ground alert, but by the first week of November, this number had increased to 84. The SAC ICBM force, comprising Convair SM-65 Atlas, Martin SM-68 Titan and new Boeing LGM-3 Minuteman missiles, also came to readiness.

Although the crisis was a direct confrontation between the US and the USSR and the latter had not consulted its allies, the European allies of both sides became embroiled in the situation because a US attack on Cuba would almost certainly have triggered a Soviet annexation of West Berlin. Warsaw Pact forces were ordered to an increased state of readiness on the morning of 23 October. At the same time, leave for military personnel was cancelled in the USSR and the missile forces were brought to the 'highest combat readiness.' US Air Forces Europe (USAFE) tactical nuclear aircraft, such as the F-100D of the 20th TFW based in the UK, were strike-loaded. Non-US NATO forces remained at their usual peacetime states of readiness, but Canadair Argus (RCAF) and Avro Shackleton (RAF) maritime patrol aircraft (MPA) were active in tracking Soviet submarines in the North Atlantic.

The USAF started low-level reconnaissance sorties over Cuba on 22 October, using the Vought RF-8A Crusader of naval squadron VFP-62 and the RF-101 Voodoo from the 363rd TRW. Tensions rose steadily over the next four days and the crisis reached a climax on 27 October. On that day a U-2 flown by Maj Anderson was shot down over Cuba. By then the USAF had nearly 1,500 bombers either airborne or loaded on ground alert and these were supported by 1,000 AAR tankers. On the same day the alert status of UK strategic forces was also discreetly increased. At all Vulcan, Victor and Valiant units, aircraft were loaded with nuclear weapons and the QRA aircraft were brought to five minutes' readiness at cockpit alert. Normally the RAF kept some 40 of their 60 Thor missiles at 15 minutes' readiness state, but on 27 October 59 missiles were generated

The prototype English Electric Canberra B(I)8 prototype. The interdictor aircraft served with three RAF squadrons in Germany and was armed with the US-built Mk 7 nuclear weapon. (Crown copyright)

to the increased readiness level and a number of them were readied and held at eight minutes to launch.

The following day, First Secretary Nikita Khrushchev agreed to remove Soviet missiles from Cuba, in exchange for the removal of US missiles from Italy and Turkey. The crisis had been defused but it was far from over: strategic and air defence forces on both sides remained at advanced states of alert. SAC remained at DEFCON 2 until 21 November and the Soviet missile forces likewise remained at full combat readiness until the same date. On 27 November, US forces stepped down from DEFCON 3 after they had monitored and verified the withdrawal of the missiles and bombers from Cuba. The Jupiter missiles were withdrawn from Italy and Turkey in early 1963. The crisis marked the highest point of tension during the Cold War and once again the USSR had misjudged US resolve.

THE USSR AND THE WARSAW PACT, 1962–64

By 1964, 30 regiments of the IA-PVO were equipped with the delta-winged Su-9. A short-range interceptor

armed with the RS-2-US radar-guided AAM [AA-1 Alkali], the Su-9 delivered an impressive performance, but it suffered from chronic unreliability. In particular the Lyulka AL-7F engine lasted only for a few flight cycles. An improved version of the aircraft, the Su-11 [Fishpot-C], entered PVO service with 393 GvIAP at Privolzhskiy, near Astrakhan, in 1964 and was in widespread front-line service early the following year. Like the Su-9, the Su-11 was compatible with the Vozdukh-1 GCI system which could send secure data-linked commands to the aircraft, making the interception process less vulnerable to communications jamming. The PVO procedure was for all interceptions to be closely controlled from the ground-based control post, using radar GCI. Apart from centralizing control, perhaps at the expense of initiative and independence on the part of the aircrew, this system worked for a pilot force with little tactical experience or flexibility. Unlike western air-defence forces where aircrew were converted onto operational aircraft types at a dedicated conversion training unit, the PVO sent its pilots to operational regiments directly from flying schools.

The Mach 2 capable Convair B-58 Hustler became operational in 1960 and replaced the Boeing B-47 Stratojet. A total of 116 were built and served with the 43rd BW and the 305th BW. The aircraft was flown by a crew of three and both weapons and extra fuel were carried in the large pod under the fuselage. (USAF)

The Martin B-57B was developed from the English Electric Canberra, but had various improvements, including a tandem 'fighter type' cockpit. The B-57E variant was originally produced as a target-towing aircraft, but a number were converted for night surveillance operations over Vietnam. (USAF)

The training of new pilots was then left to the discretion of the unit commander and, with only 60-90 flying hours a year (the NATO standard was double this), the tactical training of PVO aircrew was limited.

Another aircraft type which joined the inventory of the PVO in 1964 was the Yakovlev Yak-28P [Firebar]; the two-seat configuration of this aircraft made it more suitable for low-level interceptions than the single-seat type, in which the pilot workload was much higher. Like the Su-11, the Yak-28P was armed with R-8MR [AA-3 Anab] semi-active and R-8MT infra-red seeking AAMs, but whereas the Su-9 and Su-11 were point-defence systems because of their limited range, the longer range of the Yak-28 suited it to remote regions, where the air defences had to cover large expanses of territory. Thus, while most PVO armies had only one regiment of Yak-28P, the 10th Independent PVO army which covered the Kola Peninsula had three (174th GvIAP at Monchegorsk, near Murmansk, 641GvIAP at Petrozavodsk-Besovets, near Lake Onega and 524 IAP at Letneozerskiy, near Arkhangelsk). Detachments from Yak-28P Polki were also periodically based forward at Rogachevo on Novaya Zemlaya to provide air defence of the Arctic region.

The introduction of the S-75 SAM system, with its ability to defend the high-level airspace, had forced the US and NATO air forces to switch to low-level tactics to reach targets in the USSR and Eastern Europe. Meanwhile, the PVO missile forces had been further strengthened by the S-125 Neva [Sa-3 Goa] SAM system which was effective against targets as low as 1,000ft. Since US/NATO aircraft practised flying at 250–500ft, there was still a gap that would have to be covered by interceptors. This caused the PVO a number of problems. Firstly, because each GCI site could only control its fighters if both interceptor and target were visible to the same radar, but low-level targets might either get lost in 'ground clutter' and become invisible to the radar, or, because of the short radar pick-up ranges at low-level, a high-speed target might move swiftly into the coverage of a neighbouring radar unit. Secondly, no PVO fighter was fitted with pulse-Doppler radar capable of 'look down,' so the final stages of a low-level interception would, in any case, have to be carried out visually. Finally, PVO pilots were required to carry out very few low-level interceptions: just one interception below 1,500ft had to be completed every six months, and most practice intercepts took place above 3,000ft.

The Soviet strategic policy switched dramatically in 1960 from the manned bomber to the ballistic missile as the prime nuclear attack force. As a result, bomber production and deployment were curtailed in favour of missiles. The three VAs of the DA were renamed

Raketnaya Armiya (missile armies), and re-equipped with ballistic missiles. Instead, the long-range manned bomber force was re-organized into three OTBAK: the 2nd OTBAK based in Ukraine, the 6th OTBAK in western Russia and the 8th OTBAK in the Far East. Manufacture of the Tu-95 [Bear] and Mya-M4 and 3M [Bison] bombers ceased in the early 1960s after only about 300 Tu-95 and less than 100 M-4/3M airframes had been completed. Small numbers of both types remained in service as bombers armed with free-fall bombs, but, reflecting the new emphasis on missiles, some 70 aircraft from the Tu-95 fleet were either modified or rebuilt to Tu-95KM [Bear-C] (*Kompleks Modernizirovany* – complex upgraded), standard; these were capable of launching the Raduga Kh-20 [AS-3 Kangaroo] nuclear Air-Launched Cruise Missile (ALCM) and were also equipped for AAR to increase their reach still further. The majority of the Mya-M-4 and 3M aircraft were also converted to become AAR tankers to support this weapons system. Both the Tu-95 and the Mya-3M were also used in the ELINT and reconnaissance role.

In the DA medium bomber force, the new emphasis on missiles caused the withdrawal of the Il-28 from front-line service in DA regiments, leaving the Tu-16 as the mainstay of the force. Many of these aircraft, beginning with those operated by 200 and 402 TBAP, were converted to Tu-16K standard so that they could carry the KSR-2 ALCM [AS-5 Kelt], and its KSR-5 Anti-Radiation Missile (ARM) variant. Some 43 Tu-16 tankers were also converted to the 'probe and drogue' configuration, becoming the Tu-16NN, to be compatible with other receiver types. Amongst those was the Tu-22A [Blinder-A], the first supersonic bomber used by the DA, which was first issued to 203 TBAP at Baranovichi, in the Byelorussian SSR,

An ex-RAF Canadair-built F-86 Sabre in service with 2° *Stormo* of the Italian Air Force. The type was replaced by the Fiat G-91 in the early 1960s. (Jarrett)

First observed in 1967, the Tupolev Tu-95RT [Bear-D] electronic intelligence aircraft was operated by the *Aviatsiya Vogenno Morskogo Flota* (AV-MF – Soviet naval aviation). The type was frequently found operating near NATO naval exercises. (Paxton)

in 1962. Apart from the bomber, two more variants of the Tu-22 entered service almost simultaneously: the Tu-22R [Blinder-C] reconnaissance version, issued to 121 and 290 *Otdel'nyy Dal'nerazedovatel'nyy*, (ODRAP – independent long-range RAP), and also the Tu-22P *Postanovshchikpomoyek* (P – jammer) electronic warfare aircraft.

Bomber regiments of the DA periodically carried out training in the Arctic during the early 1960s. The so-called *aerodromy podskoka* ('bounce' airfields), at Olenya, Vorkuta, Norilsk, Tiksi, Cheruvka, and Mys Schmidta, also Nagurskoye were amongst 16 airstrips used to extend the range of Soviet bomber aircraft targeting North America. The airfield at Anadyr on the Chukotka Peninsula in the north-eastern USSR, which was home to a MiG-17 detachment from 529 IAP, was used as a forward operating base for Tu-16 units. From the late 1950s, pairs of the bombers often flew close to the Alaskan border, but it was not until 5 December 1961 that F-102 Delta Daggers of the 317th FIS based in Alaska made a successful interception. Probing of NORAD defences continued and on 14 March 1963 two Tu-95s were able to penetrate some 45km into Alaskan airspace without being intercepted; two F-102A interceptors which were launched from the forward alert strip at King Salmon were unable to catch the intruders.

The policy switch from manned aircraft to missiles also affected the FA. Tactical missiles took the place of 'assault aircraft' and organic SAMs provided close-in air defence. Between 1960 and 1961, the FA was reduced to half its former strength, but at the same time, and after having been the lowest priority amongst the Soviet air arms for modern equipment, the FA received two new aircraft types: the Sukhoi Su-7B specialized ground-attack aircraft and the Mikoyan-Gurevich MiG-21 air-superiority fighter. Both aircraft were short-range types, but they offered the VVS tactical forces a

Above:
Of the 250 Tupolev Tu-22 [Blinder] aircraft built, only some 20 were the bomber variant. The majority of those in service were equipped for reconnaissance and electronic warfare. The Tu-22K [Blinder-B] missile carrier could be armed with the Raduga Kh-22 [AS-4 Kitchen] anti-shipping missile. (Getty)

Left:
The Tupolev Tu-16KS [Badger-B] was adapted to carry the Raduga KS-1 Komet [AS-1 Kennel] anti-shipping missile. (Sputnik)

Above: The Mikoyan-Gurevich MiG-21PFM [Fishbed-F] variant was introduced in 1968. Seen here undergoing maintenance, one major change was the introduction of a sideways opening canopy: earlier variants were hinged at the front. (Sputnik)

Right: A line of Soviet Air Force Mikoyan-Gurevich MiG-21 PFM fighters. In the foreground, a MiG-21UM [Mongol-B] operational training aircraft is being readied for flight. (Sputnik)

A MiG-21PFM being towed by a Ural APA5-D airfield starter vehicle, which carried a generator unit which supplied power for engine start. (Sputnik)

significantly improved operational capability over the MiG-15 and MiG-17 which they replaced. By 1965, the combat elements of the 24th *Vozdushnaya Armiya* (VA – air army) in the DDR were fully equipped with the Su-7B and MiG-21. However, during the 1960s, variants of the MiG-17 remained the most numerous type of fighter-bomber in service with non-Soviet Warsaw Pact (NSWP) countries, including the Polish-built PZL-Mielec Lim-6P which was optimized for the ground-attack role. The various versions of the MiG-21, the MiG-21F-13 (*Forsirovannyy* – uprated, compatible with the K-13 missile system), the MiG-21PF [Fishbed-D] (*Perekhvatchik* – interceptor) and the MiG-21PFM [Fishbed-F] (*Modernizirovannyy* – modernized) were also supplied in large numbers to become the standard day fighter of the Warsaw Pact air forces. The preponderance of the MiG-21 in the FA reflected the Soviet doctrine of '*gospodstov v vozdukhe*' (air supremacy), rather than close-air support of ground forces being the priority for tactical aircraft over the battlefield.

During the early 1960s, the differing interpretations of Communist ideology in post-Stalin USSR and in China caused a rift – the 'Sino-Soviet split' – between the two countries and their respective allies. Albania openly sided with China and as a result, the USSR broke off diplomatic relations in December 1962, withdrawing its military aid from the country. Although Albania did not formally leave the Warsaw Pact, it became de facto a non-aligned country from 1962 and the *Forcës Ajrore* (FAj – Albanian Air Force), re-equipped with the Chinese-built Shenyang J-5, a licence-built MiG-17F, and the Shenyang J-6 version of the MiG-19S. Romania, too distanced itself from the USSR and from 1962 it no longer participated in Warsaw Pact exercises. In fact, something of a divide had opened between the

Northern and Southern TVDs: in contrast to the air forces of the DDR, Poland and Czechoslovakia which received modern aircraft and sustained a ground-attack capability, those of Romania, Hungary and Bulgaria became largely air defence forces with fewer modern types.

USA AND NATO, 1963 – 64

As a counter to the growing effectiveness of the PVO interceptor and SAM forces, the SAC bomber force had changed its tactics in the late 1950s from high-altitude attacks to low-level penetration. In the case of the B-47, weapon delivery was from a LABS or pop-up profile. Unfortunately, this new environment took its toll of the B-47, which had not been designed for the stresses imposed by low-level flight. Metal fatigue cracks were found in the wings of some aircraft, necessitating expensive modification to a type that was already obsolescent. The Berlin and Cuban Crises gave the B-47 a stay of execution, but the aircraft began to

The two-man crew of a McDonnell CF-101B Voodoo interceptor rush to their aircraft. The aircraft carries the 'Canadian Armed Forces' markings which were introduced after the amalgamation of the Canadian Army, Navy and Air Force in 1968. (USAF)

be phased out of SAC service in 1963 and the last had left the frontline by 1966. By 1964, a total of 37 of the SAC bombardment wings were equipped with the B-52, albeit that some wings comprised just a single squadron. Apart from free-fall nuclear bombs, the B-52 could also carry two of the North American-built AGM-28 Hound Dog ALCM. If necessary, the engines of the missiles could be used to assist the eight engines of the B-52 for a heavy-weight take-off; once airborne the missile could then be refuelled from the aircraft's main fuel tanks. Throughout the 1960s, SAC also operated the Convair B-58 Hustler, which equipped the 43rd BW at Carswell AFB, Texas and the 305th BW at Bunker Hill AFB, Indiana.

The BMEWS became operational in 1961. Three sites at Clear, in Alaska, Thule, in Greenland and Fylingdales, in the UK, provided warning of attack by Soviet missiles. Warning of attack by bombers was still provided by the DEW-line, whose radar feeds were linked into the NORAD SAGE data-processing

The Canadair-built CF-104 Starfighter equipped the three wings of the 1st Canadian Air Division Europe from 1963. The aircraft were used in the nuclear strike and tactical reconnaissance roles. (USAF)

Right:
During the 'Cuban Missile Crisis' of 1962, the USAF deployed the McDonnell RF-101C Voodoo to fly low-level reconnaissance missions over the island. (USAF)

system. However in March 1963, an incursion into Alaska by Soviet Tu-95 bombers demonstrated that for all the sophistication of the DEW-line, SAGE and the Bomarc/Nike Hercules SAM systems, NORAD still needed to be equipped with manned fighters capable of intercepting high-performance targets. NORAD command noted that 'overflights of the Alaskan NORAD region by Soviet aircraft in March 1963 clearly showed the inadequacy of the F-102.' The long-term solution was to procure the McDonnell F-4C Phantom, but in the short-term an eight-, and later ten aircraft F-106 detachment from the 325th FIW was deployed to Elmendorf AFB under Operation *White Shoes*. Two F-106 were kept at five-minute readiness at each of the forward operating bases at King Salmon and Galena. The first successful F-106 interception took place on 8 September 1963, when two Tu-16 bombers were intercepted over the Bering Sea. Operation *White Shoes* became a rolling detachment until 1970, with each F-106 wing taking its turn to provide the personnel.

The Canadian contribution to NORAD was enhanced in 1962 with the replacement of the CF-100 with the CF-101B Voodoo. The improved effectiveness of the type was reflected in the reduction from nine CF-100 squadrons to five CF-101B squadrons, and by 1964 the number of squadrons had been reduced further to just three: 409 Sqn at Comox, near Vancouver,

A McDonnell F-101C Voodoo of the 92nd TFS at RAF Bentwaters, Suffolk. In USAFE service during the first half of the 1960s, the F-101 was deployed in the nuclear strike role. (USAF)

416 Sqn at Chatham, New Brunswick, and 425 Sqn at Bagotville, Quebec. The units of 1 Air Division Europe also underwent a major re-equipment in the same timescale. In the late 1950s one of the Sabre day fighter squadrons in each wing had been replaced by a CF-100 all-weather squadron, but in 1962 the CF-100 squadrons were disbanded and the Sabre was replaced by the Canadair-built CF-104 Starfighter. The new aircraft type also marked a switch from the air-defence role to that of tactical nuclear strike using the US-built Mk 28 and Mk 57 bombs. Since non-French nuclear weapons had been excluded from French soil, 2 Wing at Grostenquin was disbanded and its squadrons were redistributed between 3 Wing at Zweibrucken and 4 Wing at Baden-Solingen. However, 1 Wing, which was dedicated to the reconnaissance role, remained at Marville.

The re-equipment of 1st Air Division Europe reflected a general re-equipment programme throughout NATO forces in Europe. The F-84G Thunderjet, which had been the backbone of NATO air forces through the 1950s, was replaced by the Lockheed F-104G Starfighter in the BRD, the Netherlands, Belgium and Italy. These aircraft were 'multi-role' fighters which could fulfil both the air defence and ground-attack roles; in the latter the aircraft could be armed with a US-built Mk 61 tactical nuclear weapon under the 'dual key' system, whereby the weapon remained in US custody until they were released by SACEUR. The USAFE nuclear-armed units included the 36th TFW at Bitburg equipped with the F-105, the 20th, 48th and 50th TFW (at Wethersfield, Lakenheath and Hahn respectively) with F-100D and the 81st TFW at Bentwaters with the F-101C.

The F-104G was also introduced into service with the Danish Air Force, which had also procured the F-100D. Both the Greek Air Force and Turkish Air Force also operated the F-104G, although the F-84F (or the F-84Q variant) remained in widespread service with both forces.

In the early 1960s, the air defence forces within Europe were largely equipped with the F-86F Thunderstreak day fighter and F-86D/K Sabre all-weather interceptor. However, the air forces of Denmark

Black smoke from the Avpin starting system billows under a Gloster Javelin FAW 6 from 29 Squadron on the flight line in the summer of 1960. (Masterman via Author)

After being withdrawn from the nuclear bomber role, the Vickers Valiant saw useful service as an AAR tanker. A Gloster Javelin FAW9 all-weather interceptor from 23 Squadron has linked to the hose and awaiting the fuel to be pumped. (Miller)

and the Netherlands also operated the Hawker Hunter and the Belgian Air Force briefly used the CF-100. USAFE air-defence units on the continent were equipped with the F-102, while RAFG replaced the gun-armed Javelin FAW4 with the missile-armed Javelin FAW9 and then, from 1965, with the Lightning F2.

RISE OF SOVIET NAVAL AVIATION

At the end of World War II, the Soviet Navy was a small coastal force, but over the next decades it expanded into a formidable blue water force. Of particular concern to NATO was the large submarine force of the Soviet Northern Fleet, which included vessels armed with SLBMs: from just 38 submarines in 1963, the force had increased to 158 by 1967. The main base for these submarines was at Severomorsk, near Murmansk, which meant that they had to sail past the Norwegian coast and then transit the Greenland–Iceland–UK Gap (GIUK Gap) before reaching their operational areas in the North Atlantic. This, in turn, made them vulnerable to being located and tracked (and attacked) by NATO maritime patrol aircraft. Much of this work fell to the seven Avro Shackleton-equipped squadrons of RAF Coastal Command, most of which were based in Northern Ireland. Additionally, US Navy Lockheed P-2 Neptune units operated along the eastern seaboard of the USA as well as from Argentia, Newfoundland and Keflavik, Iceland; they were augmented by 404 Sqn, 405 Sqn and 415 Sqn of the RCAF maritime air command, which operated the Canadair CP-107 Argus. In the early 1960s, the P-2 was progressively replaced by the Lockheed P-3 Orion.

Like the submarine force, the *Aviatsiya Voyenno-Morskogo Flota* (AV-MF – Soviet naval aviation), also increased in size and capability in the late 1950s. In the mid-1960s, the air arm of the Northern Fleet, which was also representative of the Baltic, Black Sea and Far Eastern fleets, comprised a division of three Tu-16K-equipped *Morskoy Raketonosnyy Aviatsionnyy Polki* (MMAP – maritime missile aviation regiments), two independent reconnaissance regiments and an anti-submarine regiment. Most of the units were positioned at the three air bases at Severomorsk. The anti-submarine unit, 403 *Otdel'nyy Protivolodochnyy Aviatsionnyy Polk* (OPAP – independent anti-submarine aviation regiment), was equipped with the Beriev Be-6 [Madge] flying boat, while 392 ODRAP was

The Douglas B-66 Destroyer, a development of the A-3 Skywarrior in service with the US Navy, a was designed to replace the Douglas B-26 Invader light bomber. However the type proved more suited to the reconnaissance role which resulted in the production of the RB-66B. It was used for night photographic missions in Vietnam; 'Photoflash' flares, to illuminate a target, were carried in the bomb bay. (USAF)

equipped with the Tu-95RT *Razvedchik Tseleukazatel* (RT – reconnaissance targeting) aircraft which provided targeting information for the SLBM systems. As the decade progressed, the Tu-95RT and variants of the Tu-16 flown by the AV-MF became increasingly common over the Norwegian and Mediterranean Seas and the peripheries of the North Atlantic and also the North Pacific Ocean.

ANOTHER SHOOTDOWN

The Cold War had reached its closest point to becoming World War III during the Cuban Missile Crisis of 1962 and although political tension had dissipated in the subsequent months, it still remained relatively high. The military forces on both sides remained on alert, ready to respond to any perceived threat. This was particularly the case on either side of the IGB. Dawn on 10 March 1964 heralded a foggy morning at Zerbst air base and although the fog lifted a little in the early afternoon, the visibility remained poor in thick industrial haze. Despite the poor weather, *Kapitán* V.G. Ivannikov, the senior pilot of the squadron, and *Kapitán* B. Sizov, of 35 IAP were holding QRA alert with responsibility for the southern sector of the DDR. At around 16:45hrs, a Douglas RB-66 Destroyer from the 10th TRW based at Toul-Rosière strayed into East German airspace, possibly as a result of a faulty compass. By unfortunate coincidence, however, it overflew a major Soviet army exercise that was taking place on the ground near Magdeburg. A MiG-19S flown by *Kapitán* F.M. Zinoviev from the Wittstock-based 33 IAP was airborne on a defensive patrol in the northern sector and it was immediately vectored towards the intruder. At the same time the Zerbst QRA flight was scrambled. As Ivannikov and Sizov climbed through the haze in full afterburner, Zinoviev had already intercepted the RB-66 and ordered the US aircraft to follow him. However, the RB-66 turned away from him onto a westerly heading and Zinoviev was instructed to engage it. He had just fired a burst from his cannons when the Zerbst-based aircraft arrived. Sizov engaged first, but did not receive authorisation to fire until he was too close, so he broke off and Ivannikov closed on the target.

RB-66 SHOOTDOWN

Capt F.M. ZINOVIEV
33 IAP

I was on the runway in a matter of seconds. Visibility was half the runway length, so I could take off... and immediately the controller called: "717th, take off in afterburner!" In fact, the afterburner of the MiG-19 was rarely used on take-off. We usually took off in maximum dry power because if the afterburners did not light simultaneously, with the thrust of 3,250 kg on each engine and a take-off weight of 7,500 kg, the aircraft could easily swing out of control. I remember that the speed increased so quickly that the aircraft left the ground on its own... I had not even retracted the gear when I heard "Steer course 330, the target is hostile, arm your weapons." I will not lie - I was quite apprehensive. Although Sizov took off after me, he was vectored onto the target first, when it reversed onto a westerly heading... After the attack by Kapitán Zinoviev the bandit slowed to about 200kts, descending to 4,000m altitude; it seems likely that this was due damage, but the aircraft remained intact and continued to fly to the west. We were a couple of dozen kilometres to the border when I heard the command to open fire and shoot down the intruder. The "RS" switch stood for "single salvo". Only four S-5s came out and all of them hit the target, damaging the fuselage and the left engine. My instinct of self-preservation prevailed: a further rocket salvo would have been unsafe as the consequences would be unpredictable if all thirty-two RSs hit. Instead I fired the 23-mm cannon in a rear-quarter attack from below as the target passed ahead of me. I finally ceased fire

The Mikoyan-Gurevich MiG-19 [Farmer], which was capable of supersonic speed in level flight, was the front-line interceptor in service with Soviet and Warsaw Pact air forces in the late 1950s and early 1960s. The aircraft is armed with four Kaliningrad K-8 (R-8) [AA-3 Anab] AAM. (Jarrett)

The two-seat North American F-100F Super Sabre was used extensively during the Vietnam War by forward air controllers (FAC) known as 'Misty'. The F-100F was also used for the first 'Iron Hand' missions which targetted enemy air defences. (USAFM)

In 1963, 4° *Stormo*, based at Grossetto near Elba, became the first wing in the Italian Air Force to be equipped with the Lockheed F-104G Starfighter. Eventually six wings would operate the type. (Getty)

about ten kilometres from the border. The enemy aircraft exploded and in the haze of the setting sun, three red-and-white parachutes blossomed. The earth was already quite dark. Visibility in the Zerbst region had now deteriorated below the minimum, so I was ordered to divert to the alternate airfield... on the landing run the Command Post warned me: "Beware, slow down, the right wheel is smoking." In fact, it turned out to be a fuel vapour escaping through a hole in the right-hand drop tank, which looked like smoke. After I taxied into the disarming bay the engineer came up to me, called me to the right wing and pointed to a 15-centimeter fragment crushed into the pylon of the drop tank. With this trophy and the gun camera film cassette, I arrived at the Command Post and reported to the regiment about the results on the sortie. From launching to the end of the engagement, the whole flight had lasted no more than 5 to 7 minutes.

FLEXIBLE RESPONSE

In the early 1960s, NATO strategy, as expressed in the military committee document MC-48, was that 'In the event of aggression [the USSR] will be subjected immediately to devastating counter-attack employing atomic weapons.' However, the U-2, Berlin and Cuban crises showed that a more flexible approach was needed to deal successfully with smaller scale threats which could be resolved at a lower level of force rather than all-out nuclear war. This led to the concept of 'Flexible

Above:
A Lockheed F-104G Starfighter of 306 Squadron of the RNAF. The unit was based at Twenthe and served initially as the conversion unit before being assigned to the tactical reconnaissance role. (USAF)

Left:
In 1963, the Turkish Air Force took delivery of 48 new-build F-104G Starfighters to establish four squadrons based at Murted. (USAF)

The French EC 3/7 'Languedoc' operated the Dassault *Mystère* IV in the ground-attack role from Nancy-Ochey during the late 1960s. (Bannwarth)

Response', which was explained in a document, MC 14/3 of 1967, establishing that 'the main deterrence to aggression short of full nuclear attack is the threat of escalation which would lead the Warsaw Pact to conclude that the risks involved are not commensurate with their objectives. Should an aggression be initiated, short of a major nuclear attack, NATO should respond immediately with a direct defence.' From the perspective of NATO air forces, the new strategy put a greater emphasis on conventional capability and on the tactical nuclear forces. Nuclear-capable aircraft in particular played an important role in gradual escalation by selective use of individual weapons as a show of resolve.

Soviet strategy remained more ambivalent towards nuclear weapons, which were seen as an integral part of the whole arsenal available to battlefield commanders. However, a CIA report on Soviet general-purpose forces in 1967 reported that 'the army, air, and naval forces of the Soviet Union are large but poorly structured for the role being cast for them. Molded in the early 1960s as an adjunct to the missile forces in a nuclear war, the general-purpose forces were given short shrift in budget deliberations. As a result, they now represent a compromise between what the military wanted and what the government granted. With the resources allowed them, the military purchased large quantities of weapons systems such as tanks, supersonic fighters, and submarines, but failed to provide the means of sustaining their forces in extended offensive operations. Ostensibly designed for attack in a general nuclear war, the Soviet general-purpose forces are in fact better suited for defense in non-nuclear conflicts.'

Both NATO and the Warsaw Pact faced significant challenges to their integrity in the mid-1960s. In the case of NATO, the first of these was the decision of France to leave the integrated military structure in 1966. French units were repatriated the following year: the F-100D units EC 3 and EC 11 left Lahr and Bremgarten respectively for Toul and Luxeuil. Moving in the opposite direction, the Canadian CF-104 reconnaissance squadrons at Marville moved to Lahr. Similarly, the USAF 25th, 26th and 66th TRWs were evicted from their bases at Chambley, Toul and Laon. The 25th TRW was disbanded, while the 26th TRW, equipped with the RF-4C, moved to Ramstein and the 66th TRW, with the RF-101C, moved to Upper Heyford. However, although it had left the integrated structure, France remained a member of the alliance. The second challenge for NATO was conflict between

Greece and Turkey in 1967, caused by political developments on Cyprus. As a result, US nuclear warheads were removed from both countries, but once again the alliance held.

The challenge to the Warsaw Pact was more fundamental; in early 1968, the election of a liberal government in Czechoslovakia heralded the 'Prague Spring' and with it the possibility of Czechoslovakia leaving the Eastern Bloc, followed perhaps by other countries. Diplomatic manoeuvring to re-establish Soviet control over the country continued throughout the summer, during which the Warsaw Pact Exercise *Sumava* practised the invasion on three fronts of 'a NATO country' which was simulated by Czechoslovakia. In fact, the exercise served as a dress rehearsal for Operation *Dunay*, a full-scale invasion of the country, which started in the early hours of 21 August. Some 20 divisions, mainly from the Soviet Army but including contingents from Poland, Hungary and Bulgaria, entered Czechoslovakia simultaneously from north, east and south. The operation, which included airborne assaults on airfields, was accompanied by electronic warfare support, including jamming and chaff corridors sowed by Tu-22PD EW aircraft of the 226 ODRAP. Fighters and fighter-bombers from the 4th VAP, based in Poland, blockaded Czech airspace and a number of units were deployed forward to Czech air bases. These included the MiG-17-equipped 42 GvIAP which deployed to Hradec Králové, as well as MiG-21 regiments from 6th and 11th GvIAD moving to airfields at Zatec, České Budějovice, Brno and Bratislava. Reconnaissance aircraft such as the Yakovlev Yak-27R were operated by 932 OGvRAP from Hradčany and by 164 RAP from Pardubice. No resistance was offered by the Czech forces, which were, in any case, completely overwhelmed and a new government, approved by the Soviet hierarchy, was installed in Prague. Once again, the Warsaw Pact was held together by coercion, although Romania was vociferous in denouncing the invasion.

Below:
A North American F-86K from EC 3/13 'Auverne' of the Armée de l'Aire (French Air Force) on the approach to Colmar in the early 1960s. The type was eventually replaced by the Dassault Mirage III. (Bannwarth)

Dassault Mirage IV A strategic bombers of the *Commandement des Forces Aeriennes Strategique* (CFAS – strategic air force command). In the late 1960s, the French nuclear deterrent was upgraded with the introduction of the AN-22, a 60-70kT free-fall bomb. (Dassault Aviation)

A line of Armée de l'Aire (French Air Force) SNASCO *Vautour* [Vulture] IIB light bombers of the, showing the interesting access to the bombardier's front cockpit. The type could carry a nuclear weapon, but was replaced in this role by the Dassault Mirage IV. (Jarrett)

The Soviet invasion forces remained in Czechoslovakia and in October the *Central'naya Gruppa Voysk* (CGV – central group of forces) was re-formed for service in the country. The air component of the new CGV was provided by the 131st *Smeshannaya Aviatsionnaya Diviziya* (SAD – mixed aviation division), comprising two regiments of MiG-21PF and one regiment of MiG-21R.

BRITISH AND FRENCH STRATEGIC & AIR DEFENCE FORCES, 1965 – 69

Although the four Canberra interdictor squadrons of RAFG and the four Canberra bomber squadrons of the Middle East Air Force (MEAF) Strike Wing based in Akrotiri, Cyprus, were armed with US tactical nuclear weapons under the 'dual key' system, the UK was an independent nuclear power in its own right. At its peak strength in 1960, the British strategic nuclear force comprised 18 squadrons within Bomber Command equipped with the Valiant, Victor and Vulcan, known collectively as the 'V-Force.' Unfortunately, the Valiant, like the B-47, had not adapted well to the low-level environment and the fleet was grounded in late 1964 after fatigue cracks were found in the wing spars. However, the Victor and Vulcan were unaffected and two squadrons of Victor B2BS, 100 Sqn and 139 Sqn at Wittering, and three squadrons of Vulcan B2A, 27 Sqn, 83 Sqn and 617 Sqn at Scampton, were charged with maintaining the British independent nuclear deterrent with the Blue Steel stand-off weapon. The V-Force/Blue Steel system was replaced in mid-1969 by the

WE WILL BURY YOU! 1960-69   119

Left:
Throughout the 1960s the air defence of northern France was provided by the 30e Escadre de Chasse Tout Temps (all-weather fighter wing), from bases at Creil and Reims. The unit was equipped with the SNASCO *Vautour* IIN, all-weather interceptor. (Bannwarth)

Lockheed UGM-27 Polaris A-3 Submarine Launched Ballistic Missile (SLBM) operated by the Royal Navy. The Thor IRBM had been withdrawn from RAF service in 1963 as had also the majority of the Bloodhound SAM units. By 1964, Fighter Command defended the British Isles with six squadrons of Lightning, based at Wattisham, Leconfield and Leuchars. A sole Javelin FAW9-equipped squadron at operated from Binbrook.

France pursued its own independent nuclear force in the late 1960s having successfully detonating a warhead, *Gerboise Bleue* (Blue Jerboa), in 1960. Over the next five years the weapons and a suitable delivery system were developed and the French independent nuclear deterrent entered service in 1965.

The independent strike force, the CFAS – strategic air force command expanded from one *Escadre de Bombardment*, (EB – bomber wing) 92, equipped with the SNASCO *Vautour* IIB, to include a further three wings. These were EB 91, EB 93 and EB 94, each of which comprised three strike *escadrons* of Dassault Mirage IV, armed with the AN-11 weapon, and supported by one *escadron* of Boeing C-135F tankers. The entire force was dispersed over France, with each *escadron* based at a different airfield. Meanwhile, the air force had also replaced most of the US and British types in its inventory with French-built aircraft. The F-84F and F-100D remained in service in the ground-attack role within *Commandement de la Force Aérienne Tactique* (FATac – tactical air command), but they were being steadily replaced by the Dassault Mirage III. However, by 1965 the *Commandement des Forces de Défense Aérienne* (CAFDA – air-defence command) had been completely re-equipped with the Dassault *Mystère* and Super *Mystère* day fighters and the *Vautour* IIN all-weather interceptor.

SOVIET STRATEGIC & AIR DEFENCE FORCES, 1965 – 69

From the mid-1960s, the DA began to practice long-range missions in regiment-sized formations to simulate attacks on targets in the USA. The first of these was flown, on 1 October 1965, by 23 Mya-3M [Bison] from 79 TBAP. From their base at Ukrainka, near Seryshevo on the border with north-eastern China, the formation transited to rendezvous with tanker aircraft over Kamchatka before descending to low-level and heading for the Aleutian Islands. From here they flew northwards following the border between the USSR and the USA and then returned to drop their weapons

The Sukhoi Su-15 [Flagon-A] interceptor entered service with the PVO-Strany in 1965, replacing the Sukhoi Su-9 [Fishpot] and Su-11 [Fishpot-C]. The aircraft was capable of Mach 2.2 and carried up to four Kalingrad K-8 [AA3 Anab] missiles. (Sputnik)

A Myasishchev 3MD [Bison-C] at the air show which marked the 50th Anniversary of the October Revolution at Domodedovo airport near Moscow in 1967. A number of new types including the Mikoyan-Gurevich MiG-23 [Flogger] and MiG-25 [Foxbat] and also the Sukhoi Su-15 were seen in public for the first time. (Jarrett)

on the bombing range at Litovka in Primorskiy Kray. The mission, which lasted over 11hrs, demonstrated the capability of the DA bomber force to reach into the USA.

Deliveries to DA units of the Tu-22 continued through the late 1960s and by the end of the decade there were some 257 of the type in service. From 1966, this included the Tu-22K [Blinder-B] variant, which could be armed with the Raduga Kh-22 air-to-surface missile (ASM). Throughout the second half of the decade, Tu-16, Tu-20 and Tu-22 aircraft from the DA, as well as the AV-MF, continued to actively probe the defences of the USA and NATO.

The continuous upgrade of the PVO-Strany continued and the air defences of the 'high north' were bolstered with the arrival of the Tu-126 [Moss] Airborne Early Warning (AEW) aircraft and the Tu-128P [Fiddler] long-range interceptor. The Tu-126 was operated by a single unit, 67 *Otdel'naya Aviaeskadril'ya Dal'nego Radiolokatsionnogo Obnaruzheniya* (OAE DRLO – independent long-range radar surveillance squadron), which was based at Šiauliai in Latvia. From here, the aircraft would typically transit three hours northwards to remain on station for two hours 30min patrolling the area of Novaya Zemlaya and Franz Josef Land. These missions involved working closely with the Yak-28P interceptors of 641 GvIAP, which maintained a detachment of aircraft operating from Rogachevo on Novaya Zemlaya and Tu-128P interceptors of 518 IAP based at Talagi, Arkhangelsk. Additionally, in the summer 67 OAE DRLO detached two aircraft to operate from Olenya on the Kola Peninsula. Rather than controlling interceptors directly, the radar feed from the Tu-126 was fed into the PVO data system by secure data-link; the interceptors were then controlled via the Vozdukh GCI system. In this way the PVO hoped to detect and intercept incoming US bombers while they were still at high-level over the Arctic Ocean before they descended to their low-level ingress routing.

The Tu-128P, which was armed with the R-4R [AA-5 Ash] semi-active radar and R-4T infra-red AAM,

served with three regiments in the Arctic north, 72 GvIAP at Amderma, 445 IAP at Savatiya near Kotlas and 518 IAP at Talagi. Another new type to see service in the late 1960s, the Sukhoi Su-15 [Flagon], was also introduced as a gradual replacement for the Su-9, Su-11 and MiG-21PFM. The first unit to receive the type was 611 IAP in the Moscow PVO district; by the end of the decade eight regiments around the periphery of the USSR had been re-equipped.

US AIR FORCES, 1965 – 69

In 1964 the number of USAF ICBM on ground alert equalled, for the first time, the number of manned bombers on alert. From that time the importance of the *Chrome Dome* airborne alert force declined sharply: the Minuteman and Titan II ICBM were becoming more numerous and offered far more cost-effective way to maintain a nuclear alert force. In 1965, a proposal by the US Secretary of Defense Robert S. McNamara to discontinue *Chrome Dome* was challenged by the USAF commanders, but as a compromise the operation was scaled down dramatically. By 1967, it was limited to four nuclear-armed aircraft carrying out airborne alert indoctrination (training) flights over the Thule monitor route. Unfortunately, on 22 January 1968, a B-52G of the 380th SBW armed with four live B28 nuclear weapons suffered a fuselage fire and crashed close to

A McDonnell F-4C Phantom armed with two Martin AGM-12 Bullpup AGM. The missile was guided via a radio link to the weapons systems operator (WSO) in the back seat of the Phantom. (USAF)

Thule, causing an international scandal in regard to nuclear safety. This was not least because the USA had ignored the explicit ban by the Danish government of nuclear weapons from all of its territories and airspace, including that of Greenland. As a result, airborne alert was suspended immediately and the SAC bomber force was held instead at ground alert. In 1968, the original dispersal plan for the B-47 force was revived for the B-52 so that aircraft would be widely scattered in the event of a crisis, making them more difficult to target. The reduced requirement for airborne alert coincided with US involvement in the Vietnam War during which Operation *Arc Light*, which ran from 1965 to 1970, deployed the B-52 in the tactical bombing role in Vietnam.

Much of the burden of operations in Vietnam was borne by TAC. Beginning in 1965, four F-100D wings were deployed to South Vietnam to carry out airstrikes against Việt Cộng (VC) forces in South Vietnam, Cambodia and Laos. Later the F-100D and F-100F were used as 'Misty'; fast FAC directing interdiction missions against VC supply routes and also as 'Wild Weasel' defence suppression aircraft over North Vietnam. Deep strike missions into North Vietnam were flown by two F-105D Thunderchief-equipped wings, the 355th TFW at Takhli and the 388th TFW at Korat, in Thailand. The F-4D Phantom-

Opposite:
An image that epitomises the frontline of the RAF in the late 1960s: an Avro Vulcan B2 strategic bomber of 50 Squadron is escorted by English Electric Lightning F6 interceptors of 5 Squadron. (Crown Copyright)

equipped 8th TFW based at Ubon, Thailand provided fighter sweep/escort and was armed with Raytheon Air Intercept Missile (AIM)-7D/E Sparrow semi-active radar missile and the Raytheon/General Electric AIM-9D Sidewinder infra-red seeing missile. By 1970, the F-4 had replaced the F-105 in the bombing role and the RF-4 was being used for reconnaissance missions over North Vietnam by the 432nd TRW at Udorn. Meanwhile, most of the F-100-equipped wings based in the USA had also been re-equipped with the F-4C/D, although in 1967 the 474th TFW at Cannon AFB, New Mexico, received the General Dynamics F-111A all-weather strike aircraft.

Also in the continental USA, the F-101, F-102 and F-106 interceptors of ADC, reinforced by ANG units, continued to maintain alert under the command of CONAD and NORAD. The requirements of TAC, especially in relation to operations over Vietnam, meant that the F-4C/D could not be spared to replace the interceptor force in Alaska, as had been requested by CONAD in the early 1960s. Instead, Operation *White Shoes* (later renamed Operation *College Shoes*) continued and the F-106 alert aircraft in Alaska were frequently scrambled to intercept Soviet long-range aircraft operating close to the coast. In late 1968, there was also increased Soviet aerial activity off north-eastern Canada, and in response, a detachment of aircraft from the F-106-equipped 27th FIS was deployed to Goose Bay from November. The Soviet aircraft were probably not expecting to encounter any fighters in this remote region, but on 13 May 1969 two F-106 scrambled from Goose Bay and intercepted two Tu-95 bombers off the coast of Labrador.

EUROPE AND CANADA, 1965 – 69

The late 1960s was a period of consolidation for the air forces of northern Europe, although most experienced some decrease in size because of budgetary restrictions. In the UK, the RAF amalgamated the three functional commands, Bomber, Fighter and Coastal Commands, into the single entity of Strike Command in 1968. In the same year all three Canadian services were amalgamated to become the Canadian Armed Forces (CAF). The Canadian 1 Air Division had already lost two squadrons from its strength (434 Sqn and 444 Sqn) in 1967; in 1969, 3 Wing at Zweibricken closed and its two remaining squadrons were divided between those at Lahr and Baden-Solingen.

Earlier in the decade, most of the European air forces operating the F-84F, F-86E and F-100D sought a replacement for these obsolescent types. Unlike the earlier replacement of the F-84G with the F-104, there was no consensus and each country made a different choice. The Belgian Air Force acquired the Dassault Mirage V, the Netherlands Air Force purchased the Northrop NF-5 Freedom Fighter, whereas the Danish Air Force procured the Saab F-35 Draken (dragon); all of these new types entered squadron service in 1970. Meanwhile the Norwegian Air Force had taken delivery of the Northrop F-5A, which eventually equipped six squadrons. Both Turkey and Greece also received the F-5, each air force operating five squadrons of the type.

The replacement for the F-100D and the F-102A in USAFE was the F-4C/D, which eventually equipped nine fighter wings in Europe: From 1966 the 401st TFW was based at Torrejon, near Madrid, Spain. Previously the airfields of Torrejon, Morón and Zaragoza had been used by SAC as forward operating bases for the B-47 under Operation *Reflex*. Between 1960 and 1964, air defence of these bases had been undertaken by an F-102 detachment of the 497th FIS.

Throughout the NSWP air forces, the various marks of the MiG-21 were upgraded to more modern variants. The Polish *Wojska Obrony Powietrznej Kraju* (WOPK – national air-defence forces) also underwent a re-organization in 1967, when some units were disbanded and others were re-designated. Amongst these was 5.PLM-Sz based at Bydgoszcz, which became 3.PLM-B and moved from 8.DLM-Sz to report directly to the *Dowództwa Lotnictwa Operacyjnego* (DLO – operational aviation command), at Poznan. This arrangement had become necessary because in a major change of policy, the USSR had decided to equip some of the more dependable NSWP forces with tactical nuclear weapons. The 3.PLM-B was therefore equipped with the Sukhoi Su-7BM (*Bombardirovschik Modernizeerovanniy* – modernized bomber) which could carry the Soviet 6U-57 weapon. Polish pilots and ground crews began training for the nuclear strike role at the Soviet training facility at Krasnodar, near the Black Sea port

The Dassault Super Mystère remained in service with the 12e EC well into the 1970s. The aircraft began to be camouflaged in the closing days of the 1960s. (Bannwarth)

of Novorossiysk during 1964 and became operational two years later. During the Warsaw Pact Exercise *Lato-67*, held across Poland and East Germany in 1967, a Su-7 delivered an IAB-500 *Imitatsionnaya Atomnaya Bomba* (imitation atomic bomb), which simulated a nuclear burst using liquid fuel, phosphorous and high explosive. The live nuclear weapons were held under Soviet control and initially they were stored in Russia, to be transported forward only once they were required for combat use. However, this arrangement proved to be impractical and under Project *Wisła*, nuclear storage sites were secretly built in Poland. The Arab-Israeli 'Six Day War' of 1967 occurred almost simultaneously with *Lato-67* and it delivered some important lessons on tactical air power, including the vulnerability of aircraft on the ground. As a result, the WOPK was one air force which started to practice the dispersal of aircraft and *Drogowe Odcinki Lotniskowe* (DOL – highway strip operations).

THE SECOND DECADE

At the beginning of the 1960s it had seemed that missiles would soon replace the manned bomber and interceptor. However, as both sides of the Cold War recognized the need to be able to respond to minor aggression with a limited conventional response rather than a full-blown nuclear strike, the inherent flexibility of manned systems ensured their survival. Nevertheless, the development of strategic bombers on both sides had ceased and the remaining 1950s designs, in the shape of the B-52 and Tu-95, were to remain the mainstay of SAC and the DA until the end of the Cold War. The story for tactical and air-defence aircraft was different: the revolution in aircraft design that had taken place in the late 1950s was reflected in the supersonic fighters designed and built in the 1960s and similar innovation in the latter part of the decade would also spawn a new generation of aircraft which entered service in the 1970s.

Meanwhile, in Western Europe, NATO forces re-organized as a result of France withdrawing from the integrated military structure, while in Eastern Europe the Warsaw Pact reflected on the consequences of the Czechoslovakian uprising. In Southern Europe, Turkey and Greece continued to regard each other suspiciously while political events on Cyprus drew them towards inevitable conflict.

Above:
A Northrop F-5A Freedom Fighter of 338 Skv of the RNoAF based at Øland. In the anti-shipping role, the aircraft could be armed with the AGM-12 Bullpup missile. (Luftfartsmuseum)

Left:
A Republic F-84F Thunderstreak of 36° *Stormo* based at Gioia del Colle. The wing re-equipped with the F-104G Starfighter in the mid-1960s, but the F-84F remained in Italian service into the early 1970s.

CHAPTER 3
FREEZING FRONTIERS 1970-79

"The Cold War with its sterile paradox of freezing frontiers without eliminating the risk of conflict did not point the way to a solution." Willy Brandt, 1971

No-one knew it at the time, but 1970 marked the chronological half-way point of the Cold War. It was also a watershed, preceded by two decades of international crises and rising tensions, and followed by two more decades of slow improvement in international relations. Diplomatic initiatives to work towards a mutually peaceful coexistence started under US President Richard Nixon and First Secretary of the USSR Leonid Brezhnev, who adopted a policy of détente between the two sides. Nixon visited Moscow in 1972 and a return visit to Washington was made by Brezhnev the following year. The Strategic Arms Limitation (SALT) talks began in 1972, the Mutual and Balanced Force Reduction (MBFR) talks commenced in Vienna in 1973 and in the same year, the Conference on Security and Cooperation in Europe (CSCE) opened in Geneva. The final act of CSCE, issued in Helsinki two years later, stated that 'the participating states recognize the interest of all of them in efforts aimed at lessening military confrontation and promoting disarmament which are designed to complement political détente in Europe and to strengthen their security.'

However, all of these negotiations took place against a background of Mutual Assured Destruction (MAD) in the event of a nuclear war and of a huge concentration of force in Europe. The air forces which had evolved during the 1950s and 1960s had matured by 1970 and most of the front-line units and their bases remained extant from then until the end of the Cold War. The main focus of air power remained in Europe: two-thirds of the tactical aircraft strength of the VVS FA was concentrated in the DDR, Poland, Hungary and Baltic, Byelorussian and Carpathian military districts and both the UK and the US maintained sizeable tactical air forces in the BRD. Furthermore, both sides were continuing to develop and improve the equipment and training of their forces.

US AND SOVIET STRATEGIC & DEFENSIVE FORCES, 1970-74

In the early 1960s, the ballistic missile had overtaken the strategic bomber as the main delivery system for nuclear warheads in both the US and the USSR. By 1974, the US had a strategic missile inventory of 1,054 ICBM and 656 SLBM, while that of the USSR included 1,575 ICBM and 720 SLBM. Both sides still retained sizeable forces of manned bombers, although

A full salvo of 68mm SNEB (Societe Nouvelle des Etablissements Edgar Brandt) rockets are fired from a Hawker Siddeley Harrier GR3 at a target on the air weapons range at RAF Holbeach. During the 1970s, the typical armament for the Harrier comprised the SNEB rocket and the Hunting BL755 Cluster Bomb. (Richard Cooke)

the composition of these forces changed little through the late 1960s and early 1970s. In the US, SAC operated around 440 B-52D, G and H variants which were supplemented by a further 66 General Dynamics FB-111. A strategic bombing version of the F-111 tactical bomber, the FB-111 replaced the B-58 in SAC and equipped the 380th BW at Plattsburgh AFB and also the 509th BW at Pease AFB. Throughout the 1970s an almost continuous modification programme to the B-52 ensured the type continued to be combat effective. The night/adverse weather capability at low-level was improved by the addition of Low-Light Television (LLTV) and Forward Looking Infra-Red (FLIR) systems and the defensive Electronic Counter Measures (ECM) suite was also enhanced. The AGM-28 Hound Dog of the 1950s was replaced by the Boeing AGM-69A short-range attack missile (SRAM), 20 of which could be carried by a B-52. The SRAM, with a range of some 1,060km, did not have the reach of the Hound Dog, which had nearly eight times the range, but it was considerably more accurate than its predecessor.

Although the SAC line-up changed little in the new decade, the air-defence forces of CONAD were upgraded and many of the F-102 and F-106 units were re-equipped with the F-4. One F-4E squadron, the 43rd TFS, deployed from Florida to Elmendorf AFB in 1970, to take responsibility for the air-defence of Alaska. The unit also maintained QRA from the forward operating bases at King Salmon, Galena, and Eielson AFB. Although the F-4E represented a major improvement in capability over the F-102, the airframes did not cope well with the particularly cold conditions of the winter of 1970/71. In a reversal of the trend in the early 1960s for missiles to replace aircraft, the BOMARC SAM system was decommissioned in 1972.

In the USSR, the composition of the DA forces, like those of SAC, were virtually unchanged in the early 1970s. The DA operated only about 100 Tu-95 and 35 Mya-3M long-range bombers; its main strength was the 450 Tu-16 and 170 Tu-22 medium-range bombers. During this period, bomber units trained intensively in delivering ASMs, including live firings of Kh-22 [AS-4 Kitchen] missiles. At the same time, the air-defence forces of the PVO-Strany continued the progressive replacement of older interceptors with the Su-15. From 1972, the IA-PVO inventory also included the

The General Dynamics FB-111A replaced the Convair B-58 Hustler in SAC. The aircraft had an internal weapons bay (which could accommodate two AGM-69A SRAM) and four on under-wing pylons. The two outer pylons did not rotate, so the wings could not be swept if they were used to carry extra fuel tanks. (USAF)

MiG-25P [Foxbat], which could sustain speeds up to Mach 2.8 and reach an altitude of 78,000ft. The aircraft had originally been designed to counter supersonic US bomber aircraft such as the B-58 and the ill-fated North American XB-70 Valkyrie and it caused some concern in US intelligence circles because of its assumed capabilities. It was indeed an impressive machine, but when Lt V.I. Belenko landed a MiG-25 at Hakodate in Japan on 6 September 1976 the intelligence services discovered that they had significantly over-estimated its capabilities. Although various prototype versions of the aircraft had been flying since the mid-1960s, the MiG-25P first entered operational service with 764 IAP at Perm in 1971; in the same year the 61 IAP at Baranovichi (near Minsk) and 786 IAP at Pravdinsk (near Gorky) also converted to the type. Three more PVO Polki re-equipped with the type over the following three years.

The Arab-Israeli War of 1973 caused a brief international crisis when the USSR indicated that it would intervene to prevent the destruction of the Egyptian 3rd Army which had been surrounded by Israeli forces in the Sinai desert. Nuclear warheads were reported to be en-route to Egypt. On 25 October 1973, US forces were brought to DEFCON 3, the highest readiness state since the Cuban Crisis just 11 years previously. The situation was swiftly resolved, but the conflict led to the oil crisis of 1973–74, when Arab nations applied an oil embargo on the US and other countries that had supported Israel. Between October 1973 and March 1974, the price of oil rose from $3 to $12 a barrel. The shortage of oil during this period directly affected NATO air forces, which were forced to reduce their flying hours dramatically. Air forces on both sides of the Cold War were already implementing lessons learned from the 1967 Arab-Israeli conflict and in particular the vulnerability of aircraft on the ground to pre-emptive air attack. Programmes of 'hardening' and 'toning down' were being implemented across both NATO and Warsaw Pact airfields: aircraft were no

During the 1970s, AAR support for Soviet long-range aviation was provided by Myasishchev 3MS-2 [Bison-B] tankers. A total production of the Mya-M4 and 3M was only 92. (Sputnik)

A Tupolev Tu-16K [Badger-C] refuelling from a Tu-16Z [Badger-A] tanker. The refuelling hose is streamed from the right wingtip of the tanker and is connected to the left wingtip of the receiver. The spherical bob-weight on the end of the hose is visible behind the wing of the receiver. (Luftfartsmuseum)

Soviet pilot Lt V.I. Belenko, serving with the 513 IAP based at Chuguyevka, some 190km north-east of Vladivostok, defected on 6 September 1976. He landed the Mikoyan Gurevich MiG-25 he was flying at Hakodate airport (Japan), but ran off the end of the short runway. The aircraft was subsequently dismantled and flown to the USA where it was examined in forensic detail, then reassembled and test flown. (Getty)

longer parked in straight lines along taxiways, but were housed in concrete Hardened Aircraft Shelters (HAS) which were also camouflaged to make them a difficult target. The 1973 war emphasized many of the lessons of Vietnam, such as the vulnerability of tactical aircraft to SAMs and the need for them to be fitted with Radar Warning Receiver (RWR) equipment and to be fitted with on-board ECM.

CENTRAL REGION TVD & WESTERN TVD, 1970 – 74

The RAF, which had streamlined its command structure in the late 1960s, underwent a major re-equipment programme in the early 1970s. Perhaps the most radical initiative was the introduction of the Hawker Siddeley Harrier, the world's first vertical/short take-off and landing (V/STOL) combat aircraft. The Harrier was introduced to 1 Sqn at RAF Wittering, as well as 3 Sqn, 4 Sqn and 20 Sqn at RAF Wildenrath in Germany, and tasked with Close Air Support (CAS) of the army. The Harrier force quickly established procedures for 'field operations' away from conventional airfields, making them an almost impossible target for counter-air operations. The strike/attack and reconnaissance units of RAF Germany also replaced the aging Canberra with more modern types: three Phantom FGR2 squadrons formed at RAF Brüggen and one Phantom and two Hawker Siddeley Buccaneer S2 squadrons formed at RAF Laarbruch. In the nuclear strike role, the Phantom was armed with the US-supplied B57 weapon and the Buccaneer with the British-designed WE177; both were designed to reach targets in the DDR and western Poland. Another three Phantom squadrons based at RAF Coningsby were not nuclear-capable, but instead were designated for tactical support of the UK Mobile Force. In the

Yakovlev Yak-28PM [Firebar] supplemented the Tupolev Tu-128 as an all-weather interceptor in the Arctic high north. The 641st GvIAP operated the type from Rogachovo Air Base on Novaya Zemlaya Island until the mid-1980s. (Sputnik)

event of hostilities, the UK-based Harrier squadron was expected to deploy to Norway and the Phantom squadrons at Coningsby to Denmark.

The RAF maritime forces were also completely re-equipped. Four squadrons of Hawker Siddeley Nimrod replaced the Shackleton in the maritime patrol aircraft role, greatly increasing the effectiveness of the RAF anti-submarine capability, and two squadrons of Buccaneers were formed to operate against Soviet maritime surface forces. The V-Force now comprised four squadrons equipped with the Vulcan (44 Sqn, 50 Sqn, 101 Sqn and 617 Sqn) at RAF Waddington and RAF Scampton which retained a tactical nuclear role with the WE177 bomb. Also there were three Victor AAR tanker squadrons (55 Sqn, 57 Sqn and 214 Sqn) at RAF Marham and a Victor-equipped strategic reconnaissance squadron (543 Sqn) at RAF Wyton. Two nuclear-capable Vulcan-equipped squadrons (9 Sqn and 35 Sqn) were based in Cyprus forming the NEAF Strike Wing.

The UK was also host to USAFE tactical fighter units including two wings of F-4D (the 48th and 81st TFW) based at Lakenheath and Bentwaters/Woodbridge and the 20th TFW at Upper Heyford, which was equipped with the F-111E. All of these units were nuclear-capable and while the F-111 had the range to reach deep into the Eastern Bloc, the F-4 units might expect to deploy into Germany in the event of conflict. Based in Germany were a further three USAFE ground-attack wings of F-4C/D (36th TFW at Bitburg, 50th TFW at Hahn and 52nd TFW at Spangdahlem) and an F-4C/D all-weather fighter wing, the 86th TFW at Ramstein. Learning from the experience of Vietnam, the 81st TFS at Spangdahlem was equipped with the EF-4C Wild Weasel IV. This variant of the F-4 was fitted with the AN/APR-25 Radar Homing and Warning System (RHAWS) and the Texas Instruments AGM-45 Shrike anti-radiation missile, so that it could locate and destroy the SNR-75 target tracking radar of the S-75 SAM system. Also in the 4 ATAF area, the Canadian air presence in Europe was reduced further in 1971, with 1 Wing at Lahr being disbanded, which left only three squadrons (421 Sqn, 439 Sqn and 441 Sqn) of CF-104 at Baden-Solingen to form the new 1 Canadian Air Group (1 CAG). The reduction in the number of squadrons was due at least in part to the high attrition rate of the CF-104 during routine training. When formed, 1 CAG relinquished the nuclear strike role but continued as a conventional ground-attack unit.

Although the 86th TFW was part of the USAFE contribution to 4 ATAF, one of its constituent units, the 32nd TFS, continued to be based at Soesterburg to bolster the air-defence forces of the Netherlands. The Dutch airspace was defended by two squadrons,

322 Sqn and 323 Sqn at Leeuwarden, which operated the F-104G in the all-weather fighter role; two other Starfighter units, 311 Sqn and 312 Sqn at Volkel flew in the ground-attack role. The NF-5A, which had replaced the F-84F in the inventory of four squadrons, was also employed as a ground-attack aircraft. Like the Dutch, the Belgian Air Force also had two F-104G all-weather fighter units, 349 Sqn and 350 Sqn at Beauvechain, and two F-104G ground-attack units, 23 Sqn and 31 Sqn at Kleine Brogel. Like the Dutch, the balance of the Belgian force, two wings of Mirage V, was dedicated to ground-attack.

During the 1960s, the Luftwaffe had increased in both strength and importance. It was the largest operator of the F-104G, with seven wings of the type based at Nörvenich, Lechfeld, Büchel, Memmingen, Hopsten, Neuburg and Wittmund. Five of these were ground-attack units, which also had a nuclear role. They were supplemented in the conventional ground-attack role by three *Leichten Kampfgeschwader* (LeKG – light bomber wings), equipped with the Fiat G-91.

Two wings, JG 71 and JG 74, flew the F-104G as an all-weather fighter until they were re-equipped with the F-4F Phantom II in 1973. Two ground-attack wings, JaBoG 35 and JaBoaG 36 also converted to the F-4F in 1975, but the first Luftwaffe Phantom-equipped units were in fact the two *Aufklärungsgeschwade* (reconnaissance wings), AG-51 and AG-52, which received the RF-4E in 1971.

Started in the early 1960s, the NATO Air-defence Ground Environment (NADGE) project was finally completed in 1973. Using the latest computer technology, the NADGE system was a semi-automatic early warning and weapon controlling system linking the air-defence forces of Norway, Denmark, the Netherlands, Belgium, the *Bundesrepublik Deutschesland* (BDR), France, Italy and Greece also Turkey. It represented a major leap forward in capability from the previous generation of non-integrated manual systems in each country. The NADGE had a system of 84 ground stations and covered a front from Norway to Turkey: some 4,800km. Apart from the manned

The RAF developed a unique ability to deploy off-base to dispersed field sites with the STOVL capability of the Hawker Siddeley Harrier GR1. These aircraft are from 1 Squadron based at Wittering. (Bramall)

interceptors, the system also controlled a belt of MIM-14B Nike-Hercules SAMs, covering the Hi-MEZ (High Missile Engagement Zone) along its length and a further belt of MIM-23 HAWK, covering the Lo-MEZ which stretched across Denmark and the BDR. The French air-defence system was incorporated into the NADGE, but French combat forces remained under French national, rather than NATO, control. Similarly, UKADGE the British equivalent system remained separate from, but compatible with NADGE.

Although the French forces were no longer included in the NATO integrated military structure, French Air Force units were expected to supplement 4 ATAF in time of crisis. By 1970, all units flew French-built aircraft: the ground-attack units of *Force Aérianne Tactique* (FATac – Tactical Air Force) were equipped with the Mirage IIIE or the SEPECAT Jaguar A, while the air-defence units of CAFDA had begun to be re-equipped with the Mirage F1C. The FATac also benefitted when a contract to supply the Mirage 5F to Israel was cancelled and the aircraft were delivered to EC 3/13 (and later EC 2/13) at Colmar. In 1972, FATac also gained a tactical nuclear role, with the deployment of the AN-52 nuclear weapon, which could be carried by the Mirage III and also the Jaguar.

On the other side of the Iron Curtain, the air force of the DDR, the LSK/LV, like that of its western counterpart, had expanded and increased in importance. Six wings were equipped with the MiG-21, with the main variants in East German service being the MiG-21 SPS (*Sduv Pogranichnovo Sloya* – boundary layer wing flap blowing) and MiG-21SPS-K (*Kanone* – cannon), both of which were sub-variants of the MiG-21PFM. The LSK/LV was predominantly an air-defence force, but as the MiG-21 replaced earlier types in service, so aircraft became available to form 31.*Jagdbombergecshwader* (JBG – ground-attack wing) (later re-numbered JBG-37) was formed in 1971 at Drewitz with the MiG-17; the first East German ground-attack unit.

By far the most important air force based in the DDR was the Soviet 16th VA (renumbered from the

The Ballistic Missile Early Warning System (BMEWS) consisted of three radar sites at Clear in Alaska, Thule in Greenland and Fylingdales in the UK. Two McDonnell Douglas F-4M Phantom FGR2 interceptors of 56 Sqn are seen overflying the 'golf ball' radomes covering the radar heads. (Richard Cooke)

A Handley Page Victor SR2 strategic reconnaissance aircraft of 543 Sqn at RAF Wyton. The equipment pallet could carry four F49 survey or eight F96 reconnaissance cameras. Additional fuel tanks were fitted at either end of the pallet. The nine Victor SR2s remained in service until 1974. (Crown Copyright)

24th VA in 1968). It was equipped with the most modern types and comprised five regiments of MiG-21SMT [Fishbed-K] (*Sapfir Modernizirovannyy Toplivo* – modernized, Sapfir-21 radar and increased fuel capacity) and MiG-21PFM and, from 1973, three regiments of the Mikoyan-Gurevich MiG-23 [Flogger] variable-geometry fighter. There were also six regiments of Su-7B/BM ground-attack aircraft in East Germany. These were backed up by another three fighter regiments of MiG-21SM/SMT and three ground-attack regiments of Su-7BM or Sukhoi Su-17M of the 37th VA based in Poland. Entering service in 1970, the Su-17M [Fitter-C] was a variable-geometry derivative of the Su-7, with improved take-off and landing performance over the latter. The export version of this aircraft, the Su-20, was used in the tactical reconnaissance role by 7.*PLB-R of the Wojska Lotnicze* (Polish Air Force) based at Powidz. Although the *Wojska Obrony Powietrznej Kraju* (Polish Air-defence Force) had undergone restructuring in 1967, further changes were made four years later; in particular, and in an unusual step, 40.PLM at Świdwin replaced its MiG-21PF fighters with the older Lim-6bis ground-attack aircraft. The new structure of the Polish Air Force included two *Brandenburską Dywizję Lotnictwa Szturmowo-Rozpoznawczego* (Brandenburg assault and reconnaissance divisions), each comprising two ground-attack regiments of LiM-6bis plus one reconnaissance regiment, and the *Pomorską Dywizję Lotnictwa Myśliwskiego* (Pomeranian Fighter Division), consisting of three regiments equipped with the MiG-21PF/M.

In Czechoslovakia, the post-1968 government had become one of the most ruthlessly oppressive of the Eastern Bloc regimes and was therefore trusted by the Soviet leadership. As a result, the Czech Air Force was spared the fate of the Hungarian Air Force and, having been purged of any 'dissident elements,' it remained a formidable force fulfilling both air-defence and ground-attack functions. It was mainly equipped with modern variants of the MiG-21, but also included Su-7BM ground-attack aircraft and the Czech-built Aero L-29R Delfin [Maya] reconnaissance aircraft.

During wartime, the Warsaw Pact tactical air forces in the Western TVD planned to establish a number of air supremacy corridors, some 50km wide, extending into the BRD, overwhelming the local air-defences –

both aircraft and SAM systems – so that the ground forces could advance unmolested by NATO aircraft. The role of the Soviet FA aircraft did not extend to deep interdiction, for example to neutralize NATO nuclear forces, since this was the remit of surface-to-surface missile (SSM) forces. However, Soviet FA forces deployed in the DDR and Poland did have a secondary nuclear capability: fighter regiments such as 35th IAP at Zerbst, 159th IAP at Kluczewo-Stargard and 871st IAP at Kołobrzeg included pilots who were combat ready in the nuclear strike role.

NORTHERN REGION TVD & NORTH-WESTERN TVD, 1970–74

The security of the North-western TVD was of two-fold importance to the USSR: firstly, it included the strategic naval base at Severomorsk, near Murmansk and secondly it covered potential trans-Polar attack routes from North America. The paucity of airfields in a region consisting largely of uninhabited tundra and the waters of the Arctic Ocean was reflected in the long-range Tu-128P and Yak-28P interceptors operated by the 10th *Otdel'naya Armiya* (OA PVO – independent PVO army), which operated from bases around Murmansk and Arkhangelsk. Additionally, the airfield at Rogachevo on Novaya Zemlaya in the high north was home to the MiG-17PF-equipped 991st IAP; however, the obsolescent MiG-17 was replaced by the more suitable Yak-28 when 641 GvIAP moved permanently to Rogachevo from Petrozavodsk, near Lake Onega in 1972.

As well as the 10th OA PVO, the North-western TVD also included the 76th VA of the Leningrad VO, and the 35th *Protivo Lodochnyy Aviatsionnyy Diviziya* (PLAD – anti-submarine aviation division), of the AV-MF based at Fedotovo, near Vologda. The latter division comprised three regiments of Tu-142 [Bear-F] naval MPA. Based on the original Tu-95 design, the Tu-142 was optimized for long-range maritime reconnaissance and anti-submarine warfare operations. While the PVO forces in the TVD were intended to provide defence against air attack, the units of the 76th VA were equipped to support ground forces defending

The AdA operated the North American F-100D Super Sabre through the early 1970s. EC 3/11 'Corse,' based at Toul-Rousières, kept their aircraft in this silver finish until 1975, just before the unit re-equipped with the SEPECAT Jaguar A. (Bannwarth)

In the mid-1960s, some 30 PVO-Strany regiments were equipped with the Sukhoi Su-9 [Fishpot] interceptor, but the type was replaced by the Mikoyan MiG-25P [Foxbat] and Sukhoi Su-15 [Flagon] during the early 1970s. (Getty)

the region. A tactical reconnaissance regiment (98th GvRAP) equipped with the Yak-28R was based at Monchegorsk, near Murmansk. Three ground-attack regiments of MiG-17, MiG-21SMT and Su-7BM operated from bases around Leningrad.

Soviet submarines sailing from Severomorsk, or Tu-142 MPA flying from Fedotovo would first have to round North Cape before transiting through the GIUK Gap and then in to the Atlantic Ocean. The nearest of NATO air forces to the Soviet border was the RNoAF: two squadrons in particular 331 Skv and 334 Skv based at Bodø, were equipped to counter the expected threat. The former, equipped with the F-104G was an air-defence unit, while the latter flew the F-5A armed with the Martin-Marietta AGM-12 Bullpup ASM in the anti-shipping role. A single ASW unit, 333 Skv, operating the Lockheed P-3B Orion MPA was based at Andøya: F-5-equipped ground-attack units at Rygge, Sola and Ørland completed the combat elements. After detection and interception by

FREEZING FRONTIERS, 1970–79 141

A flight of Mikoyan Gurevich MiG-23M [Flogger-B] interceptors taxi out for a training sortie during Exercise *Karpaty*, in the Carpathian Military District (Ukraine), 1977. The MiG-23M was introduced into VVS/PVO service in 1970. (Sputnik)

Right:
The Mikoyan-Gurevich MiG-21 SMT [Fishbed-K] was fitted with an enlarged and distinctive dorsal fuel tank. This aircraft was operated by 296 IAP at Altenburg, East Germany during the 1970s and early 1980s. (Getty)

Below:
A double brake parachute was fitted to the Sukhoi Su-7B [Fitter-A] because of the high approach speed of the aircraft, thanks to its 63° swept wings. This Su-7 has just landed at an airfield near Moscow in 1970. (Sputnik)

Norwegian forces, the submarine or MPA would be handed over to NATO aircraft operating from the UK or Iceland. Keflavik was home to the USAF 57th FIS, which operated the F-102A until 1973, after which it was re-equipped with the F-4C. The interceptor force was supported by a permanent detachment of Lockheed EC-121 Warning Star aircraft from the 551st AEW&C wing. A permanent P-3 detachment assembled from USN units on six-monthly deployments from their permanent bases in the US, also operated from Keflavik. These aircraft were frequently augmented by CAF CP-140 MPA detached from their bases in Canada. During ASW operations all of these forces would work closely with RAF Nimrod MPA of 120 Sqn, 201 Sqn and 206 Sqn flying from RAF Kinloss. Soviet aircraft flying into the UK Air Defence Region (UK ADR would be intercepted by the RAF Northern QRA force at Leuchars, comprising 43 Sqn with the Phantom FG1 and 111 Sqn with the Lightning F3. These aircraft might be directed by fighter controllers using the ground-based radar head at Buchan or Saxa Vord, or by the crew of an Avro Shackleton AEW2 airborne radar aircraft of 8 Sqn; additionally, AAR support for the interceptor squadrons was provided by Victor K1 tanker aircraft.

In time of crisis, the ground forces on the NATO Northern Flank would be reinforced by close-support aircraft such as the Harrier GR1 from 1 Sqn RAF and the Canadair CF-116 (also known as the CF-5) from 434 Sqn and 435 Sqn of the CAF which would deploy from their bases in Canada. The security of the Baltic approaches was primarily the responsibility of the Royal Danish Air Force (RDAF) although their squadrons would be reinforced by RAF Phantom squadrons from Coltishall and supported by the Luftwaffe units in northern Germany and also two Marineflieger F-104G wings, MFG-1 and MFG-2.

The most numerous interceptor in the PVO-Strany organisation during the 1970s was the Sukhoi Su-15TM [Flagon-F], seen here armed with R-98MR [AA-3 Anab] radar guided missiles The Su-15TM variant, which entered service in 1971, was equipped with the Taifun-M radar and additional aerodynamic modifications. (Sputnik)

Two English Electric Lightning F6 interceptors from 5 Sqn refuel from a Handley Page Victor K2 over the French Alps. The two squadrons of Lightnings based at RAF Binbrook, deployed to Cyprus each year for an air-to-air firing camp. (Paxton)

QRA LAUNCH

23 APRIL 1970
Fg Off S.W. GYLES, 23 SQN RAF

It was about 04:00hrs that morning when the squawk box crackled into life with the familiar "Leuchars, this is Buchan, alert two Lightnings." In the event, only one aircraft was scrambled with my flight commander Squadron Leader 'Chalkie' White at the controls. Meanwhile, mayhem was breaking out on the station. Squadron personnel were being called in to ready more aircraft. The crew of the Victor tanker on the Operational Readiness Pan (ORP) was brought to readiness, and I was getting inundated with telephone updates from Buchan.

Squadron Leader White had just returned from his sortie, shadowing two Bear Ds in the pitch black when the squawk box crackled into life again: "Leuchars, alert two Lightnings and as many more as you can get. We have 80 unidentified tracks rounding North Cape."

Within 5min and in total RT silence I was cleared onto the runway by a green from an Aldis light from ATC and I was thundering off in the early light of dawn. Lift off speed was around 175kts; I cancel [after]burners almost immediately to conserve fuel; drag the throttles back to cruise nozzles (some 88 percent) then advance to 95 percent, just below the rpm when the nozzles would close again, then a cruise climb at M0.9 to 36,000ft. With the radar, nav aids and IFF also switched off I headed off north to a position far, far north-east of the Scottish

Two Blackburn Buccaneer S2 maritime strike aircraft performing 'buddy-buddy' refuelling. Two squadrons of these aircraft were also based at RAF Laarbruch, Germany in the overland strike/attack role. (Paxton)

A Beriev Be-12 [Mail] amphibious Maritime Patrol Aircraft photographed in 1967. The type entered service in 1960 and remained on the AV-MF inventory until the end of the Cold War. (Sputnik)

mainland. Twenty minutes later I reckoned I was there and switched on went the radio, radar and IFF. What I saw staggered me. My B-scope display was swamped with contacts from 20 out to 60 miles. A radio check with Saxavord determined that there were some 60 contacts in my area. At that point I made visual contact with the 'enemy'. There were finger-four formations of Badgers and Bears everywhere: I did not need the radar any more, since it was just a matter of latching on to the nearest formation and start taking photographs, moving up from the rear of the formation; one photograph either side and the underside of each aircraft. I had photographed three of that first formation when a shadow went over my cockpit. I glanced up to see another four-ship of Badgers cross over me about 500ft above.

At about this time I was advised that our tanker was in the vicinity. A check of my fuel gauges showed that a bit of juice [fuel] would not go amiss. I asked for 'pigeons' (heading and distance) to the tanker, to which the controller replied that he had not a clue since he had some 60 contacts in close proximity and all heading south-west. I called the tanker to turn 180°, to which he replied could I hold on for 5min as he was intercepting three Bears. He eventually turned around; I got my fuel and returned to the melee, to be joined by another Lightning. For another 90min we again mixed with the huge formations with just the occasional interlude to get fuel. By the time all three of us had to break off and head back to base on minimum fuel I had intercepted and photographed three Bear Ds, six Badger Ds and one Badger C. The other Lightning,

flown by Graham Clark, had intercepted seven aircraft, and the Victor had accumulated three. But that was not the end of the story.

Quite conveniently, the tanker pilot reported that he was sitting with a Bear D that was heading straight for Leuchars and did we have any film left to record the event for posterity. So, we went to join him and expended the last of our films in various three-ship formations. At around 200 miles to go to base the Bear rocked his wings and turned gently away.

SOUTHERN REGION TVD AND SOUTH-WESTERN TVD, 1970 – 74

In the southern region, *Grupo Operacional* (operational group) 501 of the *Força Aérea Portuguesa* (FAP – Portuguese Air Force) continued to operate the F-86F from a base at Monte Real. In 1974, a military coup in Portugal – the 'Carnation Revolution' – brought in a socialist government which both distanced itself from NATO and withdrew from the various colonial wars in Guinea, Mozambique and Angola. As a result, the FAP was greatly reduced in size and a number of FIAT G-91 aircraft were repatriated. These were used to form a new unit, Esc 62, at Montijo.

In contrast to the obsolescent types operated by the Portuguese, the Italian Air Force was fully equipped with modern types. These included the Aeritalia-built F-104S (S – *Super*), an improved version of the F-104G, with more thrust and the capability to carry the Raytheon AIM-7 Sparrow semi-active AAM. The F-104S replaced the F-104G in six *Stormi*, while three further *Stormi* retained the F-104G. Another Italian-designed and built type, the two-engine FIAT G-91Y, equipped 8° *Stormo* at Cervia and also 32° *Stormo* at Brindisi in the ground-attack role.

After the withdrawal of the Fairey Gannet AEW 3 early warning aircraft in the early 1970s, some 12 Shackleton MR2 aircraft were modified to carry the AN/APS-20 radar from the Gannet in order to continue early warning radar coverage of the UK – Faroes – Iceland Gap in the North Atlantic. (Lee)

Two McDonnell F-101B Voodoos from the 136th FIS of the New York ANG fly over Niagara Falls. Air National Guard units shouldered much of the responsibility for the air defence of the USA within NORAD. (USAF)

FREEZING FRONTIERS, 1970–79 149

The THK underwent a re-organization in 1972 when *Filo* (squadron) numbers were changed to match the numbering of the *Ana Jet Üs* (jet air bases). The THK combat element included six F-100C/D-equipped *Filo*, one F-104G *Filo*, two F-102A *Filo* and five F-5 *Filo*.

In 1973, when King Constantine II of Greece was deposed by a military junta, the *Ellinikí Vasilikí Aeroporía* (Royal Hellenic Air Force) was renamed the *Ellinikí Polemikí Aeroporía* (EPA – Hellenic Military Air Force). By then the service had expanded to 11 *Moira* (squadrons) operating F-5A, F-104G and F-102A as well as the long-serving F-84F. However, the political manoeuvring continued in Greece until 15 July 1974 when the Greek junta orchestrated a military coup in Cyprus, which overthrew the Cypriot President, Archbishop Makarios. This in turn precipitated an invasion of northern Cyprus by Turkish forces. Operation *Attila* was launched at dawn on 20 July 1974 with a pre-strike reconnaissance by an RF-84F of 184 *Filo* which had been deployed forward to Inçirlik for operations. At 06:00hrs, Turkish paratroops being carried in Douglas C-47, Lockheed C-130 and Transall C-160 transport aircraft began an airborne assault at Gönyeli, some 16km from Nicosia. An hour later, amphibious landings were made to the west of Kyrenia, and during the course of the afternoon two further waves of paratroops were dropped near Nicosia. On the first day of operations, the F-100 and F-104 units of the THK flew over 115 ground-attack missions in support of ground forces. These accounted for the destruction of at least four Soviet-built T-34 tanks used by the Cypriot National Guard. One RF-84F from 184 *Filo* was shot down and the pilot, *Üsteğmen* (Leiutenant) I. Karter was killed. At the end of the day the THK had also lost two F-100 (from 132 *Filo* and 171 *Filo*) and a number of the paratroop-carrying aircraft had been damaged by Cypriot anti-aircraft fire. Meanwhile, the EPA was unable to join the fighting due to the distance between Greece and Cyprus – and the presence of the US 6th Fleet, which attempted to contain the hostilities; a force of seven newly delivered F-4E Phantoms was launched from Iraklion to attack Turkish positions on Cyprus, but this was recalled when it was made clear that they would be intercepted by USN aircraft. The RAF Vulcan bombers of the NEAF Strike Wing were also evacuated from Akrotiri to Malta to prevent any further escalation of the conflict. Turkish air operations continued early the next morning with attacks by F-100s on a road

An Aeritalia-built F-104S Starfighter of 102° *Gruppo*, 5° *Stormo* of the AMI based at Rimini. The F-104S, which entered service in 1969, was powered by a FIAT-built J79-GE-19 engine. The type was capable of carrying the AIM-7 Sparrow radar-guided air-to-air missile (AAM). (Schleiffert)

FREEZING FRONTIERS, 1970-79

Above:
The mediocre performance of the FIAT G-91 was addressed in the two-engined FIAT G-91Y 'Gino' which also had an improved wing. This aircraft is in service with 101° *Gruppo* of 8° *Stormo* which was based Cervia, near Rimini, and operated the G-91Y from 1971. (Thomas)

Left:
A Republic RF-84F Thunderflash tactical reconnaissance aircraft of 348 *Moira* of the EPA – Greek Air Force, based at Larissa. Greece was the last operator of the RF-84F, with their aircraft remaining in service until the early 1980s. (Schleiffert)

Thirty-two examples of the remarkable Lockheed SR-71 Blackbird strategic reconnaissance aircraft were built. The aircraft, which was operated by the 9th SRW, was capable of sustained flight at speeds above Mach 3. (USAF)

convoy attempting to reinforce the front-line forces of the Cypriot National Guard. An unfortunate incident occurred during the afternoon of 21 July after a Greek naval flotilla was reported to be off Paphos. A force of 12 F-100C from 181 Filo, 16 F-100D from 111 Filo and 16 F-104G from 141 *Filo* were launched to attack, but the ships that they engaged were actually from the Turkish Navy. Two destroyers were damaged and another, TCG *Kocatepe* (D-354), was sunk. During 21 July, some 200 ground-attack sorties were flown by the THK, for the loss of two F-100s and one F-104 to ground fire. The first intervention by the EPA was on 22 July when a two F-5A from 337 *Moira* intercepted a two THK F-102s over the Aegean Sea near Limnos. In the ensuing combat each side fired two missiles but despite claims by both sides to have shot down the other,

there were no casualties on either side. However, on the same day a further two Turkish F-100s were lost to ground fire. Seventeen F-104s from 141 *Filo* attacked Nicosia airport, before a ceasefire was declared that evening. The immediate result of the conflict was an embargo by the US on arms to Turkey and in particular the sale of F-4E aircraft and F-102 spares. As a result, the Turkish Air Force had to source new aircraft instead from Italy, in particular the F-104S.

Like the NATO southern flank, the south-western TVD of the Warsaw Pact was also less homogenous and harmonious than its northerly counterpart. Hungary was still distrusted by the Soviet leadership, and the Hungarian Air Force remained the smallest air force in the Warsaw Pact, comprising just three regiments of MiG-21 air-defence fighters and a single reconnaissance squadron. The main instrument of air power in Hungary was the Soviet 36th VA which fielded three fighter regiments and four ground-attack and reconnaissance regiments. The fighter regiments included 515 IAP with the MiG-21SMT at Tököl and 14th GvIAP at Kiskunlachaza with the MiG-23M, both of which also fulfilled a secondary nuclear strike role. Neighbouring Romania remained a full member of the Warsaw Pact, but had distanced itself from the USSR and did not permit foreign forces to be based within its borders. The *Fortele Aeriene ale Republicii Socialiste Romane* (Romanian Air Force) comprised two *Divizia Aviație Vânătoare Tactica* (tactical fighter divisions), each comprising a fighter-bomber regiment equipped with MiG-17 or S-102, two fighter regiments and a reconnaissance squadron equipped with variants of the MiG-21. In Romanian service, the MiG-21PF was designated the MiG-21RFM (*Radar Forțaj Modernizat* – radar; reheat upgraded), the MiG-21PFM version was known as the MiG-21RFMM (the additional 'M' – re-engined) and the MiG-21R became the MiG-21C (*Cercetare* – reconnaissance).

In contrast to Hungary and Romania, Bulgaria remained closely aligned to the USSR and was rewarded accordingly with its own tactical nuclear capability. This involved the same weapon custodianship arrangement as that in Poland and it was discharged by 2 IAE/19 IAP, equipped with the MiG-21M, based at Graf Ignatiev. In the mid-1970s, pilots from this unit began their nuclear training in the USSR.

SOVIET A-BOMB DELIVERY

1976

Lt S. POPOV, BULGARIAN AIR FORCE

'The weapon delivery manoeuvre was the most difficult task and we usually performed it in at the end of the course. We did that at Krasnodar. Approaching the range, we accelerated to a speed of 1,050kph (560kts) and then started the pull-up manoeuvre. This was a loop, during which we dropped the bomb. The aircraft started the profile from about 100m altitude and the top of the loop was about 3,000m. In a 45º release, the bomb would fly forward for 7km, but when performing a 106º drop, however, it would eventually fall directly back onto the release point. You make a half-roll to recover and run for the deck. The bomb falls for about a minute or two. During this time, you have to get away safely so that the shock wave does not reach you. A very difficult task. The measure of excellence was an accuracy within 500m of the bullseye'

The Boeing KC-135Q was specifically designed to support SR-71 operations. The SR-71 used JP-7 a less-volatile fuel, so that, unlike the 'standard' KC-135, the give-away fuel had to be kept separate from the JP-4 fuel used by the tanker. (USAF)

In 1972, 21st IAP based at Uzundzhovo withdrew its MiG-19S aircraft and replaced them with the older MiG-17PF. The reason for this apparently backward step was the poor reputation of the MiG-19 in Bulgarian service. The RD-9B engines of the MiG-19 proved to be very unreliable and the Bulgarians experienced a high accident rate with these aircraft, losing almost half of their inventory of the type through accidents.

ATTRITION

The Bulgarian experience of a 48 percent attrition rate with the MiG-19 was not entirely untypical of the accident rates among combat aircraft at that time. The F-104 gained a notorious reputation as a 'widow maker' thanks to an attrition rate of 30 percent with the Luftwaffe and of 46 percent with the RCAF/CAF. The loss rate for the Lockheed F-104 in both the Dutch and Belgian service was around 35 percent and the Danish lost a similar proportion of their F-100D force. The lost rate for the MiG-21F-13 in Hungarian service was also around 37 percent. However, accidental losses were also dependent on a number of factors including the flying rate and the role of the aircraft: for example, the Canadians flew more hours per CF-104 than other nations flew their F-104G fleets and they did so exclusively in the high-risk low-level environment. Statistics can be presented in a number of ways, one being the loss rate per 100,000 flying hours. Using this measure, the Bulgarian MiG-19 rate was 100 aircraft lost per 100,000hrs, the F-104G was 139 aircraft, the RAF lost 41 Lightning aircraft and the MiG-21F in Soviet service was 30 aircraft. Between 1971 and 1975, the comparable rate for the McDonnell F-4 Phantom II F-4 in USAF service was 50 aircraft lost. But whichever way the statistics might be presented, there can be no doubt that the life of fighter aircrew at the height of the Cold War was challenging and often dangerous. One unfortunate accident occurred on 14 July 1970 during the Exercise *Zenit-70* when a Polish MiG-21PFM flown by *Kapitan* (Captain) H. Osierda from 11.PLM intercepted a Czech Air Force Su-7BKL; forgetting that he was flying a live-armed aircraft, he fired a K-13R AAM which destroyed his target. Fortunately, the Czechoslovak pilot, *Kapitán* F. Kružík ejected safely.

US AND SOVIET STRATEGIC & DEFENSIVE FORCES, 1975 – 79

Perhaps the most spectacular development in US strategic forces was the introduction of the Lockheed SR-71 Blackbird reconnaissance aircraft, which was capable of sustained cruise at Mach 3.2 at 85,000ft. The type was first introduced to the 1st SRS, 9th SRW at Beale AFB, California in 1968 and was used for reconnaissance missions over North Vietnam. From 1977, Detachment 4 was formed at RAF Mildenhall to carry out reconnaissance over the Baltic and the Barents Seas. The aircraft on these missions were supported by a Boeing KC-135Q Stratotanker, which carried the special fuel required by the Pratt & Whitney J58 engines of the SR-71. Two routes were flown: the first followed the Norwegian coast to the North Cape and into the Barents Sea, before turning to run towards Murmansk/Severomorsk then turning once more to fly parallel to the coastline of the Kola Peninsula, remaining in international airspace just 20km off the coast. These missions collected important data on the Soviet forces in the Murmansk area and in particular the activities of the Soviet Northern Fleet. The second profile, known as the 'Baltic Express' crossed Denmark over the Baltic Sea and ran along the Polish coast, past Kaliningrad towards the Lithuanian SSR and the Latvian SSR. The route then looped around the island of Gotland to pass through the narrow corridor of international airspace between it and the island of Öland to turn back towards Danish airspace. Flying at great height and speed, the SR-71 was virtually invulnerable to interception and could cover large areas of interest with its on-board sensors.

The line-up of the SAC bomber force remained virtually unchanged through the second half of the decade, although improvements to the B-52 bombing and navigations systems continued. In 1975, four SAC wings operated the B-52D, ten operated the B-52G and seven more flew the B-52H, a total of some 400 aircraft. In the second half of the decade, the number of aircraft reduced to 338, partly due to attrition and partly because of limitations derived from the SALT negotiations. During this time CONAD and TAC both underwent substantial re-organization. In 1975 CONAD was disestablished and Air Defense Command (ADC) took over as the US element of NORAD.

Two Bitburg-based McDonnell Douglas F-15A Eagle air superiority fighters from the 525th TFS, 36th TFW pass over Cochem castle on the River Mosel. The 36th TFW was responsible for the air defence of the 4ATAF region of southern Germany. (USAF)

However, this arrangement was short-lived as ADC was disestablished in 1979. The aircraft strength of ADC was transferred to the command of TAC, becoming Air Defense, Tactical Air Command (ADTAC). This re-organization combined with a major re-equipment programme with high-quality aircraft types which had been born out of the lessons learned in Vietnam. That conflict had highlighted the vulnerability of relatively large and un-manoeuvrable aircraft like the F-105 and F-4 in contrast to the smaller and more agile MiG-21; aircraft losses had also demonstrated the lethality of ground fire over the battlefield to conventional fighter-bombers. The McDonnell-Douglas F-15A Eagle interceptor and air superiority fighter entered service with the 1st TFW at Langley AFB, Virginia in January 1976 and the following year with the 49th TFW at Holloman AFB, New Mexico. The F-15A represented a departure from 'traditional' interceptors in that the previous 'Century Series' fighters had tended to sacrifice manoeuvrability in favour of performance: with a design that had been influenced by the overestimates of the capabilities of the MiG-25 prototypes first seen in the late-1960s, the F-15 benefitted from excellence in both performance and manoeuvrability. US air-defences were further improved with the introduction of the Boeing E-3 Sentry Airborne Warning and Control System (AWACS), which also represented a quantum leap in performance over the propeller-driven EC-121 that it replaced. Tactical Air Command (TAC), also received the first General Dynamics F-16A Fighting Falcon light-weight fighters which were issued to the 388th TFW in January 1979. These short-range but ultra-agile aircraft were intended to supplement the larger F-15 in establishing and maintaining air superiority over enemy escort fighters. Another new type to enter TAC service in the late 1970s was the Fairchild A-10 Thunderbolt, which was optimized for CAS to ground forces. In particular, it was intended to kill Main Battle Tanks (MBTs) such as the T-64 and T-72 which equipped Warsaw Pact armoured formations in Europe. The first combat ready A-10 unit was the 354th TFW at Myrtle Beach AFB, South Carolina in 1977.

Along with new equipment came new training regimes, including the establishment of

FREEZING FRONTIERS, 1970-79

The long-serving Boeing B-52G was updated in the early 1980s with the addition of the AN/ASQ-151 electro-optical viewing system (EVS) comprising low-light television (LLTV) and forward looking infra-red (FLIR) systems, which can be seen in the port and starboard turrets respectively under the nose. (USAF)

Exercise *Red Flag* at Nellis AFB, Nevada. Born from the experience of the Vietnam War that most combat losses occurred in the first ten sorties of an operational tour, Exercise *Red Flag* sought to simulate wartime missions over Eastern Europe as closely as possible, so that USAF aircrews could, in effect, fly those first ten sorties in peacetime. Realistic targets including replicas of Eastern European airfields, armoured columns and industrial targets were set up on the Nellis weapons ranges in the desert to the north of Las Vegas; these were defended by Soviet SAM systems and Northrop F-5 aircraft flown by the aggressor squadron, using standard Soviet tactics. Both SAM systems and aggressors used film rather than live weapons to make their claims and every exercise mission was debriefed in great detail so that aircrews could learn the lessons. The first Exercise *Red Flag* was held in 1975 and two years later participation was also opened to the RAF.

The Vietnam War had also demonstrated the need for defence-suppression missions to support operations against targets defended by SAMs and this was further borne out by the experiences of Arab and Israeli air forces during the Yom Kippur War of 1973. The 'Wild Weasel V' programme resulted in the appearance in 1978 of the F-4G Phantom, which could be armed with the AGM-45 Shrike and the AGM-78 standard ARM. The F-4G was issued to the 35th TFW at George AFB, California in 1978 and to the 52nd TFW at Spangdahlem, Germany, the following year. Operating in a pair with an F-4E 'missile carrier,' the F-4G would

orbit near the SAM engagement zone ready to attack any missile systems that it detected. Although the VVS also included Suppression of Enemy Air-defenses (SEAD) aircraft, the Soviet doctrine differed from the US approach, with dedicated aircraft embedded within the attack force and targetted against specific pre-identified missile systems. Types utilised included aircraft such as the Tu-16P (Pilon – pylon) which could fire up to 12 chaff-dispensing RPZ-59 rockets to establish a corridor through defences and the Tu-22KPD, which was armed with the Raduga Kh-22P anti-radar missiles (ARM). They were supplemented by the Yak-28PP (*Postanovschshik Pomekh* – jammer), which would escort the attack aircraft through the corridor, jamming enemy air-defence radars.

The Soviet DA began to replace the Tu-16 with the Tu-22M2 [Backfire-B], a variable-geometry supersonic long-range bomber in the mid-1970s. The 185 GvTBAP at Poltava became operational with the new type in 1975 and it was followed by the 840 TBAP at Solsty near Novgorod. These aircraft could with AAR, reach mainland US and carried up to three Kh-22 ASM; however, the VVS initially removed the AAR equipment so that the type would not be counted as long-range bomber in the SALT negotiations. The Tu-22M2 also saw service with the AV-MF. Meanwhile, the integration of the MiG-25 into the IA-PVO defences continued through the second half of the 1980s with another three regiments being re-equipped with the type. From 1978, new aircraft were completed to the

Originally conceived as a lightweight air superiority fighter, the General Dynamics F-16 Fighting Falcon had, by the end of the 1970s, become a capable ground-attack platform. This aircraft from the 4th TFS, 388th TFW is carrying one AIM-9L and one AIM-9J Sidewinder, a 2,000-lb Mk 84 bomb and an auxiliary fuel tank on each wing, with an ALQ-119 electronic countermeasures pod on the centreline. (USAF)

The USAF 81st TFW, based at RAF Woodbridge and Bentwaters, Suffolk converted from the McDonnell Douglas F-4C Phantom to the Fairchild A-10 Thunderbolt. In wartime, the six A-10 squadrons of the wing would deploy forward to bases in Germany. (USAF)

MiG-25PD [Foxbat-E] (*Dorabotannyy* – upgraded) standard, which included the Sapfir-25 (sapphire) radar, giving the aircraft a look-down shoot-down capability against low-level targets. Aircraft already in service were retrospectively modified to the same standard, becoming the MiG-25PDS (*v Stroyou* – in service). The original PVO plans had been to replace obsolescent interceptor aircraft such as the Su-9, Su-11, Yak-28P and MiG-21PFM with the Su-15 such that by 1975 there would be 41 regiments, representing half the PVO fighter strength, equipped with the Su-15. However, Su-15 production was halted in 1976 with only 29 front-line regiments operating the type. Nevertheless, from the late 1970s the Su-15 remained as the most numerous type of interceptor in PVO service. The remaining units, starting with 401st IAP at Smolensk-Senerny, were re-equipped instead with the MiG-23P [Flogger-G] and MiG-23ML (*Legkiyy* – lightweight), both of which were fitted with the Sapfir-23 radar.

An operational trial to simplify the command and control of FA and PVO units within the same military districts commenced in 1977: until then the fighter units in each organization were controlled by parallel command structures which did not coincide geographically. During the trial, all fighter units in the Baltic and Leningrad military districts whether PVO or VVS units, were placed under the tactical control of the local military district commander. Dual-role aircraft in FA service, such as the Mikoyan Gurevich MiG-21 and MiG-23, could thus be switched between roles, depending on the tactical situation within each district. This arrangement would later be adopted for most regions, leaving just five independent air-defence force armies covering strategically important areas.

EUROPEAN THEATRE, 1975–79

The dramatic increase in the capability of tactical aircraft during the late 1960s and early 1970s gave the Soviet military leadership reason to reconsider how FA assets might be used in a conflict. For example, the Su-7B of 1960 could carry some 2,000kg of ordnance over a combat radius of just over 160km in daylight and good weather, whereas the Sukhoi Su-24 [Fencer] of 1975 could carry 4,000kg of ordnance over a radius of 480km by day or night and in all-weather conditions. In the traditional Soviet doctrine, a combined arms ground offensive would be preceded by massive artillery bombardment followed by an assault by armoured forces leading to a breakthrough and rapid advance by tanks and armoured infantry. The role of the FA would be to establish air superiority over the frontal area and isolate the enemy front-line forces from their reserves and re-supplies. Deep interdiction and close support functions would be left to the artillery and missile forces. Each Front, comprising two armies and one air army, would execute two such thrusts and in the Western TVD three Fronts would attack NATO forces in the Central Region. The use of artillery and missile forces reflected the doctrine that the use of nuclear weapons was inevitable and, indeed, integral to any European conflict.

However, the Soviet military thinking of the mid-1970s recognized the inflexibility of the 1960s approach and the concept of the initial air operation was established in 1975. It was expected that the offensives by all three Fronts would open simultaneously, so that six corridors, each requiring a first wave of some nine to ten regimental missions (or around 350 sorties per corridor), would need to be established at the same time. The first wave, comprising of around 1,000 Su-7, Su-17/20 and/or MiG-17, would punch through the NATO frontlines and target the Hawk SAM belt and tactical nuclear delivery systems; they would be closely followed by a second wave of around 875 aircraft to consolidate the corridor, while a third wave of long-range aircraft would follow shortly afterwards to attack NATO nuclear-capable airfields and nuclear storage facilities in the rear areas.

During the late 1970s, large-scale exercises were held each year; high-level exercises such as *Zapad* (west) and *Soyuz* (union) tested the strategic command and control functions and occasionally incorporated smaller tactical exercises for front-line forces. Exercise *Granit* (granite) gave the air-defences of all Warsaw Pact countries the opportunity to practise their operational procedures against simulated targets. In the more tactically-based Exercise *Shchit* (shield), the aircraft of the FA and nuclear strike tactical air forces practised

The Convair F-106 Delta Dart remained in front-line USAF/NORAD service through the 1970s. This aircraft, from the 194th FIS, California ANG has fired a Douglas AIR-2A Genie missile. (NARA)

Learning lessons from combat during the Vietnam War, the USAF began to use 'adversary' aircraft to train aircrew in dissimilar air combat. The Northrop F-5E Tiger, a MiG-21-sized aircraft, was flown by US and UK-based 'Aggressor' squadrons using Soviet tactics and operational doctrine. (USAF)

the procedures for the initial air operation; for example, Exercise *Shchit-76* involved the forces of the USSR, Poland the DDR and Czechoslovakia. The scenario for most exercises involved an attempted NATO invasion of Eastern Europe using nuclear weapons followed by a counter-offensive by Warsaw Pact (WP) forces advancing across Western Europe as far as the English Channel. This would typically involve the use of around 600 nuclear weapons, of which approximately 33 percent would be delivered by aircraft. Although aircraft co-operated closely with ground forces, the degree of co-ordination was very basic and tended to rely on carefully pre-planned manoeuvres carried out at specific times. While WP aircrew performed well in such exercises, there was no evidence that they would be able to cope if the tactical reality was at odds with their rigid plan or if there was any slippage in the pre-planned time-line for the ground operation.

NATO forces also carried out frequent exercises: for example, Exercise *Central Enterprise* was an annual event involving all tactical air forces in the central region. Various local air-defence exercises were also mounted such as Exercise *Blue Moon* in Denmark, Exercises *Elder Joust/Elder Forest* in the UK and Exercise *Datex* in France. Additionally, a system of Tactical Evaluations (Taceval) tested the ability of each unit to generate sufficient combat ready aircraft to meet their wartime commitments and then required them to demonstrate their wartime role over two or three days. Taceval was run as a no-notice exercise by COMAAFCE (Commander Allied Air Forces Central Europe) evaluation teams. Most scenarios involved an initial attack by WP forces including chemical weapons and an escalation to nuclear war in a three-day timescale. NATO air forces also had pre-planned operations, for example under 'Option Alpha' all airfields in the DDR, western Poland and Czechoslovakia would be neutralized. However, unlike the WP air forces, subsequent operations were extremely flexible and tasking for CAS or air interdiction missions would be provided from the Air Tactical Operations Centres (ATOC) based on the requirements of ground and air commanders. CAS missions would be integrated into the battlefield by FAC, while long-range aircraft would have free routing beyond the ground commander's Fire Support Co-ordination Line (FSCL).

For NATO air forces, the advances in technology gave their aircraft a qualitative edge over their WP counterparts. Inertial navigation systems and improved weapon aiming systems enabled ground-attack aircraft to locate and attack their targets accurately while pulse-Doppler radars gave air-defence aircraft a look-down

A Dassault/Dornier Alpha Jet from *Jagd-Bomber Geschwader* (JaBoG) 49 taxies out for a weapons training sortie from Fürstenfeldbruck. The type, which replaced the FIAT G-91 in Luftwaffe service, is armed with a 27mm Mauser BK-47 cannon fitted in a pod mounting carried under the fuselage. (AirDoc)

Developed from the Mikoyan Gurevich MiG-25 interceptor, MiG-25RBS [Foxbat-D] reconnaissance aircraft was fitted with sideways looking airborne radar (SLAR) sensor to gather data. (Luftfartsmuseum)

shoot-down capability against low-level intruders. The USAF units in Europe where systematically upgraded during the late 1970s. The F-15A replaced the F-4E in the 36th TFW at Bitburg in Germany in 1977 and the following year saw the A-10 deployed to the 81st TFW at Bentwaters/Woodbridge in the UK. At the same time, the F-4C Phantoms based at Keflavik were replaced by the F4E and the E-3A was also deployed to Iceland. For the RAF, the introduction of the SEPECAT Jaguar GR1 into service at Coltishall and Brüggen in the mid-1970s released the Phantom FGR2 for the air-defence role, in which it replaced the obsolescent Lightning. In Norway, the F-5A was replaced in 334 Skv by the CF-104 in 1975, although replacement of the F-104 in the air forces of Norway, Belgium, the Netherlands and Denmark was aleady in the pipeline. All of these countries had chosen the F-16 to replace the F-104 and the first European unit to receive the F-16 was 349 Sqn of the Belgian Air Force, based at Beauvechain,

in January 1979. The left-leaning government of the Netherlands also took this opportunity to amend its contribution to NATO air forces, by limiting the RNAF to conventional air support operations (and thereby withdrawing from the nuclear strike role) and local air superiority.

FOXBAT INTERCEPT

28 FEBRUARY 1979
Maj ROLF NOEL, 334 SKV RNoAF

On 28 February 1979, I was launched from QRA at Bodø, leading another F-104G to investigate three Soviet Il-38 May anti-submarine aircraft that were operating in the Barents Sea, some 130km northeast of the

An early variant of the Tu-22M2 [Backfire-B], note the rounded air intakes, is intercepted over northern Norway by a RNoAF Canadair-built CF-104 Starfighter of 334 Skv operating from Bodø. (Luftfartsmuseum)

North Cape. After identifying the 'bogies', we turned back towards our forward operating base at Banak in the northernmost part of Norway; this by now was some 240km away. I led us down to low-level to carry out a reconnaissance on some shipping on the return leg. At 200ft over the sea, we were out of radio contact with the GCI controller. Suddenly I caught sight of a contrail coming towards us, high above and almost on a reciprocal course. It was moving fast; should we go for it. A quick fuel check said 'no', but with over 2,000hrs operational experience on the F-104, my brain said 'yes'. I told my wingman to shut down his radar, IFF and TACAN and follow me in silence. I gave him the sign to go into afterburner and we accelerated to 620kt. Then we pulled up into a slightly skewed 'Immelman', following a lead pursuit curve all the way up to whatever altitude we needed to catch the contact. Halfway through the manoeuvre we came back into radio coverage and the GCI controller suddenly broke in with some unnecessary chatter. It was very distracting, so I called 'Judy' (meaning that I did not need his help) and silence reigned once again. At this stage, my wingman fell out of formation and ended some trailing me by 16km, so I told him to head back towards Banak. The manoeuvre worked out perfectly for me since I arrived directly underneath the contact at 36,000ft and Mach 0.96. I could not believe my eyes: Was it really a Foxbat: Yes it was a MiG-25 Foxbat C. However, I was going in completely the wrong direction with my fuel getting critically low, but I knew that I had to take some photographs if I was going to be believed and took some ten images in around 15sec, ending up on his starboard side. Then he saw me and accelerated away, manoeuvring violently. I turned back towards the coast, picked up my wingman and we both landed at Banak with less fuel than I care to mention. Unfortunately, the

GCI controller was given credit for the intercept, even though it had been a completely self-positioned independent manoeuvre on my part. In reality it was only thanks to my own experience, judgement and also a healthy disrespect for fuel regulations – that we caught the Foxbat!

NATO aircrew were also able to practise low-flying regularly: they could fly as low as 500ft over most of western Germany and down to 250ft in formal Low Flying Areas (LFA). A transit route through the Netherlands, flown at 250ft, linked the German low-flying system with the coastal weapons ranges at Vliehors and Noordvaarder. Aircraft based in the UK could use a 250ft low-level link route that ran around the periphery of the UK as well as a number of small LFA inland, which were also linked by transit corridors. A similar arrangement existed in France for the AdA. The UK low-flying system was expanded in 1979, to include most of the UK in order to meet the demand for low-flying training and also to spread the noise nuisance over a wider footprint. In addition to low-flying within the UK, the RAF Vulcan squadrons carried out training detachments to Goose Bay in Canada, where vast LFA over sparsely-populated regions of Labrador provided an ideal opportunity for tactical flying. Air weapons ranges in Germany, Belgium, France and the Netherlands, plus, for UK-based aircraft, the UK, provided ample opportunity for ground-attack aircraft to practise weapon delivery profiles. For the Luftwaffe, the Italian Air Force, RAF Germany and USAFE units, these ranges were supplemented by the Air Weapons Training Installation (AWTI) at Decimomannu, Sardinia. The AWTI had originally been established by the RCAF in the late 1950s to use the air weapons range at Capo Frasca on the west of the island, but the Canadians left in the mid-1970s. From 1979, the AWTI included the

During the 1960s and 1970s, the Polish-built Aero Vodochody L-29 Delfin [Maya] was the standard training aircraft used by Warsaw Pact air forces. Over 2,000 were supplied to the USSR and the type could also be used in the light attack role. (Getty)

The first RAF Germany unit to equip with the SEPECAT Jaguar GR1 in 1975 was 14 Sqn based at Brüggen. This photograph, taken ten years later, also gives an impression of operations from a 'flight line' before the advent of dispersed Hardened Aircraft Shelters (HAS) to protect aircraft from attack. (Lee)

Air Combat Manoeuvring Instrumentation (ACMI) range, which used data-link to enable complex air combat training sorties to be debriefed properly.

In the AFSOUTH area, the air forces of Portugal and Italy remained unchanged, but those of Greece and Turkey continued to be modernized. As a result of the US arms embargo after the invasion of Cyprus, the THK found it increasingly difficult to operate the F-102 without spares support. Replacing the type in 182 *Filo* with the F-104S purchased from Italy provided enough spares for 142 *Filo* at Murted to continue flying the F-102 until 1979, by which time the embargo had been lifted. An order for the F-4E order placed before the invasion of Cyprus was then completed. The Greek EPA was unaffected by embargoes and took delivery of the first F-4E to 117 PM at Andravida in 1974; in addition, the Ling-Temco-Vought A-7H Corsair II was procured for 115 PM at Souda, where the type replaced the obsolete F-84F. The British presence in the Mediterranean was greatly scaled down following the government's decision in the mid-1970s to withdraw its permanent forces from the region. As a result, the Vulcan equipped squadrons (9 Sqn and 35 Sqn) and Lightnings of 56 Sqn left Akrotiri to return to the UK in January 1975. A Nimrod squadron (203 Sqn) and a Canberra PR7/9 reconnaissance squadron (13 Sqn) remained at Luqa, Malta for the next few years, but these had also been withdrawn by 1978. The introduction

of the Sukhoi Su-24 to 4th GvBAP and 63rd BAP at Chernyakhovsk, Kalingard in 1974 brought with it a quantum leap in the deep interdiction capability of the FA. Equipped with terrain avoidance radar (as opposed to the more complex Terrain Following Radar [TFR] used by the USAF F-111) the Su-24 was the first all-weather low-level strike aircraft to enter VA service. For shorter-range tactical operations the Mikoyan-Gurevich MiG-27 [Flogger-D], based on the MiG-23 airframe but optimized for the ground-attack role, started to be issued to FA units. Meanwhile export versions of the MiG-23 were delivered to NSWP air forces. The first service to receive these aircraft the Bulgarian VVS in late 1975, but deliveries were soon made to the air forces of Poland, Czechoslovakia, the DDR, Hungary and Romania. Nevertheless, variants of the MiG-21, the most modern being the MiG-21bis, still formed the backbone of the Warsaw Pact air forces in the late 1970s.

TACTICAL AIR-TO-GROUND WEAPONRY

Even during the 1970s, the 1950s-type general-purpose free-fall bomb still remained the simplest and most numerous air-to-ground weapon. Most NATO air forces used the US-supplied Mk 80-series of bombs which ranged from the 250lb Mk 81 to the 2,000lb Mk 84, while most Warsaw Pact air forces used the

A Lockheed F-104G Starfighter of JaBoG 34 based at Memmingen on the landing roll-out. During the 1970s, the Luftwaffe operated four wings of F-104G in the nuclear strike role. (Grondstein via AirDOC)

Soviet FAB-250 and FAB-500 (*Fugasnaya Aviatsionnaya Bomba* – high-explosive aviation bomb: 250kg and 500kg respectively). However, these weapons were not particularly effective against massed armour formations: unguided rockets or cluster bombs were more suited to such a large-scale mobile target. The French-built SNEB 68mm rocket was in widespread use with European air forces, while Canadian forces used the 70mm CRV-7 on the CF-104. Warsaw Pact forces used the S-5 rocket from the UB-32 launcher: like the US-built 2.75-inch Mighty Mouse system, this rocket had originally been intended as an air-to-air weapon, but while it proved too inaccurate for that role, it was very suitable for air-to-ground firing. However, rockets required careful aiming and a whole salvo might be required to kill a single tank. If a rocket might be compared to a rifle, then a cluster bomb, which could scatter bomblets over a wide area, would be likened to a shotgun and therefore be more appropriate for moving or widespread targets. The RAF introduced the BL-755, a cluster bomb specifically designed for use against Warsaw Pact vehicles, into service in the early 1970s; unlike a general-purpose bomb it did not require pinpoint accuracy and a single weapon had a kill footprint of some 75m by 20m, within which it might disable a number of targets. Thus, a 'stick' of four bombs dropped in a single pass could potentially destroy a large number of vehicles. In a similar role, the USAF fielded the CBU-24 (Cluster Bomb Unit), while the USSR developed the RBK-250 (*Razbros Bomba Konteynor* – scatter bomb container).

Other contemporaneous Soviet developments included the Kh-23 *Grom* (thunder) [AS-7 Kerry] and Kh-25 [AS-10 Karen] missiles which were based on the R-8 AAM. Unlike western AAMs which tended to be of slender design with relatively small warheads, the Soviet AAMs were large rockets which could be adapted to carry heavier warheads. Potentially, any tactical aircraft (such as the MiG-23) capable of carrying the R-8 could also carry the air-to-ground variant. The Kh-23 used radar guidance, and the Kh-25 used laser guidance. The equivalent US weapon was the AGM-65 Maverick, which used a TV-optical guidance system; some 35,000 Maverick missiles were delivered to the USAF in the 1970s.

The RAF Hawker Siddeley Nimrod maritime patrol fleet was upgraded to the MR2 standard in the late 1970s. The improved variant, seen here, featured the EMI Searchwater radar and the 'Yellow Gate' electronic support measures (ESM) carried in wingtip pods. (Lee)

Based on the Mil-8 [Hip] transport helicopter, the Mil-24D [Hind-D] was a purpose-built assault helicopter which saw service with Warsaw Pact air forces from the early 1970s. (MoD Russia/Wikimedia)

NATO military forces were trained and equipped to operate in a chemical environment, but NATO did not have chemical weapons in its inventory. However, Warsaw Pact did keep a stock which could be delivered by artillery, missiles or aircraft. Like nuclear weapons, their chemical munitions were regarded as being an intrinsic part of military operations. Tactical aircraft could be armed with the KhAB-250 variant of the FAB free-fall bomb.

THE RISE OF THE ASSAULT HELICOPTER

Both NATO and the Warsaw Pact deployed jet fighter-bombers for close air support of the ground forces, but it was increasingly recognized in the 1970s that the helicopter might prove a better weapons platform against armoured units. Slower moving and able to take advantage of even the smallest amount of ground cover, the helicopter could find target acquisition easier on the battlefield than its fast-moving counterpart. Attack helicopters could also escort tactical transport types to their landing sites during an assault, where they could also provide supporting firepower. The US experience in Vietnam had confirmed the tactical usefulness of the armed helicopter and the US Army had deployed the Boeing Vertol AH-1G Cobra in Europe. The British Army also armed its Westland Scout helicopters with the French-built Nord AT-11 ATGW (wire-guided anti-tank missile). However, it was the Soviet forces which fully embraced the offensive potential of the helicopter. The Mil Mi-8TVK [Hip-E] gunship variant of the tactical transport helicopter was operated in large numbers by Warsaw Pact air forces and from 1974, both FA and NSWP units in Europe also operated the Mil

After an embargo was placed on Israel in 1967, 50 Dassault Mirage 5Fs which were originally destined for the Israeli Air Force were diverted to the AdA and were operated by the 13 ième EC based at Colmar. (Bannwarth)

Mi-24D [Hind-D], a purpose-built assault helicopter which was armed with a Gatling-type gun as well as rockets and the 9M17 [AT-2 Swatter] *Skorpion* (scorpion) ATGW. The Soviet tactical concept was to use massed helicopter assaults to capture or neutralize important targets ahead of advancing armoured columns. Whereas the attack helicopter was regarded in NATO forces as being part of the army organic firepower, it was operated by the tactical air forces of the Warsaw Pact.

THE THIRD DECADE

Despite the optimistic starting points of SALT, CSCE and MBFR, the decade ended with deteriorating international relations after the Soviet invasion of Afghanistan in the last days of 1979. A number of other factors were beginning to come into play including the failing health of the Soviet leader Leonid Brezhnev, a simmering unrest in Poland and economic recession on both sides of the Iron Curtain. During the decade, the air forces of all the nations had continued the cycle of re-equipment: the combat aircraft of the late 1970s were more versatile than their predecessors, offering manoeuvrability with performance and the capability to operate at low-level in all weather conditions. Training exercises became ever more complex and realistic while the command and control arrangements evolved into more effective organizations. In Europe, aircraft operated from camouflaged airfields and both air and ground-crews were fully trained to work in conditions of Nuclear Biological and Chemical (NBC). To many of the participants, it seemed as if the Cold War had reached self-sustaining momentum and that the force structures established over the previous three decades had become permanent fixtures.

A McDonnell Douglas Phantom FGR2 of 56 Squadron armed with four British Aerospace Skyflash and four AIM-9 Sidewinder AAMs. The 'air defence grey' colour scheme was adopted by the RAF in 1978. (Lee)

CHAPTER 4
TEAR DOWN THIS WALL! 1980-89

"If you seek peace, if you seek prosperity for the Soviet Union and Eastern Europe if you seek liberalization: come here to this gate! Mr. Gorbachev, open this gate! Mr. Gorbachev, tear down this wall." Ronald Reagan, 1987

In first few years of the 1980s it seemed that much of the diplomatic progress of the previous decade had been reversed. The Soviet invasion of Afghanistan provoked a decision by the US not to ratify the SALT-II agreement which had been reached between First Secretary Brezhnev and President Jimmy Carter. Carter himself was replaced in 1981 by President Ronald Reagan, who took a much more confrontational stance against the USSR than his predecessor had done. At the same time, the Soviet Union itself entered a period of political uncertainty: when Brezhnev died in 1982, he was followed in quick succession by two 'old guard' politicians, Yuri Andropov and Konstantin Chernenko, both of whose instincts were for an adversarial approach to international relations. Apart from causing a rift with the US, the Soviet involvement in Afghanistan proved to be unexpectedly troublesome for the USSR, with echoes of the US experience in Vietnam some 15 years earlier.

Having survived the economic recession caused by the oil crisis of 1973, the countries of the Europe and North America were faced with another economic recession in the early 1980s. As the standards of living stagnated on both sides of the Iron Curtain, popular disaffection and resentment against domestic governments grew at the very time that international relations were worsening. In Eastern Europe, cracks were once again beginning to appear in the Warsaw Pact. The establishment of the Solidarność (Solidarity) trade union in Poland in 1980 was a direct challenge to the Communist regime and enjoyed widespread popular support. Although the USSR did not intervene directly in Poland, the Warsaw Pact exercise *Soyuz-80*, held close to the borders of Poland, was designed to intimidate the Poles. Furthermore, under intense Soviet pressure, the First Secretary of the *Polska Zjednoczona Partia Robotnicza* (PZPR – Polish United Workers' Party), Stanisław Kania was replaced by the hard-line General Wojciech Jaruzelski in 1981. Later in the year, Jaruzelski declared martial law in the country, but this move did little to slow the momentum of popular protest and soon Solidarność became the largest trade union in the world.

In NATO, the recession squeezed the defence budgets of many countries just as they were struggling to honour the agreement made in 1977 for every country to increase its defence spending by 3 percent in real times year-on-year until 1984. This arrangement

A Mikoyan MiG-31 [Foxhound] long-range interceptor on the landing roll, photographed some years after the end of the Cold War. The introduction of the MiG-31 and the Sukhoi Su-27 [Flanker] marked the modernization of the Soviet air defences in the Arctic high north in the 1980s. (Sputnik)

A Boeing B-52G Stratofortress of the 43rd Strategic Wing, based at Anderson AFB on Guam in the Western Pacific Ocean, dropping Mk82 500lb 'Snakeye' high-drag bombs in 1984. The bomb tails open after release to retard the bombs so that they do not damage the aircraft by detonating directly underneath it. A B-52 could carry up to 51 of these bombs, but the 'Cold War' weapons load would be more likely to be 20 Boeing AGM-86A Air Launched Cruise Missiles. (USAF)

also coincided with major re-equipment programmes in many European air forces to replace aging aircraft types such as the F-104G and Vulcan. Cutbacks in some military budgets were inevitable and it was unfortunate that reductions to the Royal Navy that were announced in the British defence review of 1981 were misconstrued in South America as signalling a lack of resolve, which resulted in the attempted annexation of the Falkland Islands by Argentina the following year. Fortunately, a robust campaign by British forces ejected Argentinian troops from the islands and also served to clarify British military intent to any doubting observers. However, NATO found itself at odds over the US 'Double Track' policy of deploying General Dynamics BGM-109G Ground Launched Cruise Missiles (GLCM) and Martin Marietta Pershing II IRBM into Europe unless the USSR withdrew the RSD-10 *Pioner* (Pioneer), [SS-20 Saber], IRBM that had been deployed in the late 1970s. The deployment of US missiles provoked popular anti-US protest in many European countries.

NORTH AMERICAN AND SOVIET STRATEGIC & DEFENSIVE FORCES, 1980 – 85

During the late 1970s, the Rockwell B-1A strategic bomber had been cancelled in favour of new ICBM systems and modifications to the existing B-52 fleet. At the time, the prime reason given for the decision was that the B-1 programme was significantly overrunning its budget and was no longer cost-effective; what was not made public at that stage was that the budget was instead being diverted to the development of the advanced technology bomber, which would eventually become the Northrop Grumman B-2 Spirit 'stealth bomber'. However, after the change in the US government in 1981, the Reagan administration increased the funding to the SAC budget with the result that the B-1 programme was reinstated to meet the requirement for a Long-Range Combat Aircraft (LRCA) which was intended to act as a launch vehicle for ALCM. A redesigned version of the aircraft, the

A General Dynamics F-111F from the 48th TFW, based at Lakenheath, Suffolk, in 1982. The aircraft is carrying four 2000lb GBU-10 Paveway II Laser-Guided Bombs (LGB) and is equipped with an AN/AVQ-26 Pave Tack laser designator pod which protrudes slightly from the aircraft internal weapons bay. The USAF developed its capability to drop precision-guided munitions during the early 1980s. On the night of 14/15 April 1986, aircraft from the 48th TFW bombed targets in Libya with LGBs in retaliation for terrorist attacks on US personnel. (USAF)

B-1B, was developed around the Boeing AGM-131A SRAM II weapon system and the work previously carried out in the B-1A programme meant that the new system could be in service by the middle of the decade. In the meantime, the B-52D, G and H as well as the FB-111A continued to equip the front line of SAC. The unique capabilities of the B-52 ensured its retention on the frontline right through the 1980s: no other aircraft could match is range and weapon carrying capabilities and continuous upgrades to its weapons systems and defensive equipment made it irreplaceable. Although the last B-52D was retired from service in 1983, a total of 272 B-52G and H models remained in SAC service through the 1980s. The fleet underwent further improvement when 98 B-52G, the first of an eventual total of 194 aircraft, were modified to carry the Boeing AGM-86B ALCM, a nuclear-capable weapon which used a terrain contour-matching guidance system (TERCOM) and had a range of some 1,500 miles. Being a much smaller aeroplane, the FB-111A was unable to carry the AGM-86B and its main armament remained the Boeing AGM-69 SRAM. The aircraft could carry two of these missiles internally and another four on wing pylons (with a limitation to performance), but the lack of potential for further upgrade to the FB-111A in the strategic role meant that its days in the SAC inventory were numbered and its eventual replacement by the B-1B became inevitable. Air-to-air support for USAF strategic and tactical aircraft, which had been provided by the KC-135 since the mid-1950s was significantly – if somewhat belatedly – updated during the 1980s by the retrofitting of more efficient Pratt & Whitney TF-33-PW-102 and CFM International CFM56 turbofans to the KC-135 fleet. This simple step instantly added to the USAF AAR capability because the more efficient fuel burn meant that the tankers had more give-away fuel, or could fly longer ranges or both. In 1981, there was a further enhancement to the SAC AAR fleet with the introduction of 60 McDonnell Douglas KC-10 Extenders. Uniquely, the KC-10 had both a boom and a hose and drogue system, so that it could be used equally by USAF, USN and USMC aircraft (as well as those of allies such as the RAF or the French Air Force).

Within NORAD, the air defence of the USA was undertaken by ADTAC, which in 1980 comprised six Air Divisions (Air Divs) within the USA plus Air Forces Iceland and the US-manned DEW-line radar sites in Alaska, Canada and Greenland. The Air Divs were organized geographically and included both ground radar units and fighter interceptor squadrons. Initially,

Right:
A flight of four McDonnell F-4D Phantoms of the 457th TFS, 301st TFW, USAF Reserve based at Carswell AFB, Texas, refuelling from a McDonnell Douglas KC-10 Extender in September 1983. The KC-10 provided a substantial increase in capability over the KC-135, although the USAF only procured 60 airframes. (USAF)

Below:
The Boeing KC-135R Stratotanker was a modification of the original KC-135 re-engined with the CFM International CFM56. (USAF)

each Air Div contained one regular air force squadron equipped with the F-106 or F-15 supported by two or three ANG squadrons equipped with the F-101 or F-106. However, a re-organization in 1982 reduced the front-line units considerably and left just four Air Divs controlling only five regular units: three F-15 squadrons (5th, 48th and 318th FIS) and two F-106 squadrons (49th and 87th FIS) which were supported by 11 ANG squadrons. After another organizational reshuffle in 1985 ADTAC was renamed 1st Air Force. In Alaska, the 21st TFW had replaced the F-4E with the more capable F-15A in 1980 and the first interception of Soviet aircraft by the new aircraft occurred on 24 November 1982 when two F-15s operating from the forward alert strip at King Salmon intercepted a DA Tu-95. The remaining interceptor units in NORAD were Canadian, comprising the three CF-101 squadrons of the CAF: 409 Sqn at Comox, 416 Sqn at Chatham and 425 Sqn at Bagotville; these CAF units maintained 5-minute QRA readiness and 416 and 425 Squadron, based in the east of the country, often intercepted Tu-95s in the Canadian Air Defense Identification Zone (CADIZ). However, by 1980 the CF-101 was showing its age and its replacement by the McDonnell CF-188 Hornet (known as the CF-18) started in 1982.

In 1980, the Soviet DA was reorganized from the three OTBAK structure introduced in the 1960s into five air armies: the 4th and 24th VA *Verkhovnoye Glavnokomandovaniye Operativnogo Naznacheniya* (VGK ON – Operational High Command), based in Poland and Ukrainian SSR respectively and the 30th, 37th and 46th VA *Verkhovnogo Glavnogokomandovaniya Strategicheskogo Naznacheniya* (VGK SN – Strategic High Command), based in the Far East, Central USSR and the Byelorussian/Baltic SSRs respectively. On their formation, the two VGK ON absorbed the long-range all-weather tactical bombers in their respective theatres: the 4th VA VGK ON in Poland took command of

The 159th GvIAD, based at Kluczewo, near Stargard, Poland, re-equipped with the Sukhoi Su-27 [Flanker] in 1988. Apart from the N001 Mech pulsed-doppler lookdown radar, the aircraft was also equipped with an OEPS-27 infra-red search and track system, enabling it to search passively without advertising its presence electronically. This photograph records the departure ceremony of the regiment from Poland after the Cold War, when all 39 Su-27s were redeployed to Petrozavodsk on the western shore of Lake Onega. (Schleiffert)

Superficially similar to the Mikoyan MiG-25 [Foxbat], the two-seat Mikoyan MiG-31 [Foxhound] was a completely new airframe, based around the BRLS-8B Zaslon phased array radar which was designed to detect low-level targets such as cruise missiles. Like the MiG-25, the aircraft was capable of speeds of up to Mach 2.8. (Sputnik)

the 132th BAD which comprised three regiments of Su-24 based in Kaliningrad and Latvia as well as the Polish-based 149th BAD, which was in the process of re-equipping with the Su-24M. Like its counterpart in Poland, the 24th VA VGK ON in the Ukrainian SSR also included two divisions of Su-24. By 1982 the VVS contained 12 Su-24 regiments which were based within striking range of the NATO Central Region. The mainstay of the Soviet strategic medium bomber force remained the Tu-16, but these were being slowly phased out of service in favour of a smaller number of the Tu-22M: in 1980 there were nearly 290 Tu-16 aircraft equipping DA units (plus a similar number in AV-MF service), but five years later this figure had decreased to 220. Small numbers of the Tu-22 also remained in front-line service through the 1980s in the Ukrainian and Byelorussian SSRs: approximately 100 Tu-22KD and KP variants were used by the 15th TBAD in the ground-attack/strike role armed with the Rh-22P [AS-4 Kitchen], while about 50 Tu-22R and RDM variants were operated by 11th and 290th GvODRAP in the reconnaissance and electronic warfare support roles. Meanwhile, the Tu-22M fleet itself was updated in 1983,

with the introduction of the Tu-22M3 [Backfire-C]. This variant featured a redesigned fuselage incorporating more powerful engines, an improved navigation/attack system and also provision for a rotary launcher for the Raduga Kh-15 [AS-16 Kickback] missile. Thanks to its revised profile, the new version of the aircraft had much improved performance in terms of both speed and range over earlier variants. Five of the six Tu-22M regiments in DA service were based in the western parts of the USSR (52 GvTBAP at Ryazan, south-east of Moscow and others in the Estonian, Byelorussian and Ukrainian SSRs) from which locations they could easily reach targets in Western Europe.

Meanwhile, just like the B-52 in USAF service, the 1950s-vintage Tu-95 proved indispensable to the VVS as a strategic platform, because of its long range and its load-carrying capacity. Mirroring the enhanced capability of the B-52, a new version of the Tu-95, was also introduced in the early 1980s. The Tu-95MS [Bear-H], which was in fact based on the Tu-142 airframe, could carry up to 16 of the 2,500-mile range Kh-55 [As-15 Kent] ALCM. The Tu-95MS first entered service with the 1023 TBAP at Semipalatinsk in the

TEAR DOWN THIS WALL! 1980–89   185

Above:
The Boeing E-3 Sentry AWACS first entered service with the USAF in 1977. The 30ft diameter hydraulically-rotated radome housed a Westinghouse AN/APY-2 radar. (USAF)

Left:
A Sukhoi Su-25K (Frogfoot) close air support aircraft of 368 OShAP (Independent Assault Aviation Regiment) based at Tutow, near Demmin, Germany. The 368th OShAP had seen active service in Afghanistan prior to being deployed back to East Germany in 1988. (Schleiffert)

Kazakh SSR in 1983 and subsequently equipped three more regiments. However, despite the introduction of new variants, the number of Tu-95/142 aircraft in service remained almost constant at around 100, as older airframes were retired from service. Some 40 of the obsolescent Mya-3M were also still in the inventory in the early 1980s, until they were replaced by the Tu-95K-22. The last 3M bomber left front-line service with 79 IAP at Ukraïnka (near Lake Baikal) in 1985 although most of the over 30 tanker variants remained in service with the DA until the end of the Cold War.

Following a re-alignment of the Soviet VOs and in the light of the organizational trial of air defence in the Baltic and Leningrad VOs in the late 1970s, the command structure of the whole of the Soviet air defences was reorganized in 1981. The 16 VOs were divided into five geographic groupings based on TVDs: the Western, North-western, Far Eastern, Southern TVDs defended the borders of the USSR, while a Central Reserve was centred on Moscow. The Western TVD was further divided into the *Glavnoye Komandovaniye Voysk Zapadnogo Napravleniya* (GKVZN – Western Directorate High Command), and its south-western counterpart, the GKVYuZN. The ten independent PVO Armies were disbanded and the PVO-Strany was renamed the Voyska-PVO (VPVO – Air Defence Forces), losing its centralized command and control system in favour of more local command at TVD level. The VPVO also lost its independent flying training system which had been run in parallel to the VVS system: instead the VVS became responsible for all military flying training. However, the VPVO

took operational control of the FA interceptors within each VO. Meanwhile, another major re-equipment programme for VPVO units was under way during the 1980s, with the introduction of the Sukhoi Su-27P [Flanker] and the Mikoyan MiG-31 [Foxhound]. The large but exceptionally manoeuvrable Su-27P was first issued to 60 IAP at Dzyomgi in the Soviet Far East in 1985, replacing the Su-15. Re-equipment of units in the west of the USSR started in the same year with deliveries to the 831st GvIAP at Mirgorod in the Ukrainian SSR and the 941st IAP-PVO at Kilip Yavr, on the Kola Peninsula, where it replaced the MiG-23M. NATO forces got their first close view of the new type on 17 September 1987 when a Su-27 intercepted a RNoAF P-3B of 333 Squadron over the Barents Sea. After making three close passes on the P-3, the port fin of the Su-27 collided with the starboard outer propeller of P-3B. Despite being seriously damaged, both aircraft were recovered safely to their respective bases, but the incident showed a new, more independently minded attitude from Soviet aircrew.

The MiG-31 first saw operational service with 174 IAP, formerly a Yak-28P unit, at Monchegorsk on the Kola Peninsula in 1983. It was intended to supersede the obsolescent Tu-128P and Yak-28P which were responsible for the defence of the Arctic regions of the high north. The following year, the first of the Tu-128P regiments, 518 IAP at Talagi near Arkhangelsk, converted to the new type, and the other units gradually followed suit. The two-seat MiG-31 was superficially similar in configuration to the MiG-25, but was in fact a completely new airframe. The tactical heart of

The McDonnell Douglas CF-188 entered service with the Canadian Armed Forces (CAF) in 1982, replacing the F-101 Voodoo in the air-defence role and the CF-104 Starfighter in the ground-attack role with the 1 CAG at Baden-Solingen, Germany. The CF-188B was fully mission capable and was used for pilot training and standardization. (USAF)

A mixed formation representing the main air forces in West Germany. A McDonnell Douglas F-15C Eagle of the USAFE 36th TFW from Bitburg leads (in the foreground) a German Panavia Tornado IDS of JaBoG 37 from Lechfeld and a British Tornado GR1 of 14 Sqn from Brüggen. The Tornado GR1 differed from the IDS variant chiefly by having a Laser Ranger and Marked Target Receiver (LRMTS) mounted in a fairing under the nose. (USAF)

the aircraft was the BRLS-8B Zaslon (barrier), phased array radar, which had a true look-down shoot-down capability as well as the ability to track a number of targets simultaneously without having to lock onto them; this was matched with the long-range Vympel R-33 [AA-9 Amos] AAM, which had a nominal range of some 120km.

The main types in the inventory of the VPVO in the early 1980s were the MiG-23M, MiG-25P and Su-15T and TM (fitted with the *Taifun* (typhoon) and Taifun-M radar respectively). Unfortunately, a serious diplomatic incident was precipitated by the shooting down of a Korean airliner on 1 September 1983 by a Su-15TM from the 365th IAP-PVO based at Dolinsk-Sokol. The Korean Airlines Boeing 747 was operating a scheduled flight from Anchorage to Seoul when it strayed several hundred miles off course and overflew Soviet prohibited areas on the Kamchatka Peninsula and Sakhalin Island. Voyska-PVO commanders became convinced that it was a USAF ELINT reconnaissance aircraft and after the Su-15 which intercepted the aircraft in darkness was unable to contact the crew, they ordered the fighter to shoot it down. The airliner was destroyed and all on board it were killed. The event caused outrage across the world, but it also triggered another review of the structure of the VPVO; this resulted in a substantial reversing of the changes that had been instigated in the 1981 re-organization, so that by 1986 the structure of the VPVO had virtually returned to that of the PVO-Strany in the 1970s. On 27 December 1979, Soviet forces invaded Afghanistan, supported by elements of the 49th VA and 73rd VA. These included 115 GvIAP, equipped with the MiG-21bis, which deployed to Bagram and Kandahar, as well as 149 GvBAP, which flew the Yakovlev Yak-28I (*Initsiativa*-2 – Initiative, ground-mapping radar) [Brewer-C] from Kokaydy in the Uzbek SSR. Additionally, 217 APIB (the FA fighter-bomber

After the Falkland Conflict of 1982, the RAF deployed a squadron of McDonnell Douglas F-4M Phantom FGR2 interceptors to the Falkland Islands. Unfortunately, delays to the Panavia Tornado F2 programme meant that there was a shortfall in aircraft for the UK Air Defences and a short-term solution was required. As a result, 15 ex-US Navy F-4J aircraft, the closest equivalent to the F-4M, were procured and refurbished. Designated the F-4J(UK), the aircraft were operated by 74 Sqn at RAF Wattisham from 1984. (USN)

regiments had been re-designated from IBAP to APIB in 1977) deployed to Shindand in western Afghanistan in 1980 with the Su-17M3. By 1981 there were two MiG-21 squadrons at Bagram, one at Kabul and two more at Kandahar. Although the MiG-21 had originally been deployed in the air-defence role, it quickly became used for CAS to ground forces. In 1981 a new type, the Sukhoi Su-25 [Frogfoot], which was specifically designed for the CAS role, deployed to Afghanistan with 200 (OShAE – Independent Assault Squadron), for operational testing. The Soviet air effort over Afghanistan increased significantly in 1984, coinciding with an offensive in the Panjshir Valley. Heavy bombers including Tu-16 from 132 TBAP, Tu-22M from 200 GvTBAP and 1225 GvTBAP and Su-24 from 149 GvBAP were used to bomb mujahedeen positions. Close air support was provided by MiG-23MLA of 905 IAP operating from Shindand as well as Su-17 of the 34th IBAD at Mary-2 in the Turkmen SSR and Su-25 of 378 OShAP based at Kandahar and Bagram. Although only a handful of fighting units were detached from the air forces directly opposing NATO fronts (for example the Su-25-equipped 357 OShAP and 368 OShAP from the 16th VA in the late 1980s), the air campaign in Afghanistan nevertheless represented a drain on the overall resources of the VVS.

NATO AIR FORCES, 1980 – 85

The early 1980s saw two important projects for European NATO air forces: the formation of the AWACS force and the replacement of the F-104. In 1982, the first of an eventual 18 Boeing E-3A Sentry AWACS aircraft arrived at Geilenkirchen to form the NATO E-3 component. The three squadrons of the component operated the only aircraft actually owned by NATO rather than by the individual countries of the alliance, although they had to be legally registered in Luxembourg. The E-3A was intended to supplement the ground-based early warning radar systems of the NADGE via the Airborne Early Warning/Ground Environment Integration Segment (AEGIS) system. The introduction of an airborne radar system moved the NATO radar horizon considerably further eastwards, giving NATO air defences a much earlier warning of impending attack. Although the aircraft were based at Geilenkirchen, there were regular deployments to forward operating bases in Norway, Italy, Greece and Turkey.

During the 1970s it had been clear that the F-104 was obsolescent and would have to be replaced in the northern European air forces early in the next decade. Various options were evaluated by each of the F-104 operators, but they boiled down to three choices of

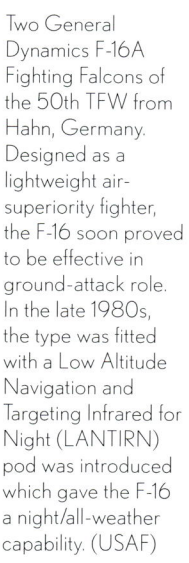

Opposite:
Three 'Wild Weasel' SEAD aircraft from the 480th TFS, 52nd TFW based at Spangdahlem, Germany. The lead aircraft is a F-4G Phantom armed with an AGM-78 SARM and an AGM-54 Shrike ARM. The type was also equipped with an AN/APR-38 Radar Homing Receiver which could detect and locate enemy radar sites. The two F-4Es carry more Shrikes – which could be launched on the instruction of the F-4G – and also bombs for attacking anti-aircraft sites. All aircraft are carrying air-to-air missiles and AN/ALQ-131 Electronic Countermeasures pods for self-defence. (USAF)

replacement aircraft: the F-18, the F-16 or the Panavia Tornado Interdictor Strike (IDS) variant. The CAF had already elected to replace the CF-101 with the CF-188 (Canadian designation for the F-18) and replacement of the F-104 by the same type would make economic sense as well as increasing their military flexibility. In 1984, 409 Sqn, which had recently converted to the CF-188, moved from Cold Lake to join 1 CAG, starting the re-equipment process at Baden-Solingen. Meanwhile, the Norwegian, Danish, Dutch and Belgian air forces had selected the F-16 as their new fighter and had formed the European Participating Air Forces (EPAF) consortium. The initial order by Belgium for 116 aircraft made their air force the largest F-16 operator in Europe, but this soon changed when follow-on orders were placed by the Netherlands. Norway and Denmark had more modest requirements, ordering 72 and 58 aircraft respectively. The EPAF aircraft were assembled in the Netherlands by Fokker for the Dutch and Norwegian air forces and by Sociétés Anonyme Belge de Constructions Aéronautiques (SABCA) in Belgium for the air forces of Belgium and Denmark. Total production by the two companies equipped 17 squadrons in the four nations.

Another consortium, this time made up of West Germany, the UK and Italy, had formed the Panavia Aircraft Gmbh to manufacture the Multi-Role Combat Aircraft (MRCA), later named the Tornado IDS. This aircraft was intended to replace a number of types in the RAF inventory and the F-104G in German and Italian service. The Tornado represented a quantum leap in combat effectiveness over the types it replaced: designed specifically for the long-range low-level strike role, the aircraft was equipped with a TFR and an attack system based around the aircraft Ground Mapping Radar (GMR), which allowed a genuine all-weather capability that had previously been lacking in European air forces. Three *Jagdbombergeschwaden* of the Luftwaffe and two ground attack *Stormi* of the AMI had re-equipped with the Tornado by 1985. However, the F-104G remained in service, as the main interceptor still equipping eight *Stormi* in the air-to-air role in 1985.

In 1982, the IDS entered service with the RAF as the Tornado GR1, replacing the Vulcan in 9 Sqn, 27 Sqn and 617 Sqn based in the UK and the six Buccaneer and Jaguar-equipped strike/attack squadrons in RAF Germany. The role of these units was tactical nuclear strike using the WE177 weapon, their secondary role was conventional attack. German-based aircraft would be armed with the Hunting JP233 runway denial weapon for operations against Warsaw Pact airfields. The remaining strength of RAFG comprised the two Harrier GR3 CAS squadrons at Gutersloh and two

Two General Dynamics F-16A Fighting Falcons of the 50th TFW from Hahn, Germany. Designed as a lightweight air-superiority fighter, the F-16 soon proved to be effective in ground-attack role. In the late 1980s, the type was fitted with a Low Altitude Navigation and Targeting Infrared for Night (LANTIRN) pod was introduced which gave the F-16 a night/all-weather capability. (USAF)

192 IN COLD WAR SKIES

Phantom FGR2 interceptor squadrons at Wildenrath, which were responsible for the day-to-day security of German airspace in 2ATAF. However, the bulk of the RAF interceptor fighter force was based in the UK, where it was charged with guarding the security of the UK ADR. In the mid-1980s, the RAF Strike Command air-defence force comprised two Lightning F6 squadrons (5 Sqn and 11 Sqn at Binbrook) and five Phantom squadrons, made up of two Phantom FG1 (F-4K) units (43 Sqn and 111 Sqn at Leuchars), two Phantom FGR2 (F-4M) units (29 Sqn at Coningsby and 56 Sqn at Wattisham) and an F-4J squadron (74 Sqn at Wattisham). A total of 15 of the latter were procured from the USN in 1984 to replace the FGR2 aircraft which had been deployed to defend the Falklands Islands after the conflict of 1982.

F-104G SIMULATED NUCLEAR-STRIKE
1981
Lt A. HARTL, JABOG 33

A single ship, four- [auxiliary] tank mission and hitting my designated target within +/-5sec was basically my daily practice mission when training for the nuclear role. Airborne from Büchel, gear up, I cancel afterburner and retract the flaps at 350kt. I then take the shortest distance to the entry point of our low-level route. I fly the route (both in and out of LFAs) at 500ft and 450kt.

The USAF Electronic Warfare suite of the 1980s included and the General Dynamics/Grumman EF-111A Raven electronic jamming aircraft. Here an EF-111A operated by the 42nd Electronic Combat Squadron, 20th TFW based at Upper Heyford, near Oxford, flies over Gibraltar harbour. (USAF)

With the four-tank configuration I have enough fuel for up to 2hrs. The F-104 is very stable at low level – the high wing loading assures a very comfortable ride, especially at over 400kt. On reaching the target, I begin the run in and at the same time accelerate to 540kt; for the last miles I drop to 250ft. I identify the target on radar for a LADD attack ['toss bombing'] and actuate the Run-in Timer according my radar display. When timer ends, I pull up at 3.5G and the timer automatically releases the bomb. After climbing at 45°, I roll the F-104 inverted and dive back to low-level, roll the aircraft upright then reduce speed back to 450kt to perform a safe egress from the target area. Returning to Büchel, I route to point 'Kilo', a prominent road bridge over the Mosel, which is also the initial point for runway 21 and enter the VFR landing pattern at 1,500ft and 320kt.

USAFE also underwent a systematic re-equipment programme in the early 1980s with the replacement of the Phantom in continental Europe. The F-4D was replaced by the F-15C in the 36th TFW at Bitburg and the 32nd TFS, which was based at Soesterburg in the Netherlands. Along with the E-3A, these aircraft represented a significant enhancement of the NATO air defences. In the ground-attack role, the 50th and 86th TFWs at Hahn and Ramstein respectively, traded the F-4E for the F-16. The F-4D was also replaced in the units based in the UK: the 48th TFW at Lakenheath re-equipped with the F-111F, while the 81st TFW at the twin bases of Bentwaters and Woodbridge was expanded to accommodate six squadrons of A-10. The electronic warfare tactics of the 1970s had also matured. The 52nd TFW at Spangdahlem comprised three squadrons of F-4G/E Wild Weasel SEAD aircraft, which from 1985 were armed with the Texas Instruments AGM-88 High-Speed Anti-Radiation Missile (HARM); in addition, the 42nd Electronic Combat Squadron (ECS) based at Upper Heyford operated the EF-111 Raven electronic jamming aircraft. In wartime, these assets would work together to neutralize Warsaw Pact air defences during NATO offensive air operations: the EF-111 could jam enemy radars in a relatively wide area while the F-4G/E combination attacked individual SAM systems which posed a threat to NATO aircraft.

In France, the Dassault Mirage 2000C, the replacement for the obsolescent Mirage III, entered service in 1983 with EC 1/2 'Cigognes' and 3/2 'Alsace'

The Dassault Mirage 2000C first entered service with the AdA in 1984, replacing the Mirage III in the 2ième EC at Dijon-Longvic. The highly-manoeuvrable aircraft was equipped with the Thompson-CSF RDI pulsed-Doppler look-down/shoot-down radar and armed with Matra Magic II and Super 503D AAM. The aircraft was fitted with a fixed AAR probe. (USAF)

Right:
The *Ejército del Aire* (EdA – Spanish Air Force) was equipped with the Dassault Mirage F-1CE (EdA designation: C.14A) and operated by *Escuadron* (Esc – squadron) 141 and Esc 142 of *Ala* (wing) 14 based at Albacete. The EdA operated 45 of these aircraft in the air-defence role. (Wikimedia)

Below:
A Franco-British collaboration, the SEPECAT Jaguar A was operated by the AdA from 1972. The first unit to receive the type was EC 1/7 'Provence' based at St Dizier.(Schleiffert)

of 2ème EC at Dijon-Longvic. While their sister reconnaissance unit, EC 2/2 'Côte d'Or', retained the Mirage IIIR and remained under command of FATac, the new Mirage 2000-equipped squadrons were transferred to CAFDA to operate in the air-defence fighter role. The last Super Mystère had been withdrawn from service in the late 1970s and the remaining squadrons within CAFDA, 5ème EC at Orange-Caritat, 12ème EC at Cambrai-Epinoy and 30ème EC at Reims, all flew the Mirage F1. The FATac inventory of ground-attack aircraft was evenly split with eight squadrons of Mirage III/5 and a further eight squadrons of the more modern Jaguar A under command.

In the late 1970s, the Portuguese Air Force underwent a re-organization as the country's armed forces readjusted its focus from counter-insurgency operations in its former African colonies to the defence of Europe. The 1ª *Região Aérea* (1st Air Region), was replaced by the *Comando Operacional da Força Aérea* (COFA – Air Force Operational Command), and a G-91 unit, Esquadron (Esq – squadron) 303, was established at Lajes, in the Azores. However, the F-86F which had equipped the fighter wing at Monte Real since the late 1950s was in urgent need of replacement. Unfortunately, Portugal was also suffering badly from the economic recession and had already reduced its defence budget by nearly 50 percent since the mid-1970s, so it seemed that it would be impossible to fund the acquisition of replacement aircraft. A solution to the dilemma was found by offsetting the operating lease for the US Navy to continue to operate from Lajes against the provision of the Ling-Temco-Vought A-7P Corsair II. The first aircraft arrived at Monte Real in 1982 to equip Esq 302 and Esq 304.

Another major development in the Iberian Peninsula was that of Spain joining NATO in 1982, but like France, Spain elected not to integrate its armed forces into the NATO command structure. The combat units of the Spanish Air Force, were divided into three commands, *Mando Aéreo de Combate* (MACOM – Combat Air Command), *Mando Aéreo Táctico* (MATAC – Tactical Air Command), and *Mando Aéreo de Canarias* (MACAN – Canaries Air Command). The combat units within each command were *Ala* (wings), each of which was subdivided

In 1981, 302 Sqn of the FAP was formed at Monte Real to operate the Ling-Temco-Vought A-7P Corsair. Portugal had procured 44 of the type and six two-seat TA-7P to replace the obsolescent F-86F Sabre. The aircraft were ex-US Navy A-7A airframes, but fitted with the TF30-P408 and also the upgraded avionics suite of the A-7E. Armament included the AIM-9 Sidewinder AAM missile and the AGM-65 Maverick ASM. (USAF)

into two squadrons. MACOM was responsible for the air defence of Spain with three wings, based at Manises (Valencia), Torrejon and Albacete and equipped respectively with the Mirage IIIE (known locally as the C.11), the F-4C (C.12) and the Mirage F1CE (C.14A). A further wing of C.14A was based at Gando, in the Canary Islands, under the command of MACAN. The final command, MATAC, comprised a single wing based at Moron with the SF-5A and SRF-5A (known as the C.9 and CR.9) for close support of the army and tactical reconnaissance. In addition to the Spanish forces, the USAFE 401st TFW remained at Torrejon, and like its counterparts in northern Europe, the wing had been equipped with F-16A which replaced the F-4C.

Both the EPA and the THK were re-equipped and re-organized in the early 1980s: aircraft deployment was rationalized in both air forces so that each airbase operated a single aircraft type. The EPA increased its combat strength from 11 to 13 squadrons, replacing the remaining F-84F with the A-7H and also forming another F-4E *Moira*. Also the F-102 was replaced by the Mirage F1CG in 114 PM at Tanagra. Meanwhile, the THK also increased in size from 18 to 20 *Filolari*, and modernized its inventory by phasing out the F-102, the RF-84F and the F-84Q. The more streamlined force now comprised eight F-4 *Filolari* based at Eskişehir, Konya and Malatya Erhaç with the F-4 and seven *Filolari* at Murte, Bandirma and Balikesir with the F-104. Two other bases, Merzifon and Diyabakir, operated the F-5 and the last of the F-100 units.

WARSAW PACT AIR FORCES, 1980 – 84

After its initial founding as a defensive force, the East German LSK/LV expanded into air-support roles with the establishment in 1981 of the *Führungsorgan Front- und Militärtransportfliegerkräfte* (FO FMTFK – Frontal Aviation and Military Transport Command). Initially, this new headquarters controlled transport and helicopter units as well as the MiG-23BN-equipped

The East German Air Force increased its ground-attack capability in 1984 with the formation of JBG-77 and the naval MFG-28, both of which flew the Sukhoi Su-22M4 [Fitter-K]. Shown is an Su-22M4 of JBG-77, with a two-seat Su-22UM3K [Fitter-G] operational trainer in the foreground. The unit was based at Laage, near Rostock. (Schleiffert)

A Mikoyan-Gurevich MiG-21MF [Fishbed-J] from JG-1 of the East German LSK/LV streams its brake parachute on landing at Holzdorf. The abbreviation 'MF' represented *Modernizirovannyy* (modernized) and *Forsirovannyy* (uprated engine). This variant of the MiG-21 was equipped with the RP-21 Sapfir (sapphire) spin/scan-type radar; although a major improvement over earlier radar systems, it was still limited by the size of the MiG-21 nose cone. (Schleiffert)

JBG-37 at Drewitz; however, from 1984 it took on two newly-formed ground-attack units, JBG-77 and MFG-28 (*Marinefliegergeschwader* – Naval Air Wing), both of which operated the Su-22M4 at Laage, as well as TAFS-47 (*Taktische Aufklärungsfliegerstaffel* – Tactical Reconnaissance Squadron). The remaining air-defence units of the 1st and 3rd *Luftverteidigungsdivisionen* (air defence divisions), were equipped with the MiG-21M or MiG-21bis, both of which were third generation variants of the MiG-21. Meanwhile, the Soviet 16th VA in the DDR had been renamed the VVS *Gruppa Sovetskikh Voysk v Germanii*, (Air Forces of the GSVG). As in previous decades, the Soviet FA regiments in the DDR were issued with the most up-to-date equipment and its force-mix reflected its main role of supporting ground forces in a mobile land campaign. By the early 1980s, seven regiments were operating variants of the MiG-23, charged in wartime with establishing air superiority over the battlefield. However, the versatile MiG-23 was a dual-role aircraft, so these regiments could be switched to ground-attack operations as and when the tactical situation warranted it. Three more regiments flew the MiG-27K ground-attack variant for the close air support of ground forces. The MiG-27 shared the same basic airframe as the MiG-23, but the radar of the latter had been replaced by laser sensors and the navigation/attack system had been optimized for the ground-attack role. Other specialist ground-attack units were based at Templin and Neurippen equipped with the Su-17 and in addition, two longer range Su-24 units, 116 GvAPIB at Brand and 497 APIB based at Grossenheim, would be used for interdiction beyond the battlefield. During the 1970s, the USSR had also established a number of S-200 Vega [SA-5 Gammon] SAM batteries in the DDR. Originally intended as a long-range defensive missile, the S-200 became now an offensive weapon, since it could directly threaten both NATO E-3 and USAF SR-71 operations, enabling the VVS-GSVG to project its power well inside NATO airspace.

Despite the civil unrest in Poland, the air force remained a well-equipped and credible force. Most of the air-defence units flew modernized variants of the MiG-21, and although the elderly Lim-6bis soldiered on in some ground-attack units, it had been replaced by the more capable Su-22M4 in both 6.PLM-SB at Piła and 40.PLM-SB at Świdwin. The Soviet 4th VA VGK ON based in Poland had also been bolstered by the introduction of the Su-24M, including the transfer from the 15th VA of two *polki* based in Chernyakhovsk, Kaliningrad and one at Tukums in the Latvian SSR.

Formed at Drewitz in 1981, JBG-37 of the LSK/LV was equipped with the MiG-23BN (Flogger-H); here in a dispersal with a Ural truck. The MiG-23BN was optimized for the ground-attack role with weapons carried on pylons fitted under the fuselage and under the fixed nibs of the inboard wings. The type also had a laser rangefinder fitted in the nose. (Schleiffert)

The LSK/LV first received its Mikoyan MiG-29A [Fulcrum] at Preschen in 1988. The aircraft were operated by 1/JG-3, the first squadron of JG-3, although the remaining two squadrons continued to operate the MiG-21MF. Note the OLS-29 Infra-Red Search and Tracking (IRST) sensor just above the nose, and the main air intake doors which have closed to prevent debris being ingested by the engines on the ground. (Schleiffert)

Thus, in the early 1980s the Soviet VVS presence in Poland had expanded in scope from being a small number of short-range units with limited capability, to becoming a powerful long-range strike force that could reach far into NATO territory.

As in Poland, the fighter units of the Czechoslovak Air Force were also mainly equipped with modernized variants of the MiG-21, while the fighter-bomber units operated the Su-7. To the south-east, the Hungarian Air Force remained the smallest in the Warsaw Pact, with just three air-defence wings, but these also operated later versions of the MiG-21. The Soviet air forces in the country, VVS *Yuzhnyy Gruppa Voysk*, (VVS Southern Group of Forces), provided the ground-attack element, including two *polki* of dual-role MiG-23 and another Su-24 unit, 727 GvBAP, at Debrecen. The Romanian Air Force had been restructured in the late 1970s so that the air-defence assets came under direct command of the *Statul Major al Fortelor Aeriene* (SMFA – air force staff), rather than through the divisional headquarters as had previously been the case. The air-defence forces comprised MiG-21 variants and, from 1983, the MiG-23ML which was operated by R57AvVt at Mihail Kogălniceanu and R93AvVt at Timișoara-Giarmata. The two divisions continued to control the ground-attack and reconnaissance functions. The reconnaissance squadron Esc38AvCc was equipped with the Harbin Hong-5, a Chinese-built version of the Il-28, but the ground-attack units R49AvVtB at Ianca and R67AvVtB at Craiova were equipped with a more modern type in the Avioane Craiova IAR-93 *Vultur* (Vulture). This joint Romanian-Yugoslav project, powered by license-built Rolls Royce Viper engines, was a manifestation of the ideological differences between the USSR and those of Romania

Introduced to the Soviet VVS in 1986, the Sukhoi Su-24M [Fencer-D] was an improved variant of the original Su-24. It included a retractable refuelling probe above the nose and the PNS-24 Tigr navigation-attack system which included the Kayra-24 TV-optical laser designator pod. The aircraft had eight hardpoints for external stores: the inner wing pylons could carry fuel tanks, while the outer wing pylons, are shown here carrying S-8 rocket pods. (MoD Russia/Wikimedia)

and Yugoslavia. Bulgaria, however, remained closely aligned with the USSR and its loyalty was reflected in a modern-equipped air force. Fighter and ground-attack units were equipped with third-generation variants of the MiG-21 and the MiG-23, and the reconnaissance unit 26 RAP based at Tolbukhin took delivery of the MiG-25RBT [Foxbat-B] in 1982.

STRATEGIC SITUATION, 1985

The government of the USSR underwent a major change in direction with the appointment of Mikhail Gorbachev as the General Secretary of the Communist Party of the Soviet Union in 1985. His twin policies of *perestroika* (restructuring), and *glasnost* (openness and transparency), were designed to eliminate corruption within Soviet political circles and to seek a less adversarial relationship with the USA. In particular, Gorbachev recognized the economic damage caused by the Cold War arms race and the drain on resources caused by the unpopular war in Afghanistan. Unfortunately, as the decade progressed the new line taken by the USSR did not meet the approval of some of the more hard-line Communist governments in Eastern Europe. In particular, the leaders of the DDR, Czechoslovakia, Bulgaria and Romania were at odds with the more liberal attitude of the leadership of the USSR; however, at the same time popular dissatisfaction with the Communist governments grew and unrest simmered across all of the countries of Eastern Europe.

After a summit meeting at Reykjavik in 1986, President Reagan and General Secretary Gorbachev reached agreement on tactical nuclear forces in Europe and as a result nuclear QRA was suspended on both sides of the Iron Curtain in early 1987. Nevertheless, both sides continued the upgrading of weapons systems throughout the rest of the decade and conventional forces were maintained at a high state of readiness. Many of the individual units in front-line Europe had been in situ since the late 1960s, but the almost continuous process of re-equipment meant that even though the order of battle had changed little in terms of unit identities and locations, the effectiveness and firepower of those units had increased greatly over the subsequent 20 years.

NORTH AMERICAN STRATEGIC, DEFENSIVE AND TACTICAL FORCES, 1986–89

After the B-1 programme was restored by the Reagan administration, the Rockwell B-1B entered front-line service in 1986 with the 337th BS at Dyess AFB, Texas. Over the next years, three further SAC BWs were re-equipped with the aircraft: 28th BW at Ellsworth AFB, South Dakota, 319th BW at Grand Forks AFB, North Dakota and the 384th BW at McConnell AFB, Kansas. Although the FB-111 remained in service after the introduction of the B-1B, its importance decreased as the number of B-1B in service increased. The B-52 retained its strategic importance, with some 210 aircraft remaining in the frontline of SAC: the ability of the B-52H to carry up to 20 ALCMs over inter-continental ranges was still unmatched by more modern types.

Within 1st AF, the air defence of the USA was progressively passed from regular USAF interceptor units to the ANG, as the ANG squadrons re-equipped with modern types such as the F-15, F-16 and F-4. By 1988, the ANG strength was nine Fighter Wing Equivalents (FWE) equipped with air-defence fighters and a similar number of ground-attack units. The last USAF F-106 unit, 49th FIS was disbanded in 1987 and two regular F-15 units were also disbanded in the late 1980s, leaving the F-15-equipped 48th FIS at Langley as one of only two regular USAF interceptor units in 1st AF; the other was 57th FIS at Keflavik, also operating the F-15, which became part of 1st AF when Air Forces Iceland was incorporated into 1st AF in 1987.

The remaining aircraft within TAC, including A-10, F-16, F-15, RF-4C and F-111, were divided between the 9th AF, covering the eastern half of the USA and the 12th AF which covered the western half. Each of these contained eight wings and most of these forces

A Sukhoi Su-17M4 [Fitter-K] of the Soviet 20 GvAPIB based at Templin/Gross Dölln, about 30 miles north of Berlin. The Su-17M4 incorporated the PrNK-54 navigation-attack system and the Klyon-54 laser target designator and rangefinder. (Schleiffert)

A Czechoslovak Air Force Sukhoi Su-25K [Frogfoot] of 30.SBoLPl undergoes servicing at Pardubice. The unit operated the MiG-15Bis until it was re-equipped with the Su-25 in 1985; the first non-Soviet Warsaw Pact air force to receive the type. The 'K' (*Kommercheskiy* – commercial) designation indicates that it is an export model. (Schleiffert)

were earmarked for deployment to Europe in the event of conflict. Amongst the forces under command of the 12th AF were the 388th ECS at Mountain Home, Idaho, equipped with the EF-111 and the 37th TFW at George AFB, California, which operated the F-4G Wild Weasel. The 9th AF included the 4th TFW at Seymour Johnson AFB, North Carolina, which received the McDonnell Douglas F-15E Strike Eagle in 1989. Based on the F-15 air superiority fighter, the F-15E was optimised for the strike-attack role, but retained an impressive self-defence capability and represented, perhaps, the very zenith of military aeroplane development in the Cold War.

An unusual flying unit was formed at Tonopah Test Range Airport, Nevada, in 1983. The 4450th Tactical Group (TG), which included an RAF presence, officially operated the A-7D for classified trials involving aircraft navigation systems. In fact, this was merely a 'cover story' and the 4450th TG was a combat unit: although it did have a number of A-7D on strength, the real equipment was the top-secret Lockheed F-117 Nighthawk stealth fighter. This strike/attack aircraft had been designed to be almost invisible to radar and remain undetected by early warning systems also it could not be engaged by radar-guided SAMs. As the existence of the F-117 was still secret, the 4450th TG flew only at night in order to hide the identity and capability of its equipment. However, this ploy was only partially successful and amid rumour and speculation in the press, the F-117 was eventually displayed to the public in 1990.

SOVIET STRATEGIC DEFENSIVE AND TACTICAL FORCES, 1986-89

Despite the demise of the Mya-3M in DA service, the number of heavy strategic bombers in VVS and AV-MF inventories had remained almost constant at around 175 aircraft. The Mya-3M had been replaced by the Tu-95K-22 and 1987 saw the introduction of a completely new type, the Tupolev Tu-160 [Blackjack], the largest supersonic bomber in the world, which had entered service with 184 GvTBAP at Priluki, Ukrainian SSR. However, the aircraft was plagued with teething problems and less than 20 of the type ever entered service. Although it was originally conceived as a 'multi-role' bomber, by the time it entered service it had become

Originally the cockpit of the Rockwell B-1A was designed as an ejection capsule, a concept similar to that of the F-111; however, during an accident in 1984 the capsule did not function correctly, and the test pilot was killed. In the B-1B, the capsule was replaced by four United Technologies Aerospace Systems (UTAS) Advanced Concept Ejection Seat (Aces) II. (USAF)

more of a stand-off platform, designed to launch long-range missiles some distance beyond the reach of the defences. Like the Tu-95MS which it complemented in the strategic bombing role, the Tu-160 was armed with the Kh-55SM (AS-15 Kent) ALCM and was intended to launch its attacks from well beyond the reach of the target defences. Its range could be extended further by the use of AAR. Perhaps surprisingly for a vast country with great distances to cover, the AAR force was relatively small and in the mid-1980s it comprised just 30 Mya-3M and about 20 Tu-16N tankers, both of which were elderly types. A more modern three-point tanker was introduced in 1987 in the form of the Ilyushin Il-78M [Midas] which was based on the Il-78 transport aircraft and incorporated three UPAZ-1M hose and drogue aerial refuelling pods. However, tanker numbers remained small and only about 50 of this new type were built. They were issued to 409 *Aviatsionnyy Polk Samoletov Zapravshchikov* (APSZ – Tanker Aircraft Aviation Regiment), within the 106th TBAD based at Uzin. By the late 1980s, the Tu-22M, which was based mainly in the western regions, made up the bulk of the DA medium bomber force, although numbers of Tu-16 and Tu-22 still remained in service.

The introduction of the Il-78M tanker was followed two years later by the arrival of the Ilyushin-Beriev A-50 [Mainstay] AWACs aircraft, which supplanted the Tu-126 in 67 OAE DRLO. Both the Il-78M and A-50

worked closely with the long-range interceptors of the VPVO such as the MiG-31 and Su-27 in the remote areas of the high north. Deliveries of both of these latter fighter types continued through the late 1980s, but despite the introduction of these highly-capable modern aircraft, the greater part of 2,000 interceptors on the VPVO strength still consisted of the 890 MiG-23 and 500 Su-15 that remained in service across the USSR. By the second half of the decade, the changes to the VPVO that were introduced in 1981 had been completely reversed, leaving the VPVO, once again, as a completely independent military service with a centralized command and control structure. Meanwhile, within the VVS, the FA consolidated its ground attack strength with the MiG-27 and Su-25. Both of these types were designed specifically for the attack role, but the Su-25 was further optimized for CAS of ground forces. The introduction of the Su-25 brought with it the reintroduction of the assault regiment, designation which had previously disappeared with the demise of the Il-10 in the 1950s. The FA also began to receive a new fourth-generation air superiority fighter, the Mikoyan MiG-29 [Fulcrum]. The MiG-29 was first issued in great secrecy to 234 GvIAP at Kubinka, near Moscow, in late 1983 and to 968 IAP at Roś, in the Byelorussian SSR the following year. The aircraft was similar in performance to the F-16, but a helmet-mounted sight also gave the MiG-29 pilot a significant

The Rockwell B-1B entered operational service in 1986 with the 337th BS (Heavy), in the 7th BW, based at Dyess AFB, Texas. Capable of speeds up to Mach 1.2, the aircraft could carry 24 AGM-69 SRAM on rotary launchers in the internal weapons bay, or up to 84 conventional 500-lb Mk 82 bombs. (USAF)

Capable of Mach 2.1, the Tupolev Tu-160 *Belyy Lebed* (White Sawn) was the world's largest supersonic bomber. The aircraft entered service with the 184th GvTBAP based at Priluky in the Ukrainian SSR in 1987. (Sputnik)

tactical advantage in air-to-air combat. The deployment of the MiG-29 was a closely guarded secret and despite being the aircraft being introduced to service in 1983, it was not until the summer of 1986 that the MiG-29 made its first public appearance, at an air show in Finland. Aircraft of the VVS were busy supporting operations in Afghanistan until the Soviet withdrawal in early 1989. Most of the work was carried out by FA Mil-24D helicopter gunships, as well as Su-25, Su-17 and MiG-23 aircraft operating from Kabul, Kandahar, Bagram and Shindshand. The pace of air operations had increased in the mid-1980s as the ground forces became more reliant on air support: air weapon expenditure doubled between 1984 and 1986. In addition to the in-country air assets, Su-17 and long-range Su-24 units operated from Mary-2 across the border in the Turkman SSR. In addition, DA aircraft, including Tu-16, Tu-22 and Tu-22M, also participated in operations over Afghanistan. The 185 TBAP, equipped with the Tu-22M3, deployed to Mary-2 in the autumn of 1988; they were supported by the Tu-22PD electronic warfare aircraft of 341 TBAP. After a three-month tour, these units were relieved by the 402 and 203 TBAP respectively.

NORTHERN REGION/NORTH-WESTERN TVD AND ARCTIC AIR DEFENCE, 1986 – 89

The Soviet Northern TVD included the 10th PVO Armiya of the VPVO, which defended the Kola Peninsula, Arkhangelsk and the High North. Its modern equipment reflected both the strategic importance, and long-range nature, of its commitments: three polki were equipped with the MiG-31 (174 GvIAP at Monchegorsk, 72 GvIAP at Amderma and 518 IAP at Talagi) and two with the Su-27P (941 IAP at Kilip Yavr and 641 IAP at Rogachevo in Novaya Zemlaya). The remaining units on strength were two MiG-25P *polki* based in the Arkhangelsk VO and two Su-15TM *polki* near Murmansk and in the Karelian SSR. As well

TEAR DOWN THIS WALL! 1980–89   207

as routine operations from their home base, the two Su-27P units also deployed regularly to the ice airfield on Graham Bell Island, part of the Franz Josef Land archipelago, far into the Arctic Circle. The Soviet approach to the problem of early warning in the Arctic was very different to that taken by the US and Canada: instead of establishing a continuous line of sensors like the DEW Line, the Soviet method was to identify key strategic areas and establish a defensive system around each of them. Thus, while the Soviets had commissioned a number of radars, such as the Duga (OTH – Over the Horizon) system, which provided the entire country with warning against ballistic missile attack, radar detection of aircraft depended instead of separate radar sites grouped around strategically important areas. Although radar data from all sites were collated at the central VPVO control in Moscow; radar coverage, particularly at low-level, remained sketchy in some remote areas.

Responsibility for North American air defence in the Arctic was split within NORAD between the 21st TFW in Alaska, equipped with the F-15C and the CAF air-

The Tu-160 [Blackjack] could carry six Raduga Kh-55 [AS-15 Kent] cruise missiles on rotary launchers in each of the two internal weapons bays, but it suffered from major teething problems and only 19 of the type were built. (Sputnik)

A Tupolev Tu-22M3 [Backfire-C] taking off, showing the revised air intakes for the Kuznetsov NK-25 jet engines. This version of the aircraft, which became operational in 1981, was capable of Mach 1.8 and could carry three Raduga Kh-22 [AS-4 Kitchen] missiles. For conventional missions, such as those flown in Afghanistan between 1987 and 1988, the aircraft could carry up to 24,040kg of ordnance. (Sputnik)

Right:
The 1960s-vintage Tupolev Tu-95KD [Bear-B] was designed to carry the Kh-20 [AS-3 Kangaroo] air launched cruise missile. This version of the Tu-95 remained in VVS DA service until the mid-1980s. (Luftfartsmuseum)

Below:
A Mikoyan MiG-27K [Flogger-J2] of the Soviet 19 GvAPIB getting airborne from Mirov-Larz, East Germany. (Schleiffert)

defence forces which comprised four CF-188-equipped squadrons: 416 Sqn and 441 Sqn at Cold Lake and 425 Sqn and 433 Sqn at Bagotville. The interception coverage might seem sparse for such a large geographic area, but effective early warning systems meant that the aircraft could be directed accurately to ensure their efficient and effective use. In 1988, a five-year programme initiated the replacement of the obsolescent DEW line with the North Warning System (NWS). The new system replaced the DEW line radars with more modern technology and improved automation. The NWS eventually consisted of 15 long-range radars, of which 11 were in Canada, including eight former DEW line sites, which were updated.

The eastern flank of the NORAD Arctic region was covered by the F-15C/D interceptors of 57th FIS at Keflavik and the NATO defensive line was anchored in the ACE Northern Region by the aircraft of the RNoAF. Two squadrons of F-16A (331 Skv and 334 Skv), were based within the Arctic Circle at Bodø, and were frequently the first NATO aircraft to intercept Soviet aircraft flying around the North Cape and over the Norwegian Sea. Further to the south, 338 Skv, based at Ørland converted from the F-5A to the F-16A in 1986, generating four front-line F-16A squadrons. Armed with the Kongsberg Defence Systems (KDS) Penguin anti-shipping missile, these aircraft could also be used, if necessary, for maritime attack. The F-5A remained in Norwegian service with 336 Skv, while 333 Skv was based at Andøya flying the P-3C in the anti-submarine warfare role. Further south again, the Danish Air Force retired its last F-104G in 1986 when Esk 726 finally converted to the F-16A. Like its Norwegian counterpart, the force now included four F-16 squadrons. It also had

Tupolev Tu-16RM (*Razvedka Morskaya* – maritime reconnaissance) [Badger-D] of the Soviet AV-MF is intercepted by a General Dynamics F-16 Fighting Falcon of the RNoAF. (Luftfartsmuseum)

Ilyushin Il-78M [Midas] tanker aircraft trails its centre hose for a Tupolev Tu-160 [Blackjack] supersonic bomber. The Il-78M was equipped with three UPAZ-1A (*Unifitsirovaniy Podvesnoy Agregat Zaprahvki* - standard aerial refuelling unit) hose drums, two underwing pods and a centre pod; which was actually mounted on the port side of the rear fuselage. (Sputnik)

on strength two Saab F-35 Draken squadrons which were used in the ground- and maritime-attack roles and could be armed with the AGM-12 Bullpup missile.

CENTRAL REGION & WESTERN TVD, 1986 – 89

The pattern of re-equipment also continued across the central region, as the F-16 programme rolled out across the remaining F-104 and F-5 operators. In the Netherlands Air Force, 313 Sqn and 315 Sqn at Twenthe converted from the NF-5A to the F-16, making a total of seven F-16A squadrons. Of those units, 322 Sqn and 323 Sqn based at Leeuwarden operated primarily in the air-defence role, while the others concentrated in the strike/attack role. The Belgian Air Force also continued to acquire the F-16 through 1988 and 1989 when 1 Sqn and 2 Sqn started their conversion from the Mirage V to the F-16. At the same time, there was a re-organization to rationalise each of its bases to operate a single aircraft type. Florennes became an all-F-16 base after 1 Sqn moved from Bierset to join 2 Sqn there in 1989 and in a reciprocal move, 42 Sqn moved from Florennes to join 8 Sqn at Bierset, making the base home to the two Mirage V squadrons. Belgium now had a total of six squadrons of F-16, based in three wings at Beauvechain, Florennes and Kleine-Brogel.

The last Canadian CF-104 squadron, 441 Sqn was disbanded in 1986 and its place at Baden-Solingen was taken by 421 Sqn which returned to Germany after converting to the CF-188 in Canada. The wing at Baden Solingen now comprised 409 Sqn, 421 Sqn and 439 Sqn which could fulfil both the air-defence and conventional ground-attack roles. Another two CF-188 squadrons, one each from Cold Lake and

Bagotville, were earmarked for deployment to Lahr in the event of hostilities. With this increase in strength to three – possibly five – squadrons of CF-188, the Canadian air presence in Europe was re-designated 1 Canadian Air Division in 1988. The F-104 was finally phased out of service in northern Europe in 1987, when the last F-104G unit in the Luftwaffe, JaBoG 34 at Memmingen, re-equipped with the Tornado IDS, to become the fourth Tornado wing of the Luftwaffe. In Germany, there were also two former F-104G German naval units, Marinefliegergeschwaden 1 and 2 (based at Jagel and Eggebeck) which operated the Tornado IDS in the anti-shipping role, using the MBB-manufactured Kormoran missile. RAF Germany had a Tornado GR1 wing at Brüggen and another wing at Laarbruch. Consequently, by 1987 COMAAFCE had under its command eight wings of long-range all-weather strike aircraft based in continental Europe. Apart from the primary nuclear strike role, the Luftwaffe and RAF aircraft had an important part to play in the pre-planned 'Option Alpha' counter-air campaign, in which NATO aircraft would be tasked to neutralize airfields in the western areas of the Warsaw Pact. In wartime, all S-200 missile batteries in the DDR were also identified as targets for NATO interdiction aircraft.

The USAFE presence in Germany was virtually unchanged throughout the late 1980s: a wing of F-15C interceptors operated from Bitburg, two ground-attack wings equipped with the F-16 were based at Hahn and Ramstein and the electronic-warfare support wing remained at Spangdahelem. Additionally, the 26th TRS based at Zweibrucken provided tactical reconnaissance and the F-15C-equipped 32nd TFS based at Soesterburg continued to reinforce the air defence of the Netherlands. The USAFE assets based in the UK included two all-weather

The Ilyushin/Beriev A-50 [Mainstay] Airborne Early Warning and Control aircraft replaced the Tu-126 [Moss] in the 67 OAE DRLO based at Šiauliai in Latvian SSR between 1985 and 1988. (MoD Russia/Wikimedia)

A Fairchild A-10 Thunderbolt of the 18th TFS, 343rd FBW, based at Eielson AFB, Alaska photographed in 1988. The wing was responsible for close support of ground forces within PACAF (Pacific Air Force) area from 1982. The A-10, which became combat ready with the 354th TFW at Myrtle Beach in 1977 was armed with the 30mm GAU-8/A seven-barrel rotary cannon and had eight under-wing and three under-fuselage weapons pylons. (USAF)

long-range strike/attack wings with F-111 at RAF Upper Heyford and RAF Lakenheath and these would be expected to continue to operate from those bases during hostilities. Like the Tornado IDS, the F-111 units were also earmarked for conventional counter-air operations. A second wing of A-10 ground-attack aircraft had been formed when the 509th and 511th TFS moved from the 81st TFW RAF Woodbridge and RAF Bentwaters respectively to join the 10th TFW at RAF Alconbury. In the event of hostilities in Europe, these two A-10 wings would deploy forward to the continent to support ground operations. Further reinforcements to USAFE would also deploy from TAC units from the USA.

TEAR DOWN THIS WALL! 1980-89

In the UK, the early 1980s had been a time of re-equipment for the ground-attack units and in the second half of the decade it was the turn of the RAF air-defence forces to be updated. The Lightning F6 was retired from service in 1988 and the two ex-Lightning squadrons were re-formed with the Tornado F2 ADV (Air Defence Variant). During its early years in service, the Tornado F2 proved to be a disappointment, mainly due to the poor performance of the interception radar. This was resolved when the Tornado F3, an improved version, entered front-line service. Over the next few years, the type began to replace the Phantom in the air-defence role and by 1989 the RAF front-line interceptor force comprised two Tornado F3 squadrons at RAF

Two Panavia Tornado IDS strike/attack aircraft of 156° *Grupo 36° Stormo* of the Italian Air Force, based at Gioia del Colle. (USAF)

Leuchars (43 Sqn and 111 Sqn), three at RAF Leeming (11 Sqn, 23 Sqn and 25 Sqn), and two at RAF Coningsby (5 Sqn and 29 Sqn). There were also two Phantom squadrons at RAF Wattisham. The interceptors were supported by Victor K2, Vickers VC10K and Lockheed TriStar tanker aircraft. Unfortunately, the selection of a replacement type for the aging fleet of Avro Shackleton AEW 2 had been delayed by a tortuous procurement process, where the British designed and built BAe Nimrod AEW 3 competed with the Boeing E-3D. The E-3D was chosen as the replacement, but the delayed decision making meant that the Shackleton would continue in service until the end of the Cold War. Although the Nimrod AEW programme was eventually cancelled, the upgraded Nimrod MR2 maritime patrol aircraft continued to equip the RAF anti-submarine force: 120 Sqn, 201 Sqn and 206 Sqn, based at RAF Kinloss.

In France, 1988 the first of the Mirage 2000N nuclear-capable strike aircraft entered service with 4ème EC at Luxeuil-St Sauveur. The aircraft was procured as the launch platform for the Aerospatiale-manufactured *Air-Sol Moyenne Portée* (ASMP – Air-to-Surface Medium-Range nuclear missile). Eventually this aircraft/weapon system would be transferred to CFAS, as a replacement for the Mirage IV, but for the rest of the 1980s, the Mirage IV maintained its position in CFAS as the airborne delivery system for the French nuclear deterrent. Apart from the sole *escadre* of Mirage 2000N, the order of battle of FATac included Mirage III and Jaguar A; CAFDA also remained otherwise unchanged for the rest of the decade with three *escadres* of Mirage F1 and one of Mirage 2000C. During the late 1980s, French forces began to work together more closely with other NATO air forces

This Tornado F3 is operated by 23 Sqn based at RAF Leeming and is armed with four British Aerospace Skyflash semi-active air-to-air missiles under the fuselage and four AIM-9L infra-red seeking AAM missiles on the underwing pylons. The wings are fully-swept at 67°. (Paxton)

and in particular NATO aircraft regularly participated in the French *Datex* air-defence exercise.

In addition to routine daily training flights, the annual training for NATO flying units was punctuated by frequent exercises both at AAFCE and local level. During large-scale exercises, NATO air forces trained together using standardized procedures and were therefore able to operate seamlessly. On the ground all NATO forces also regularly practised operations in NBC conditions. In the late 1980s, NATO air tactics continued to be based around low-level flying and day-to-day training was carried out in the LFAs over Germany and Belgium, where a 250ft LFA covered the Ardennes region. The 250ft LFAs within the UK were available to UK-based aircraft of the RAF and USAFE, as well as the squadrons of RAF Germany. Certain areas in Scotland were also designated at Tactical Training Areas (TTA) where RAF squadrons could be authorized to fly as low as 100ft in order to train for specific exercises such as Exercise *Red Flag*. Low flying at 100ft could also be practised at Goose Bay in Canada and squadrons from the RAF, the Luftwaffe and the Netherlands Air Force all used the low-level training facilities at Goose Bay. Royal Air Force and Luftwaffe Tornado units also used the Goose Bay training areas to practise tactics using the Terrain Following Radar (TFR) system in the aircraft under real conditions of poor weather. In Western Europe, Temporary Restricted Areas (TRA) could be activated within medium level airspace for air combat manoeuvring exercises. The RAF, USAFE, Luftwaffe and the Italian Air Force also used the ACMI range at Decimomannu, Sardinia. Although the French forces were not integrated within the NATO command structure, French Air Force units frequently worked with other NATO air forces and also took part in *Red Flag* exercises in North America.

A Panavia Tornado IDS of the *Luftwaffe* of Jagdbombergschwader (Fighter-bomber Wing) 33, based at Büchel, flies at low-level over the sea. (AirDOC)

Right:
Escadron de Chasse 2/12 'Picardie' converted from the Mirage F1 to the Mirage 2000C soon after the end of the 'Cold War'. (Schleiffert)

Below:
Tactical reconnaissance for the Belgian Air Force was the task of 42 Sqn, part of 2 Wing and equipped with the Mirage V. The unit was based at Florennes. (Schleiffert)

In this view of Brüggen-based 31 Sqn Tornado GR1s in transit to an Exercise *Red Flag* work-up training sortie in the spring of 1988, the Skyshadow Electronic Counter-Measures (ECM) pod carried under the left wing and the BOZ-107 chaff and flare dispenser carried under the right wing are clearly visible. (Paxton)

EXERCISE RED FLAG

7 APRIL 1988
Flt Lt M.J.W. NAPIER,
31 SQN RAF BRÜGGEN

At 500kts, the scenery really motors past. A pair of triple-A sites attempt to snatch at us, so I stay as low as I can, using whatever terrain I can find to screen us. At 100ft above the desert floor, even the smallest fold in the ground can offer some protection. Hugging the ground, I jink the aircraft slightly, to give the guns a slightly wider berth, while keeping them in the coverage of our Skyshadow jamming pod. In the back seat [navigator], Kev punches out a cloud of chaff to confuse the radar even further. Soon we have sped past them out of range and they cannot touch us anymore. Ahead, a small knoll in an otherwise anonymous stretch of desert is the Initial Point (IP) for our attack. This is where things are very different to what we are used to. In Europe we would thumb our way along a detailed map for the last couple of minutes to find the target. With so many easily identified features in any ten-mile stretch of European terrain, map reading is pretty straightforward even at 500kts. From the backseat, too, there are usually plenty of things which will show up nicely on the radar. But not in the Nevada desert. Most of it is utterly featureless. Luckily the targets are 'Big', but even so, there is the added complication that most of the Red Flag targets had been made by bulldozing shapes in the sand, so there is no vertical extent to them. They are easily visible from 20,000ft, but not from a sweaty Tornado cockpit rocketing along just 100ft above the ground.

In the back seat, Kev does his best on the radar as we thunder towards the target area: Tolicha Peak a full-size replica of the Soviet airfield at Jüterbog, East Germany. It is just the sort of thing we would

Two Tornado GR1s from 9 Sqn based at RAF Brüggen, Germany. Each aircraft carries eight 1,000-lb retard bombs under the fuselage, also 1,500-litre fuel tanks and ECM pods under the wings. A more typical war load could be two Hunting JP233 runway denial weapons. (Brewell)

be sent against if war ever broke out in the Central Region. Today we are simulating the JP233 runway denial weapon by dropping a 'hollow stick' of two 3kg practice bombs: the first will mark the start of the trail of JP233 sub-munitions and the second will mark the end. The time-to-go circle in the Head-Up Display (HUD) unwinds swiftly, counting down the last 60 seconds before we reach the target while the desert floor continues to flash past underneath us at breath-taking speed. At 30 seconds there is a slight ridge to crest before we see the target and as we clear the ridge, a massive airfield materialises ahead of me. A thin whisp of orange smoke drifting from the far end of the runway lingers from the attacks made by the aircraft ahead of us in the formation. Kev has done a great job – we are perfectly lined up with the runway. I pull up slightly to 150ft to make sure that we do not drop the weapons from too low otherwise they will not fuse properly. Then suddenly we are locked up again by another 'Firecan' radar site. I haul the Tornado on its wingtip pulling hard, jabbing the throttles into full reheat to keep our speed. The radar breaks lock so I reverse back towards the target. There is just time to line up on my aiming point, level the wings and stabilize the speed. Bombs gone! We race straight ahead off target to clear the defences, then two hard 90° turns and we are heading for home.

On the opposite side of the Iron Curtain, Warsaw Pact air forces also continued the process of upgrading their aircraft, particularly the air defence types. The older MiG-21 variants were phased out in favour of the MiG-23 and MiG-29. In addition, the long-range Su-24 regiments were withdrawn from the frontal regions, and replaced by shorter-range aircraft such as the MiG-27. This redeployment served to protect the Su-24 from NATO strike aircraft such as Tornado and F-111 and simultaneously to increase the firepower available to support army operations, reflecting the lessons learnt in Afghanistan. In the DDR the VVS GSVG resumed its old title of 16th VA in 1988 and it remained the best equipped of the VVS tactical air forces. Its three fighter divisions re-equipped with the MiG-29, generating seven fourth-generation fighter regiments for the air superiority role. One unit in the 16th GvIAD, 787 IAP, also included a squadron of MiG-25PD, which had been deployed to Finow specifically to intercept the USAF SR-71 missions over the Baltic Sea. The two Su-24 regiments were transferred to 1st GvBAD in the Byelorussian SSR in 1989 and their places at Grossenheim and Brand were taken by 296 and 911 APIB, both of which flew the MiG-27. Thus, in the last year of the Cold War, the 16th VA fielded four *polki* of MiG-27 and two of Su-17 tactical fighter-bombers. New units introduced into the 16th VA in the late 1980s also included the Su-25-equipped 357 and 368 OShAP. The order of battle of the 16th VA in the late 1980s reflected a concentration on the short-range ground-attack role, with its assets protected by agile fighters. The East German LSK/LV also received the MiG-29 in 1988, when the aircraft were issued to 1/JG3 (ie first squadron of JG3) at Preschen. However, it was not a complete re-equipment and the rest of the regiment continued to fly the MiG-21. So, too, did the other air-defence regiments with the exception of JG-9 which retained the MiG-23ML. The ground-attack element of the LSK/LV remained unchanged in the late 1980s, comprising JBG-37 with the MiG-23 and the two Su-22 units.

In Poland, the Soviet 4th VA VGK ON consolidated itself as a powerful long-range force standing behind the 16th VA and the LSK/LV. Its offensive capability was furnished by its two divisions equipped with the Su-24 and its fighter force was greatly enhanced in 1987 with the introduction of the Su-27 in 159 GvIAP at Kluczewo and 582 IAP at Chojna. The 4th VA also included electronic warfare assets based at Brzheg, in 151 *Otdel'nyy Aviatsionnyy Polk Radioelektronnoy Bor'by* (OAPREB – Independent Electronic Warfare Regiment), and 164 OGvRAP. The former was equipped with the Yak-28PP [Brewer-E] electronic jammer, while the latter operated reconnaissance versions of the MiG-25 and Su-24 as well as the MiG-25BM SEAD aircraft, which was armed with the Kh-58 ARM. However, the MiG-25BM squadron was transferred to 151 OAPREB in 1989 when the unit was withdrawn from Poland

The McDonnell Douglas F-15E Strike Eagle became operational with the 4th TFW at Seymour Johnson AFB, North Carolina, in late 1989. The aircraft is equipped with the AN/APG-70 radar which was capable of both ground mapping and air-to-air modes, so the aircraft lost none of the air-to-air capability of the fighter variants. An extra 5,600 litres of fuel was carried in conformal tanks along the fuselage side. (USAF)

With full afterburner, a McDonnell Douglas F-15E Strike Eagle of the 4th TFW based at Seymour Johnson, gets airborne. In the event of conflict, the 4th TFW was earmarked to reinforce USAFE and was expected to deploy to Ramstein. (USAF)

to the Byelorussian SSR. Like other Warsaw Pact air forces, the Polish Air Force began to receive the MiG-29 in 1989. These aircraft were operated by 1.PLM-OPK based at Mińsk Mazowiecki. However economic conditions were deteriorating in Poland and a major re-organization of the entire WL WOPK evolved during the second half of the 1980s. At Powidz 21.PLR was disbanded in 1986 when it became clear that a planned replacement of the Lim-6bis with the Su-22 would not occur and the other Lim-6bis regiment, 45.PLM-Sz became a training unit. Two MiG-21 regiments, 39.PLM-OPK and 9.PLM were disbanded in 1987 and 1988, although the 'number plate' of 9.PLM was transferred to 26.PLM-OPK at Zegrze-Pomorski. With the decreased importance of nuclear weapons after the Reykjavik summit, 3.PLM-B lost its nuclear capability and ran down its operational readiness. Its Su-7 complement was gradually supplanted by the PZL-Mielec TS-11 *Iskra* (spark) training aircraft.

The MiG-29 was also delivered to the 11.SLPl of the Czechoslovak Air Force in 1989; previously both 6 and 20.SBoLPl had converted to the Su-22M4. Although 4.SLPl, a MiG-21 unit based at Pardubice, was disbanded in 1988, its place at Pardubice had already been taken by 30.SBoLPl, which had formed with the Su-25K three years previously. Like most Warsaw Pact air forces, the Czech force was largely made up of MiG-21 and MiG-23 regiments, with four of the former and two of the latter, each equally split between the air-defence and ground-attack roles.

Just as their NATO counterparts did, the Warsaw Pact air forces carried out extensive routine training. From 1980, this began to include training in air combat manoeuvring against visual targets, when previously fighter pilots had practised only intercepts tightly controlled from the ground. Soviet and Warsaw Pact training sorties tended to be short in length (less than one hour) and pilots might achieve between 80 and 120 hours per year, whereas NATO aircrew would expect to fly a minimum of 180 hours per year. Furthermore, Warsaw Pact training tended to be highly rehearsed and concentrate on single events; however, the US Defense Technical Information Center (DTIC) reported in 1985 that there had been an increase in the number of multi-event training sorties. The DTIC assessed that Warsaw Pact aircrew were 'proficient in aircraft handling and in execution of precisely timed pre-planned attacks' and that fighter pilots were 'increasingly proficient in complex controlled intercept sorties.'

SOUTHERN REGION/ SOUTH-WESTERN TVD, 1986-89

The deployment of fourth-generation fighters continued across southern Europe. In Spain the air force took delivery of the F-18 in 1988. The aircraft were based with *Ala* 15 at Zaragoza, where they were operated by Esc 151 and 152. The first air service to receive the F-16 in the Southern Region was the Turkish, which started to receive the aircraft in 1987, replacing the F-104G in 141 and 142 *Filo* at Murted. However, the Turkish Air Force had also received something of a bounty with the withdrawal of the F-104 in northern Europe, which provided an opportunity to purchase substantial numbers of F-104G from the Luftwaffe and CF-104 from Canada. Both 181 and 182 Filo at Diyabarkir were able to replace their obsolescent F-100D with the CF-104 and the ex-Luftwaffe aircraft enabled 6 nci AJÜ at Bandirma and 9 ncu AJÜ Balikesir to continue to operate the F-104 into the next decade. The Turkish F-5 fleet was also bolstered by the delivery of ex-Norwegian aircraft, which had been made surplus by the arrival of the F-16 in Norway.

The Greek Air Force also acquired ex-Luftwaffe F-104G aircraft, which supplemented those operated by 335 and 336 Moira at Araxos. Meanwhile, two newly-formed units at Tanagra, 331 and 332 *Moira*, had already received the Mirage 2000EG in 1988. The following year, the first F-16 arrived for the Greek Air Force and was issued to 330 *Moira* which had just formed at Néa Anghialos. With a front-line force of F-16, Mirage 2000, A-7H, F-4E, F-5 and F-104, the Greek Air Force had one of the most diverse inventories of any air force in NATO.

The order of battle in the Italian Air Force remained virtually unchanged through the late 1980s, with seven *Stormi* of F-104 interceptors and two of Tornado IDS ground-attack aircraft. However, all G-91Y light-bomber *Stormi* began to re-equip with the AMX International A-11 *Ghibli* (Desert Wind) in 1989. The aircraft, which was produced in a joint venture with Brazil, was designed to fulfil the CAS role. The first

A Boeing B-52G Stratofortress armed with AGM-86B ALCMs. The aircraft could carry six externally, three each on the two wing pylons plus a further eight on a rotary launcher in the weapons bay. (USAF)

Italian unit to re-equip with the A-11 was 103° *Gruppo* which was then moved to join 51° *Stormo* at Istrana.

Like its northern counterpart, the Soviet VVS YGV in Hungary resumed its original title, 36th VA, in 1988. The change in title also represented some organizational changes. Just as in the 4th VA, the Su-24 was moved back into the USSR and a MiG-27 unit, 88 APIB moved into Debrecen. At Kunmadaras, 1 GvAPIB traded the Su-17M2 for the MiG-27 and the MiG-21-equipped 515 GvIAP was disbanded in 1989. The reconnaissance unit, 328 GvRAP, replaced the Yak-28R in its first squadron with the Su-24MR, which left the 36 VA as a small but powerful force comprising two *polki* of MiG-23 air-defence fighters and two of MiG-27 ground-attack aircraft. The order of battle for the Hungarian Air Force remained unchanged, although delivery of the MiG-29 was expected in the early 1990s.

Romania received the MiG-29 in 1989: the aircraft were issued to R57AvVt at Mihail Kogălniceanu, where they replaced the MiG-23 in the first squadron. The introduction of the MiG-23 to Mihail Kogălniceanu and Timișoara-Giarmata air bases earlier in the decade had resulted in a surplus of MiG-21 aircraft, so a new fighter regiment, R71AvVt was formed with the

type at Campia Turzii in 1986, using these aircraft. Bulgaria also received the MiG-29 in 1989 to equip 1 IAE/15 IAP at Ravenetz. This re-equipment was part of a larger programme throughout the decade, which resulted in the MiG-23 being operated by both Eskadrila of 18 IAP in the air-defence role and by 25 IBAP at Cheshnegirovo in the ground-attack role. At the same time, 22 IBAP at Bezmer re-equipped with the Su-25K. Since both of the ground-attack regiments had previously flown the MiG-17, the introduction of these new types represented a major upgrade in combat capability.

END GAME

Although re-equipment with the latest combat aircraft continued throughout NATO and the Warsaw Pact late into 1989, it coincided with the unravelling of the Communist system of government across Eastern Europe. Free elections in Poland in the summer of 1989 gave resounding support for Solidarity and destroyed the credibility of the government. The Polish Communist Party clung to power until the following year, but the shockwaves reverberated around the Eastern Bloc. On 9 November 1989, the symbolic end to the Cold War came when thousands of East Berliners overwhelmed the military checkpoints at the Berlin Wall and flooded through into West Berlin. By the end of the year, Communist governments had collapsed in all of the Warsaw Pact countries and the Cold War had ended. In the DDR, Czechoslovakia, Hungary, Bulgaria and Poland, the changeover was peaceful, but in Romania the revolution was a violent but short one. Germany was reunified in 1990 and the Warsaw Pact was formally dissolved in Prague on 1 July 1991; by the end of that year the USSR had also ceased to exist.

Opposite: Despite the introduction of the Dassault Mirage 2000N nuclear strike aircraft in 1988, the Dassault Mirage IV continued to carry the French nuclear deterrent until the end of the 'Cold War'. This aircraft, using Jet Assisted Take-Off (JATO) rockets to improve take-off performance, is from EB 1/91 'Gascogne' based at Mont-de-Marsan. (Schleiffert)

A Dassault Mirage IV of EB 2/91 'Bretagne' based Cazaux streams its braking Parachute. Throughout the 1980s, the CFAS had a force of 62 Mirage IV bombers and 12 Boeing C-135F tanker aircraft. Crews and aircraft at Operational Alert were kept at 15 minutes readiness. (Bannwarth)

Above:
When 3.PLM-B of the Polish Wojska Obrony Powietrznej Kraju, based at Bydgoszcz, lost its nuclear role in the late 1980s, its Sukhoi Su-7BM [Fitter-A] aircraft were replaced by the Polskie Zakłady Lotnicze (PZL) TS-11 *Iskra* (spark) training aircraft. (Halun/Wikimedia)

Right:
The AMX International A-11 *Ghibli* (desert wind) light ground-attack aircraft was a design collaboration between Italy and Brazil. The aircraft entered Italian service with 103° *Gruppo* of 51° *Stormo* in November 1989. (KGyST/Wikimedia)

When the Cold War ended abruptly, so did much of the political support for military spending. It was replaced by the concept of the 'Peace Dividend' which would, in theory, be generated by the reduction in defence spending. Initially, the USA, UK and Italy were diverted by the Kuwait Crisis of 1990 and the ensuing Gulf War of 1991, but nevertheless the air forces based in Europe shrank quickly. The USAFE air base at Hahn was closed in 1991, RAF Wildenrath closed in 1992 and 1 Canadian Air Division withdrew from Baden Solingen in 1993. The former Soviet 4th VA left Poland in 1992 and the 16th VA left Germany the following year. More closures and squadrons being disbanded followed in the next few years on both sides of what was once the Iron Curtain and the air forces of all the former protagonists of the Cold War rapidly diminished in size.

Paradoxically, the Cold War was an almost unprecedented time of peace in Europe, during a century that had already seen two world wars. The threat of military force, and in particular of nuclear war, was enough to prevent hostilities and the posturing of military forces became a means of indicating political will. In this respect, air power became one of the foremost political tools because of the speed of deployment, as well as the firepower and reach, of a combat aircraft. However, deterrence and posturing could only work if the military force was credible and thus the years of the Cold War witnessed the establishment of the best-equipped air forces that the world has seen. A continuous process of re-equipment with the latest aircraft and weapon systems, as well as a comprehensive and demanding training regime, ensured that those air forces were ready for action, if required, almost instantaneously. Of course, this powerful military capability was not bought cheaply: expensive modern aircraft and training costs were a huge burden on defence budgets, but there was also a human cost, in the large number of aircrew in all the air forces of NATO, the Warsaw Pact and the non-aligned nations who lost their lives during flying operations over the 40 years between 1949 and 1989.

The Lockheed F-117A Night Hawk 'stealth fighter' was operated by the 4450th Tactical Group based at Tonopah Test Range Airport from 1984, but its existence only became unclassified in 1990. Designed to be almost invisible to radars, the F-117 was not equipped with self-defence armament, but could carry two 2,000lb GBU-10 Paveway II LGBs in an internal weapons bay. (USAF)

IN NEUTRAL SKIES

At the end of World War II, most of Europe was divided between the Soviet and US spheres of interest, but a small number of countries managed avoid the polarisation to maintain a non-aligned stance. For some of those countries such as Sweden and Switzerland, neutrality was a free choice reflecting long-standing policy, while for others, like Finland and Austria, political circumstances forced their hand. But whatever the root of their neutrality, each of the non-aligned nations had to be prepared to defend themselves and an effective air force was a necessity.

SWEDEN

"Hold the border!" Thorbjörn Fälldin, Swedish Prime Minister: 1976-82

After being a regional super-power in the previous centuries, Sweden adopted a policy of neutrality from the mid-19th Century. During World War II, large well-equipped armed forces helped to ensure that Sweden remained a non-combatant. At the start of the Cold War, the *Svenska Flygvapnet* (Swedish Air Force) had a strength of some 800 combat aircraft. The basic unit of the Flygvapnet was the *Flygflottilj* (F – air wing) which was typically made up of three *Flygdivisionen* (squadrons), each of about 12 aircraft. The *Flygflottilje* were grouped into four *Flygeskader* (E – flight squadrons), but analogous to RAF Groups. The *Första Flygeskadern* (first flight squadron – E1), controlled the four ground-attack *Flygflottilje*, which were equipped with a mixture of SAAB A21 attack aircraft and B18 medium bombers; the *Fjärde Flygeskadern* (fourth flight squadron – E4), was responsible for three reconnaissance *Flygflottilje*.

The *Andra Flygeskadern* (second flight squadron – E2) and *Tredje Flygeskadern* (third flight squadron – E3), second and third flight squadrons formed the air-defence force: each comprised five *Flygflottilje* of day fighters and in addition, E3 also contained the night fighter Flugflotillj F1. In 1950, the most numerous combat type in service with E2 and E3 was the de Havilland Vampire, known locally as the J28 (J – Jakt, fighter), which equipped six *Flygflottilje*. One unit also flew the jet-powered SAAB J21R. The balance of units flew various propeller-driven types such as the SAAB J21A, the North American F-51 Mustang, known as the J26 and the de Havilland Mosquito NF19, known as the J30. The air defence of the country was organized around five *Flygbasområde* (air base areas), each of which was centred on a major air base which was responsible for a specific geographical area. These bases were Luleå, Östersund, Stockholm, Göteborg and Ängelholm.

Like the other air forces of Europe, the Flygvapnet underwent modernization and re-equipment in the 1950s, maintaining its independent neutrality through the policy of procuring indigenous aircraft whenever possible. These were produced by the Svenska Aeroplan Aktiebolag (SAAB). The first swept-wing jet fighter to enter service was the SAAB J29 *Tunnen* (barrel), which equipped 11 *Flygflottilje* by the mid-1950s. These included some A29 (A – Attack) ground attack and S29 (S – *Spaning* [reconnaissance]) versions. However, there were still some foreign types in the inventory, including the Vampire (J28) which remained in service with *Flygflottilje* F4, F14, F15, F17 and F20. Thus, by the mid-1950s, Sweden was believed to have the fourth

Traffic waits as a SAAB AJ-37 *Viggen* (Thunderbolt) attack aircraft of Flygflottilje 15, normally based at Söderhamn/Östansjö taxis onto a roadway. Under the Bas-60 concept, Flygvapnet units regularly practised dispersed operations from highway strips. (F13/Rune Ryah)

A SAAB S-18A reconnaissance aircraft of F11 Wing. Originally designed as a three-seat light bomber, the twin-seat S-18 had such a poor safety record that it was fitted with ejection seats. The type was replaced by the SAAB S-32 Lansen in the late 1950s. (Flyghistoria)

or fifth largest air force in the world, with a combat strength of 50 *Flygdivisionen*.

Sweden, just like the members of the NATO alliance, relied on reconnaissance and ELINT to ascertain the intentions of the USSR and Warsaw Pact countries in the region. Flygvapnet reconnaissance aircraft were therefore engaged in operational activities over the Baltic Sea. In the summer of 1952 a major diplomatic incident occurred, known in Sweden as the '*Catalinaaffären*' (Catalina affair). On 13 June, a Douglas Tp79 (a DC3 variant) ELINT aircraft of the *Försvarets radioanstalt* (FRA – National Defence Radio Establishment), was shot down over the eastern Baltic by MiG-15bis fighters from Tukums airbase in the Latvian SSR, killing all of the crew. Three days later, a Consolidated Tp47 Catalina from the Flygvapnet carrying out a search for the missing aircraft was also intercepted and shot down by Soviet aircraft. Apart from the diplomatic ructions that ensued, the affair emphasized the weakness of the Swedish air defences and their lack of an integrated early warning system. As a result, an air defence QRA was established and the systems for a *Stridsledning och Luftbevakning* (STRIL – battle management and early warning service) were developed.

Deliveries of the SAAB A32A *Lansen* (lance) two-seat fighter-bomber began to F17 at Ronneby in 1956 and over the next four years it went on to equip all five of the ground attack *Flygflottilje* in E1, replacing the J29. The all-weather fighter version, the J32B superseded the de Havilland Venom (J33) night fighter in F1 at Västerås in 1960 and the reconnaissance variant, the S32C saw service with F11 at Nyköping from 1958. In 1957 a major re-organisation introduced a new command and control system, known as STRIL-50 which divided the country into 11 *Luftförsvarscentral* (LFC – air defence centres), instead of the previous five *Flygbasområde*. However, the STRIL-50 system was not in permanent use: it was only mobilized for exercises or in the event of hostilities. By this time, the J28 and J29 were becoming fast outclassed as an air-defence fighters and a stopgap was required to fill the air-defence role until the SAAB J35 *Draken* (dragon) became available. The solution was to procure 120 Hawker Hunter F50 fighters, designated J34 in Swedish service, and these equipped F8 at Stockholm/Barkarby and F18 at Stockholm/Tullinge.

In 1958 the *Bas*-60 (Base-60), concept was initiated in order to make the Flygvapnet assets less vulnerable to air attack in the coming decade. Main operating bases, known as *Ordinarie baser* (O-bas – regular bases), were enlarged in area so that aircraft and equipment could be dispersed more widely within them. In addition, a number of *Temporär baser* (T-bas – temporary bases), comprising austere operating strips that only had facilities to refuel and re-arm aircraft were established across the country. On an O-bas, a *Främre klargöringsområde* (Framom – forward readiness area) – effectively an Operational Readiness Platform (ORP) – was built at each end of the runway to house about four aircraft at a high readiness state. Approximately 2–3km away, there was the *Bakre klargöringsområde* (Bakom – rear readiness area) where up to ten aircraft could be parked in dispersals and prepared for missions. Separated by a similar distance would be the *Uppställningsområdet* (Uom – line-up area), where deep rectification work could be carried out. The various other command and support functions were similarly dispersed over the base area. Where it was possible to link taxiways to the local road network, stretches of highway were strengthened and straightened to form *Reservvägbaser* (reserve bases), or road runways. Large-scale *Flygvapenövningar* (FVÖ – air force exercises) were held every few years to ensure that all the units of the Flygvapnet were combat ready.

The arrival of the J35 Draken coincided with that of the 'Century-series' fighters in the US, the MiG-21 in the USSR and the English-Electric Lightning in the UK. The first unit to operate the Draken, F13 at Nyköping, received its aircraft in 1960 and by 1965 most of the air defence units were equipped with the new fighter. The air defence system was further upgraded in the early 1960s with the introduction of the STRIL-60, a fully automatic and computerized control and surveillance system that coordinated all the various air defence components. Apart from manned interceptors, this included Bristol Bloodhound Robotsystem 68, (Rb – missile system), and Raytheon HAWK Rb67 surface-to-air missile (SAM) batteries. The 11 LFCs used in

Two wings, F4 (based at Östersund/Frösön) and F16 (based at Uppsala/Ärna) operated the North American F-51 Mustang, known as the J-26 in Swedish service. This aircraft is fitted with skis for winter operations. The J-26s were replaced by jet fighters in 1952. (Flyghistoria)

In 1948, Sweden purchased 50 Supermarine Spitfire Mk 19s for the F11 Wing at Nyköping. In Swedish service the aircraft was designated as the S-31 and the type supplemented the S-18s in the photo reconnaissance role until the mid-1950s. (Flyghistoria)

the STRIL-50 system were consolidated and reduced to seven in number. Additionally, STRIL-60 included an integrated data-link system compatible with the Draken that enabled ground controllers to pass instructions securely to the fighter aircraft during interceptions without the need for voice transmissions. Another re-organization of the Flygvapnet command structure occurred in 1966, when the *Flygeskader* E2, E3 and E4 were disbanded and their units became administered directly by the *Flygstaben* (FS – air staff); however, the offensive *Flygeskadern* E1 was retained and it now came under the direct command of the *Överbefälhavaren* (ÖB – commander-in-chief) of the *Försvarsmakten* (Swedish armed forces). The main role of E1 became that of anti-shipping strikes because of the threat to Sweden of Soviet amphibious forces operating in the Baltic Sea. In this role, the prime armament of the Lansen was the SAAB Rb04 anti-shipping missile.

The J34 Hunter, modified in Swedish service to carry the AIM-9 Sidewinder AAM, remained in service until 1969, when the last Hunter unit, F9 at Göteborg, was disbanded. At the beginning of the 1970s, the Flygvapnet possessed eight J35 Draken-equipped *Flygflottilje* in the air defence role and two more *Flygflottilje* operating the S35E Draken reconnaissance variant. The Första *Flygeskadern* comprised four *Flygflottilje*, F6, F7, F15 and F17, flying the A32A Lansen. However, the Lansen was becoming obsolescent and its successor was the SAAB AJ37 *Viggen* (thunderbolt), which entered service with F7 at Såtenäs in 1971. Over the next decade a number of versions of the Viggen were introduced into service: the SF37 (*Spaning Foto* – photo-reconnaissance) variant, the SH37 (*Spaning Hav* – maritime reconnaissance) and the JA37 (*Jakt Attack* – interceptor/ground attack).

The first JA37 unit was F13 based at Norrköping in 1980 and the air-defence system was revised again the following year, when the number of sectors was reduced again this time to four equal-sized *Storasektorer* (big sectors), which sub-divided the country from north to south. In the 1970s and 1980s, the Swedish defence budget was subject to similar economic pressures to those of other European nations and financial restrictions resulted in a number of units being

Left:
The propeller-driven J-21A was originally procured as a fighter, but also saw service until the early 1950s as a ground-attack aircraft (designated as the A-21A). The J-21R/A-21R, powered by a de Havilland Goblin engine, was the first jet aircraft to see service with the Flygvapnet. (SAAB)

Below:
Sweden was the first export customer for the de Havilland Vampire, ordering 70 Vampire F1s (J-28A in Swedish service) in 1946 and another 310 Vampire FB50s (J-28Bs). (Flyghistoria)

Right:
Mechanics service a SAAB J-29 *Tunnen* (barrel) on the ice surface of frozen Lake Rixen in February 1955. The first indigenous Swedish jet aircraft, the J-29 saw service through the late 1950s and into the late 1960s. (SAAB)

Below:
Aircraft shelters were built into the rocks at a number of air bases. Here a Hawker Hunter F50 (the export version of the Hunter F4) is towed from one such shelter. Modified to carry the AIM-9 Sidewinder AAM, the Hunter served with the Flygvapnet until 1969. (Flyghistoria)

disbanded. By the late 1970s, the *Flygflottilje* F1, F3, F11, F12 and F15 had all been disbanded, while most of the remaining *Flygflottilje* had been reduced in size from three to two *Flygdivisionen*. From its peak strength of 50 *Flygdivisionen* in the 1950s, the *Flygvapnet* had been reduced by 1985 to just 19 *Flygdivisionen*. Of these 13 flew variants of the J37, while the remaining six, split between F10 at Ängelholm and F16 at Uppsala were still equipped with the J35F.

Throughout the Cold War, Flygvapnet fighter aircraft vigorously enforced the neutrality of Swedish airspace against incursions by NATO and Warsaw Pact aircraft alike. The high performance of the Viggen also enabled the Flygvapnet the carry out interceptions against the USAF SR-71 missions over the Baltic. Although the Viggen could not match the speed or altitude of the SR-71, the aircraft could be positioned to achieve successful missile launch parameters as the SR-71 flew close to Swedish airspace.

On 29 June 1987, a SR-71 was flying the 'Baltic Express' reconnaissance route and had turned north to loop around the island of Gotland, when it suffered a catastrophic engine failure. While the crew carried out the drills to contain the problem, the aircraft decelerated from Mach 3.0 and dropped rapidly from 80,000ft to around 25,000ft. The pilot turned south to divert to northern Germany, but their route took them directly into Swedish airspace over Gotland. Two unarmed JA-37 Viggens from F13, which were on a routine training flight over the Baltic, were immediately diverted to intercept the intruder. At the same time a further two armed AJ-37 Viggens of F6, flown by Major L-E. Blad and Lt B. Ingnell, were scrambled from the southern QRA at Ängelholm. Alarmingly, the Soviets had already dispatched a MiG-25 to intercept the SR-71 and order the crew to land or be shot down. Over the next minutes, the Soviets launched some further 20 fighter aircraft for the same mission. The first pair of aircraft located the SR-71 and began to escort the aircraft through Swedish airspace. The presence of the Flygvapnet aircraft was a sufficient deterrence to ensure that the Soviet fighters remained outside Swedish airspace. The first pair of Viggens left the SR-71 when they reached minimum fuel state, but were soon replaced on station by the QRA pair, which continued to escort the aircraft until it reached the sanctuary of Danish airspace. The SR-71 eventually landed at Nordholz Air Base.

There were three variants of the two-seat SAAB *Lansen* (Lance): the A-32A ground attack and maritime strike variant (Pictured here), the J-32B all-weather interceptor and the S-32C tactical reconnaissance aircraft. Five wings of A-32A Lansens formed the backbone of the Flygvapnet strike capability through the 1960s. (SAAB)

Right:
Like the earlier Lansen, the SAAB Viggen was built in a number of variants. The AJ-37 ground-attack aircraft replaced the A-32A Lansen from the early 1970, while in the next decade, the JA-37 fighter variant replaced the J-35F Draken. A reconnaissance/ maritime strike variant, the SH-37, also entered service in the mid-1970s. (SAAB)

Below:
Four SAAB J-35F Drakens of *Flygflottilje* 13, fly low over Stegeborg Castle, near their base at Norrköping. The Draken served as a front-line interceptor from 1960 up until the end of the Cold War. (SAAB)

SR-71 INTERCEPT

29 JUNE 1979
Maj LARS-ERIC BLAD,
FLYGDIVISIONEN 62

I was the squadron commander responsible for manning the QRA unit at Ängelholm on the west coast of Sweden and that day I was one of the pair on duty. It was a really lousy day, with low clouds, drizzle and poor visibility and I told my wingman that if we took off from Ängelholm we would probably have to land at a different base; also that if we launched it would be for something serious. So, I was a little surprised when I was told to increase the alert state from 5min to 1min. As soon as I got into the aircraft I received the order 'Scramble'. I understood that this must be something quite urgent and scrambled as fast as I could. We headed out eastwards, climbing to approximately 25,000ft, flying as fast as we could, but staying subsonic over the land. During the transit I received the information that it was an SR-71 that we were heading towards. Initially, I wondered why, but after being told the altitude of the aircraft I understood that something was wrong with it. Within a few minutes we were over the Baltic and, with good visibility and just a few clouds, got the SR-71 in sight. It was really tricky to lose the speed because the SR-71 was going quite slowly – around 300kt – so we extended past it and hooked back from the east. I could see that the aircraft was in trouble because one of the jet-pipe nozzles was fully open. I flew past the right-hand side of the SR-71 because I did not know if the crew were aware of our presence. I flew close to the cockpit to show my national markings and then flew an orbit to position myself 1km behind the SR-71, while my wingman moved into close formation to take photographs. It was almost unbelievable to fly close to this beautiful and impressive machine. We kept that position for the next 6min or so, until we reached Danish airspace. I then landed back at in Ängelholm, but my wingman landed in Karlsborg after having some minor problems with his avionic systems. Throughout the incident, my intention was to try to help fellow pilots who were in trouble.

A SAAB JA-37 Viggen taxies to a refuelling point on a roadway during a winter exercise in the late 1980s. (Jönsson)

FINLAND

"'We have reached political settlement with our superpower neighbour who has a different cultural heritage and a different social order than we have."
Urho Kekkonen, President of Finland: 1981

Finland had declared itself neutral in the inter-war years, but the country nevertheless saw almost continuous combat during World War II. During the Winter War of 1939–40, Finland successfully prevented an invasion by the USSR, although in doing so it lost most of the region of Karelia to Russia. The following year after the German invasion of the USSR, the Finns saw an opportunity to regain Karelia and in an alliance with Nazi Germany, they fought the Soviets in the Continuation War of 1941-44. This conflict was concluded in the Moscow Armistice of 1944 which permanently ceded Karelia to Russia and forced Finland to lease the naval installation at Porkkala to the USSR. Subsequently the Finns turned upon their former allies and fought the Germans during the Lapland War of 1944-45. By the end of World War II, the Finnish *Ilmavoimat* (Finnish Air Force) was an effective combat-experienced force, equipped with a diverse mixture types including the Messerschmidt Bf109 fighter and the Bristol Blenheim bomber.

In the post-war years, Finland restated its intention to remain non-aligned and after the experiences of the Winter War and Continuation War, the USSR was not prepared to intervene militarily as it had done with other neighbouring countries. The Treaty of Friendship, Co-operation and Mutual Assistance (known in Finland as the Ystävyys-, Yhteistyö- ja Avunantosopimus or YYA-agreement), signed in 1948 between the USSR and Finland gave some guarantee that neutrality would be respected by the Soviets. However, it did include an article requiring Finland to prevent attacks on the USSR by third parties from its territory. Furthermore, as a former ally of Germany, Finland was bound by the Paris Treaty of 1947, which determined the level of war reparations to be paid by former Axis members to the Allies. It also placed restrictions on the size of post-war armed forces: in the case of Finland, the Ilmavoimat was limited to only 60 aircraft, none of which could be 'aircraft designed primarily as bombers with internal bomb-carrying facilities.'

As the Cold War began, the strength of the Ilmavoimat consisted of three *Lentorykmentin* (Le.R – flight regiments), Le.R 1 at Pori, to the west of Tampere, Le.R 3 at Utti, some 129km northeast of Helsinki and Le.R 4 at Luonetjävi in central Finland. Each Le.R contained two *Lentolaivue* (Le.Lv – squadrons) of about

A MiG-21bis taking off from a *maantietukikohta*, (road base): In 1978, the Ilmavoimat received the first of 26 MiG-21bis to replace the obsolescent MiG-21F-13 in the fighter/interceptor role. This aircraft was delivered in 1980 and eight years later it was converted to an MGT (MiG *Tiedusteluversio* – reconnaissance version) for use by the *Tiedustelulentolaivue* (TiedLLv – reconnaissance squadron) based at Luonetjärvi in central Finland. (Laukkanen)

Messerschmidt Bf-109G6 of PLe.Lv.41 seen at Luonetjärvi in 1950. The fighter aircraft replaced the Bristol Blenheims when that type was withdrawn from service in 1948 because of the limitations of the Paris Treaty. The Bf-109 remined in front-line service with the Ilmavoimat until 1954. (Laukkanen)

12 aircraft. The Le.Lv were also titled according to their role: *Hävittäjälentolaivue* (HLe.Lv – fighter squadrons) were designated *Tiedustelulentolaivue* (TiedLLv – reconnaissance squadrons) and *Pommituslentolaivue* (PLe.Lv – bomber squadrons). In 1949, all three Le.R were equipped with the Bf109G-6. In addition, 13 Blenheim bombers, enough to equip a PLe.Lv, were put into storage because of the terms of the Paris Treaty. The Finnish economy struggled between 1948 and 1952 while the country made every effort to pay off in full the war reparations owed to the USSR, so there was little money to spend on the Ilmavoimat, which consequently suffered with poor serviceability and subsequently little flying.

In 1952, the last of the war reparations were paid and investment could be made once more in the armed forces of the country. The Ilmavoimat was re-organized in 1952 and each Le.R became a *Lennosto* (Lsto – air command); each *Hävittäjälentolaivue* was also re-named to become a *Hävittäjälaivue* (HävLv – fighter flotilla), with the exception of the new 1.Lsto, whose sub-unit was divided into the *Hävittäjälentue* (HävLtue – fighter flight) and the *Tiedustelulentue* (TiedLtuue – reconnaissance flight). By now very few of the Bf109s remained airworthy and they were phased out initially in favour of the Valmet-built *Vihuri* (gale) training aircraft. The last Bf109G left service in 1954. The use of the Vihuri by front-line units emphasized the point that the Ilmavoimat had been unable to train many pilots prior to 1952. The first six de Havilland Vampire Mk 52s arrived in 1953 to equip HävLv 11 and 13 at Pori. Within each HävLv, the first flight was equipped with the Vampire and the second flight with the Vihuri. These units were chosen by virtue of the fact that Pori had the only tarmac runway in Finland, the others being grass or gravel, and so it was the only airfield that could accommodate the jet aircraft. Over the next decade a runway improvement programme ensured that the Ilmavoimat had sufficient airbases suitable for jet operations.

A further nine Vampire trainers also joined the frontline in the next year. Having a dual fighter/training aircraft such as the Vampire trainer in front-line service meant that the Ilmavoimat could get the maximum use out of its treaty-limited number of aircraft. Large scale air defence exercises, which became an annual event, were started in 1956, using the Blenheims of the *TieLtue* to act as targets for Vampire and Vihuri crews, which were directed by ground-based radar controllers. The Blenheim was eventually retired from service in 1958. In 1957, the three *Lennosto* (Lsto) were renamed to reflect the regions for which they were responsible: 1.Lsto became the *Hämeen Lennosto* (HämLsto), 2.Lsto the *Satakunnan Lennosto* (SatLsto) and 2.Lsto became the *Karjalan Lennosto* (KarLsto).

While the Vampire provided the Ilmavoimat with an entry into the jet age, the type was already obsolete when it entered Finnish service and it could hardly be regarded as a credible air-defence fighter, especially when compared to such types as the MiG-15. Furthermore, under the terms of the YYA-agreement, it was entirely plausible that the USSR might demand to base its own air-defence aircraft in Finland if it felt that the Ilmavoimat fighter force was inadequate. A suitable front-line fighter was therefore sought, but choice was limited by a modest budget and a desire not to use US-supplied equipment for fear of provoking the Soviets. The choice was the Folland Gnat, which entered service with HävLv 21 (previously the HävLtue) at Luoenetjärvi in 1958. Two of the aircraft were also modified to carry reconnaissance cameras in the nose section. In 1962 there was another change of unit designation when HävLv 21 was renamed to become HävLLv 11 (and the other *Laivue* also reverted to the original title of *Lentolaivue*). Another two-seat training aircraft which could also be used as a fighter-bomber, the Fouga Magister, started to replace the Vihuri in 1958, after the latter type was grounded because of safety issues. Over the next two years, the Magister equipped the units of the SatLsto and KarLsto.

With the fast-moving advances in aircraft performance and combat capability, the Ilmavoimat was soon looking to upgrade its fleet with a truly supersonic aircraft. The USSR had unilaterally withdrawn from the Porkkala naval base in 1956 as a gesture of goodwill, but by the early 1960s, in the face of deteriorating relations with the west, the USSR felt the need to apply some political pressure to secure its relationship with Finland. As a direct result of this pressure from the USSR, the MiG-21 was procured for the Ilmavoimat

A de Havilland Vampire from 2 *Lennosto* detached to Utti in 1954. The aircraft were normally based at Pori, which had the only suitable runway for jet aircraft operations, but Utti became useable that winter after the hard snowfall solidified the asphalt. (Laukkanen)

in 1962 and 20 MiG-21F-13 aircraft were delivered to Rissala by Soviet pilots the following year. Most of these aircraft were issued to HävLLv 31, but the Ilmavoimat was unable to use all of the new airframes, so six of them were sent to Luonetjärvi for storage; they were subsequently used to form the *Tiedustelulentolaivue* (TiedLLV – reconnaissance squadron) at Luonetjärvi in the early 1970s. Meanwhile, in 1966, two Ilyushin Il-28R aircraft were purchased from the USSR for photo-reconnaissance, maritime patrol and target-towing; these aircraft were based at Utti and operated by the *Kuljetuslentolaivue* (transport squadron). The last of the Vampires were retired from service at Luoenetjärvi in 1964 and their place was taken by the Magister, which served alongside the Gnat.

During the 1950s a chain of air-defence surveillance radars had been established across Finland, giving coverage across the whole country. In the next decade the system was improved and extended with the addition of long-range early warning radars. Air-defence operations centres were also built in underground bunkers and a network of *maantietukikohta* (road bases), was also established. These enabled Ilmavoimat aircraft to operate from widely dispersed sites if necessary in times of crisis. The use of all of these facilities was exercised regularly and operating from the *maantietukikohta* became routine for all front-line units from the late 1960s. However, the 'Achilles Heel' of the Ilmavoimat was that both the MiG-21F and the Gnat were purely day fighters and an all-weather air-defence capability was urgently needed. In the early 1970s, the SAAB J35XS Draken all-weather fighter was procured from Sweden and the Gnat was finally retired in 1972.

When it re-equipped with the Draken in 1973, HävLLv 11 moved to Rovaniemi in northern Finland and at the same time the *Hämeen Lennosto* was renamed

Folland (later Hawker Siddeley) Gnat operating from a forested dispersal area at a *maantietukikohta* (road bases). (Laukkanen)

to become the *Lapin Lennosto* (LapLsto), reflecting its responsibility for the defence of Lapland. In the summer of the same year, HävLLv 31 carried out the first squadron exchange visit to the USSR, visiting Kubinka airbase, another MiG-21 operator. The visits continued over the next two decades, with the host nation alternating between the USSR and Finland. The first Soviet visitors flew the MiG-21bis to Rissala in 1974 and in following years Rissala was also visited by MiG-23 and MiG-29 units of the VVS.

The MiG-21F was replaced in 1980 by the upgraded MiG-21bis; in the same year the first of 50 British Aerospace Hawks arrived to start taking the place of the aging Magisters. However, it was also decided to purchase more fighters to equip the Satakunnan Lennosto which had only operated training aircraft since the 1960s and more Drakens were purchased. In the 1980s the pilot training system was fully integrated

Above:
These two Gnats [GN-112 and GN-113] seen at Luonetjärvi in the summer of 1966 are the two aircraft which were fitted with reconnaissance cameras in the nose. (Laukkanen)

Left:
Two SAAB J-35XS Draken fighters at low-level over the forests of northern Finland. The type was first introduced to the Ilmavoimat at Rovaneimi in 1972. (Laukkanen)

Right:
A MiG-21F-13 of HävLLv 31 is serviced under camouflage netting during dispersed operations from *maantietukikohta* (road bases) in June 1973. Off-base operations from roadways were practised frequently. (Laukkanen)

Below:
Another view of a MiG-21F during dispersed operations. (Laukkanen)

into the frontline of the Ilmavoimat: within each Hävittäjälentolaivue the first *Lentue* (flight), was fully operational, the second was the operational conversion unit and the third carried out advanced flying training with the Magister or Hawk.

RC-135V INTERCEPT
27 JANUARY 1989
Lt Col J.O. LAUKKANEN

It was another busy day at the Finnish Air Force Flight Test Centre at Halli where, other than test flying, we also covered QRA; normally a task for fighter squadrons. After lunch it was my turn for a 15-minute readiness alert duty. Besides wearing normal flight gear and an immersion suit, I also wore a pressure suit which would allow me to climb to 50,000ft with a normal flying helmet. My aircraft was MiG-21BIS (serial MG-133); the cannons were armed with live ammunition. At 13:00hrs, the fighter controller ordered me to cockpit readiness for a possible identification mission and 6 minutes later I was ordered to scramble. After a fast start-up, line-up on the runway and afterburner take-off, I became airborne at 13:08hrs and headed southwest while climbing to 33,000ft in military power. I was then instructed to hold in a race-track pattern over the sea, south of Åland. After some 10 minutes holding, the controller directed me to the south-southwest and informed me that a target was approaching from some 155 miles away. With my radar switched off, the controller vectored me to intercept the target. I began a turn to starboard and got a visual on the target, which the controller ordered me to identify.

I recognized it as a USAF Boeing RC-135V flying steadily northwards. I reduced speed and formated off its right wing and checked the fuselage number. I remained in formation as it headed north, which was homebound for me. A short time later, the fighter controller informed me of two targets approaching fast from behind; I figured on them being either Swedish Viggens or Soviet MiG-23s. Then the RC-135V turned away, back to south. By now I had been airborne for an hour and my fuel state was approaching 'Bingo', but I continued in the direction of Halli; a diversion to Turku or Pikkala would be possible. Over Turku I still had 800 litres and, with clear skies over mainland Finland, I calculated that I could just make it all the way to base. Passing over Pirkkala, I initiated an idle descent and at 14:38hrs made a smooth landing at Halli. I checked my fuel status: 450 litres remaining, just 50 litres above the minimum-landing amount of 400 litres.

The MiG-21Bis replaced the MiG-21F-13 in 1980. On its tail, the aircraft carries the crouching lynx insignia of HävLLv 31. (Laukkanen)

AUSTRIA

"With how much concern and unspoken mistrust or open mistrust by its western friends was Austria confronted with when in 1955 it chose its path of permanent neutrality." Rudolf Kirchsläger, President of Austria: 1968

After being subsumed into Germany in the *Anschluss* of 1938 and subject to Allied occupation after World War II, Austria became fully independent again in 1955. The Österreichischer Staatsvertrag (Austrian Independence Treaty), signed by Austria, the USSR, USA, UK and France declared the neutrality of Austria. It also allowed the formation of the *Bundesheer* (armed forces), but it expressly stated that 'Austria shall not possess, construct or experiment with... any self-propelled or guided missile.' This particular clause was to have significant ramifications as the Austrians attempted to secure their airspace over the next 35 years. The *Österreichische Luftstreitkräfte* (LStrKr – Austrian Air Force), was formed in May 1955 and its initial inventory reflected its urgent need to train pilots and an emphasis on air observation and liaison duties. A handful of Yak-11 and Yak-18 trainers were gifted to Austria by the USSR and some 29 Cessna L-19A Bird Dog liaison aircraft were supplied by the US.

Two years later the LStrKr received its first jet aircraft, in the form of eight de Havilland Vampire T55 trainers. These were used to form the *Jabo-Schulstaffel* (fighter-bomber training squadron), which operated from Graz-Thalerhof. However, the LStrKr was very heavily biased towards support of the army and its two *Fliegerregimenten* (air regiments), were predominantly equipped with light transport aircraft and helicopters. It was not until 1961 that the first true air-combat unit, 1 *Jabo-Staffel* (fighter-bomber squadron) was formed at Vienna-Schwechat and equipped with the SAAB J29F Tunnen. Over the next two years, 30 of these aircraft, which had been refurbished after retirement from Svenska Air Force service, were procured from Sweden. In 1962, 1 Jabo-Staffel moved to a permanent base at Linz-Hörsching and the following year, after the arrival of a second batch of J29 aircraft, *Jabo-Geschwader* 1 (1st fighter-bomber wing), was established and 2 *Jabo-Staffel* was formed at Linz-Hörsching. Unfortunately, without missile armament, the obsolescent J29F was not well suited to the air-defence role and it was used instead for ground-attack missions.

The lack of any SAM system or credible air-defence fighter meant that Austria was never able to defend its airspace effectively. The problem was identified by the *Kommando Luftstreitkräfte* (KdoLu – air force command), at the time, but with only 5 percent of the

A SAAB 105Ö over the Austrian Alps; one of 40 procured to equip front-line units of the *Luftstreitkräfte* (LStrKr - Austrian Air Force) from 1972. The 105Ö was a more powerful variant of the training/light attack aircraft in service with the Swedish Air Force, with six under-wing hard points to carry weapons for the close air-support role. (SAAB)

Like many air forces, the LStrKr joined the jet age with the de Havilland Vampire T55. Eight of the type were initially used as a training aircraft at the *Jabo-Schulstaffel*, but the arrival of the French-built Fouga Magister allowed them to be used to form a third fighter-bomber *staffel*, at Linz-Hörsching. Here all served in the light attack role until the arrival of the SAAB 105Ö. (Bundesheer)

defence budget being spent on the air force, as opposed to 40 percent in both Sweden and Switzerland, there was no political will to find a solution; so, the LStrKr simply concentrated on supporting the ground forces.

By 1963, the *Jabo-Schulstaffel* had acquired 18 Fouga Magister trainers to replace the Vampire in the training role and the Vampires were transferred to Hörsching. In 1966 these aircraft were used to form 3 Jabo-Staffel which was used for training and utility duties. The same year saw a re-organization of the operational arm of the LStrKr into the *Fliegerbrigade* (air brigade); this restructuring transferred most of the anti-aircraft units to army command. In 1968, 2.Staffel moved to Graz-Thalerhof. This airfield was now named *Fliegerhorst* (air base), Nittner after a World War I aviator and Linz-Hörsching had similarly been renamed Fliegerhorst Vogler. However, the most important event in the year was the Soviet invasion of Czechoslovakia, during which the LStrKr was unable to prevent numerous violations of Austrian airspace by Soviet aircraft, including reconnaissance overflights of Vienna. The Austrian impotence was due to insufficient investment in early warning and command and control systems, as well as the inadequate J29F, which lacked the performance and armament to be an effective interceptor. Unfortunately, the poor performance of the LStrKr during the Czechoslovak crisis was to have profound repercussions over the next years.

The crisis for the LStrKr came in 1972. The J29F, Vampire and Magister were all retired in that year and their places were taken by 40 SAAB 105Ö light-attack training aircraft. The procurement of these subsonic aircraft instead of high-performance interceptors indicated the low priority given to the air defence

Left:
In 1963, the LStrKr procured 18 Fouga CM170 Magisters to replace the de Havilland Vampire as a weapons trainer in the Jabo-Schulstaffel. (Bundesheer)

Below:
The SAAB J29 Tunnan (barrel) was the first true combat aircraft operated by the LStrKr. A total of 30 were purchased in two batches from the Swedish Air Force, and were operated by 1 Staffel and 2 Staffel. (Bundesheer)

of the country. In the same year, the KdoLu was dissolved: most of the strength of the LStrKr was transferred into the army structure, leaving only a small *Fliegerbrigade*, under army command comprising the three *staffeln* of Jabo-Geschwader 1.

The situation improved slightly in 1976 when the *Fliegerbrigade* was expanded to become the *Fliegerdivision* (air division), comprising three *Fliegerregimenten* based at Langenlebarn, Graz-Thalerhof and Linz-Hörsching. There was no increase in the number of jet aircraft: the order of battle of the LStrKr continued to comprise just the three staffeln of SAAB 105Ö. However, the air-defence radar system had been increased and upgraded under the *Goldhaube* (gold helmet) programme which provided full radar coverage of Austria for the first time. The *Überwachungsgeschwader* (ÜbwGeschw – air surveillance wing), was established within Fliegerregiment 2, with responsibility for the security of Austrian airspace; it included 2 Staffel although the SAAB 105Ö was singularly ill-suited to the role. Within Fliegerregiment 3,

1 Staffel continued in the ground-attack role, while 3 Staffel took on the reconnaissance role.

The LStrKr finally obtained a high-performance fighter in the last years of the Cold War, with the purchase of 24 refurbished SAAB J35ÖE fighters from Sweden. All pilot training was carried out in Sweden and the first aircraft arrived in Austria in 1988, when they were issued to 1 Staffel and 2 Staffel, both of which were placed under the command of the ÜbwGeschw. Once again, however, the air defences were compromised because of the restrictions established in the Österreichischer Staatsvertrag: the AIM-9 Sidewinder AAM system was removed from the Drakens before they left Sweden, leaving the Austrian interceptors armed only with two 30mm cannon. In contrast to the other air forces in Europe, the LStrKr was considerably strengthened in the post-Cold War years with the acquisition of effective aircraft and weapon systems and by the turn of the century it had finally matured into an air force that was capable of defending the airspace of its nation.

In the last years of the Cold War, the LStrKr re-equipped with another Swedish-built type, the SAAB J35ÖE Draken. In 1988, a total of 24 of these air-defence aircraft were purchased from the Swedish Air Force. All were operated by Staffel 1 and Staffel 2 of Fliegerregiment 2. (Hainzl)

SWITZERLAND

"Swiss neutrality is far more than a political attitude, although of long duration, but a regular institution of public law, which has been recognised as such by the great powers for a very long time." Hans Schaffner, Swiss Politician: 1967

Switzerland has a long history of neutrality which has been safeguarded by efficient and effective military force. During World War II, the Swiss airspace was vigorously defended against Axis and Allied aircraft alike by the *Flugwaffe Kommando der Flieger und Fliegerabwehrtruppen* (Air Force Command of Aircraft and Anti-Aircraft forces), of the *Schweizer Armee* (Swiss Army). Uniquely, the Swiss armed forces have traditionally been manned by part-time civilian *Miliz* (militia), rather than professional military personnel. This arrangement was also extended to the Flugwaffe, although the nature of military flying meant that a core of professional military aviators had to be established to ensure safety and standardization. This group of *Berufsmilitärpiloten* (professional military pilots), formed the *Überwachungsgeschwader* (UeG – surveillance wing). The *Miliz* personnel, who formed the majority of Flugwaffe pilots, were contracted to serve for an aggregate of six weeks per year with their unit and to fly at least 80 hours in that time; this included attendance at the *Wiederholungskurs* (rc), Refresher Course, which was held annually for all personnel.

In the post-World War II years, the Flugwaffe was divided between three geographically-based regiments: Regiment d'Aviation 1 (Regt Av 1) covered the south of Switzerland, Fliegerregiment 2 (Fl Regt 2) the northwest and Fliegerregiment 3 (Fl Regt 3) the east. Each regiment in turn was made up of about seven *Fliegerstaffeln* (FlSt – squadrons), of 12–18 pilots. Four of the *staffeln*, FlSt 1, 11, 16 and 17, were manned by UeG pilots, while the remaining units were *Miliz staffeln*. In 1950 the combat strength of the Flugwaffe comprised 21 *staffeln* and the inventory included the Swiss-built Eidgenössische Konstruktionswerkstätte (Federal Construction Workshop) D-3800 and C-3603, as well as the North American F-51 Mustang piston-engined fighters. The Mustangs had been procured from the US after delays to the delivery of the de Havilland Vampire which had been ordered in the late 1940s. The first 75 Vampires were delivered in March 1950 and initially equipped FlSt 7, 8 and 9. The aircraft of the Flugwaffe were held centrally, rather than being on the strength of each individual *staffel* and they were issued to flying units as required. By the

A pair of de Havilland Vampire FB6 ground-attack aircraft. The Flugwaffe continuously updated its aircraft types, as demonstrated by the 'Pinocchio' nose modification on these aircraft, which was needed to house modernized avionic equipment. (Swiss AF)

mid-1950s, eight *staffeln* flew the Vampire and another nine operated the de Havilland Venom. The decade also saw the beginning of a large project to extend and improve the infrastructure of military airfields as well as the procurement of the Société Française Radioélectrique (SFR – Radio Company of France), ER-200 early warning radar system. Unfortunately, an attempt to produce an indigenous fighter aircraft, the Flug- und Fahrzeugwerke Altenrhein (FFA), P-16 was unsuccessful and the Swiss government decided instead to procure the Hawker Hunter F58 from the UK.

In 1959 *Flugzeug-Kavernenanlagen* (aircraft cavern shelters), were opened at the six airstrips at Ambri, Buochs, Meiringen, Raron, St Stephan and Turtmann. Each *flugzeug-kaverne* extended into the mountains and contained command posts and workshops as well as storage facilities for the aircraft. Although each flying *staffel* had a wartime operating base, most of the routine flying training was carried out from the larger airfields at Dübendorf, Emmen (Lucerne) and Payerne. With the arrival of the first Hunter following year, the combat units of the Flugwaffe were entirely equipped with British-manufactured aircraft. The first *Miliz* unit to re-equip with the Hunter was FlSt 21. However, during the 1960s, the Venom still provided the main strength of the Flugwaffe, equipping 14 *staffeln*, while the Hunter equipped a further five. From 1964, the manned interceptors of the Flieger und Fliegerabwehrtruppen were supplemented by another British system, the Bristol Bloodhound BL-64 SAM.

Switzerland chose the Dassault Mirage IIIS as its front-line interceptor in the early1960s, but various modifications which were required by the Flugwaffe leadership, including incorporation of the Hughes TARAN (Tactical Attack Radar and Navigation) radar/fire control system, caused a massive cost overrun. The original budget for the project of CHF 871 million in 1961 rose by a further CHF 576 million in 1964, causing a national scandal, known as the 'Mirage-Affäre'. The aircraft order was reduced from 100 airframes to just 57, the Minister of Defence, Chief of the Army Staff and head of the Flugwaffe were all forced to resign and the structure of the Flieger und Fliegerabwehrtruppen was completely revised. Under the new system, the flying units were grouped into Flieger Brigade 31, while the functions of the airfield personnel and anti-aircraft forces were also separated into Brigaden 32 and 33. Within Flieger Brigade 31, the three *Fliegerregimenten* were each sub-divided into four *Geschwaderen* (Gesch – wings), each of which corresponded to an individual airbase within the regimental area; each geschwader consisted of two or three *staffeln*.

The first Mirage IIIS unit was FlSt 17, a UeG *staffel*, which received its aircraft at Payerne in 1967

The EKW D-3800 was a Swiss-produced variant of the Moraine-Saulnier 406 fighter. The D-3800 was obsolete by the start of the Cold War and the type was quickly replaced by the North American F-51 Mustang. However, a later model, the D-3802, remained in service with the Flugwaffe until 1959. (Swiss AF)

SWITZERLAND

Left:
In many ways the backbone of the Flugwaffe during the Cold War, the Hawker Hunter Mk 58 was used in both the air defence and ground attack roles. This particular aircraft was modified to carry the AIM-9 Sidewinder air-to air missile. (Swiss AF)

Below:
Intended as a multi-role fighter/bomber/reconnaissance aircraft, the EKW C-3603 was not a particularly successful design, but after retirement from service in the 1950s, the type continued in Flugwaffe service as a target-towing and search and rescue platform. (Swiss AF)

Right:
The Northrop F-5E Tiger began to replace the Hunter in the air-to-air role from 1979. By the end of the Cold War, the Flugwaffe operated 98 of these aircraft. (Northrop/Grumman)

and was followed by FlSt 16. The third Mirage unit was the photo-reconnaissance *staffel*, FlSt 10, which replaced the Venom FB1R with the Mirage IIIRS. The Flugwaffe Mirages were armed with the Hughes AIM-4 Falcon for the air defence role and the Nord AS.30 AGM for ground attack, while the Hunters carried the Raytheon AIM-9 Sidewinder AAM and the Hughes AGM-65 Maverick. In 1965, three Hunters were detached to northern Sweden to test-fire live Sidewinder missiles on the *Vidsel* air-weapons range. The Swiss air defence infrastructure was also upgraded in 1970 with the introduction of the semi-automated FLORIDA (FLugsicherungs Operations Radar IDentifikation Alarm – Airspace Monitoring Identification and Alerting Radar) early warning and fighter control system, which replaced the obsolescent SFR system. That year also saw the first trials operating Venom aircraft from highway strips. The Swiss autobahn (motorway) system had been built to incorporate long straight stretches of road surface that could be used as temporary runways, known as *Notlandepisten* (NOLA/NOSTA – emergency strips). After the success of this exercise, it was repeated regularly in subsequent years with Venoms, Hunters, and later the Northrop F-5.

A request for more modern ground-attack aircraft was rejected by the Federal Government in the early 1970s, but a further 30 Hunters were purchased, allowing some of the Venoms to be replaced. The UeG was also expanded to include the Mirage-equipped FlSt 18 in 1975. From the late 1970s, the Flugwaffe carried out an increasing amount of overseas training and Swiss Mirages visited the Vidsel range for live air-to-air missile firings in 1977, 1981 and again in 1986. Swiss Mirages and the F-5E, which entered service in 1979, also started to use the Air Combat Manoeuvring Instrumentation (ACMI) Range at Decimomannu, Sardinia, from 1985. The arrival of the F-5E into service in the late 1970s released more Hunters from the air-defence role, which enabled the last of the Venom units to re-equip with the Hunter. Thanks to progressive upgrades to the avionics suite, the Hunter remained in front-line service with the Flugwaffe in the ground-attack role until the end of the Cold War. Additionally, the Hunters of FlSt 24 had been converted to the *Elektronische Kriegsführung* (EKF – electronic warfare) role in the late 1970s. The last year of the Cold War saw the introduction of a new training and light attack aircraft, the British Aerospace Hawk.

Up to eight JATO (Jet Assisted Take Off) rocket motors could give the Mirage IIIS an impressive short take-off performance of about 300m. The Flugwaffe operated 36 Mirage IIIS fighter aircraft and a further 18 of the Mirage IIIRS reconnaissance variants. (Swiss AF)

YUGOSLAVIA

"We are not afraid of being alone. It would be well if only the capitalist countries were against us, but we also have the socialist countries or those who call themselves socialists against us." Josef Broz Tito, 1950

At the end of World War II, Yugoslavia was one of the closest allies of the USSR. However, over the immediate post-war years, the relationship between Josef Stalin and the Yugoslav leader, Josep Tito, soured and in 1949 Yugoslavia was expelled from the Cominform (Information Bureau of the Communist and Workers' Parties) organization. A Communist regime estranged from its ideological partners and with little in common with the NATO membership, Yugoslavia chose to become a leading light for the non-aligned nations of the world. The Non-Aligned Movement (NAM) organization was founded in Yugoslavia in 1956.

In 1950, the *Jugoslovensko Ratno Vazduhoplovstvo* (JRV – Yugoslav Air Force), was well-equipped with an inventory that reflected its previous close ties with the USSR. Its basic unit was the *Puk* (regiment), which comprised three *Avijacijske Eskadrile* (aviation squadrons). In 1950 the structure of the JRV was based around six *Avijacijske Divizije* (aviation divisions), 39 and 44 *Lovačke Divizije* (fighter divisions), 29 and 37 *Jurišne Divizije* (assault divisions), 32 *Bombarderska Divizija* (bomber divisions), and 21 *Mešovita Divizija* (mixed divisions). The mainstay of the jurišna units was the Il-2 and of the bombarderske, the Pe-2. The *Lovačk Pukovnije* (fighter squadrons), however, operated more diverse fighter types, such as the Yak-3, the Bf-109G and the Yugoslav-built Ikarus S-49.

As a non-aligned nation and a former wartime ally, Yugoslavia was able to access western aircraft in the early 1950s. Its withdrawal from the Eastern Bloc also made it eligible to receive US economic aid through the Economic Cooperation Administration (ECA); thus, from 1951 the JRV received 150 Republic F-47D Thunderbolt fighters, nearly 80 de Havilland Mosquito FB6 light bombers and 60 Mosquito NF38 night-fighters. In the same year, an improved and re-engined version of the S-49, the S-49C, entered service. Two years later, Yugoslavia also entered the jet age with the procurement of 230 Republic F-84G Thunderjets and 25 Lockheed T-33 trainer aircraft, so that by the mid-1950s, the Soviet aircraft types had all disappeared from the front-line strength of the JRV. Meanwhile, the command structure of the JRV was revised to include 3 and 7 *Vazduhoplovni Korpus* (VaK – airborne corps), to manage the activities of the *Avijacijske Divizije*: 3 VaK contained 21, 32 and 37 Divizije, while 7 VaK

Yugoslavia was the only Communist-governed country to operate the Republic F-84G Thunderjet. The RViPVO operated 230 Thunderjets, which entered service in 1953 to replace the Yakovlev Yak-3 and Messerschmidt Bf-109G. Some of the aircraft were also converted to the tactical reconnaissance role. (Maranovic)

contained 29, 39 and 44 *Divizije*. In 1956, 120 ex-RAF Canadair CL-13 (F-86E) Sabres were supplied to the JRV and four of the F-84G units, 83, 94, 117 and 204 *Pukovnije* replaced their aircraft with the Sabre.

A major reorganization of the Yugoslavian air forces, code-named *Drvar*, began in 1959. Following the Soviet model, the anti-aircraft defences were incorporated into the JRV, which changed its title to *Ratno Vazduhoplovstvo i Protivvazdušna Odbrana* (RV i PVO – air force and air defence). Radar cover of the country was improved using soviet-made radar systems and the early warning and fighter control facility, *Vazdusno Osmatranje Javljanje i Navođenje* (VOJIN – air observation reporting and control), was also upgraded and improved within the revised organization. Soviet S-75 Dvina [Sa-2 Guideline] SAM systems were also acquired. At the same time, the *Korpus/Divizija* structure replaced: this time combat units were organized into five *Vazduhoplovna Komanda* (VaK-da – air commands), which closely matched the composition of the original *Avijacijske Divizije*. Many of the F-47 and S-49C units had been disbanded in the late 1950s, so by 1960 the combat strength of the RV i PVO stood at four Sabre, four F-84G and three F-47 *Pukovnije*, plus two *Izviđačke Pukovnije* (reconnaissance regiments), equipped with the RF-84G and RT-33. Additionally, 97 *Puk*, based at Mostar, had converted from the Mosquito FB6 to the Ikarus 214 *Protivpodmornički* (anti-submarine warfare), aircraft.

The last of the F-47s were retired in 1961 with the Pukovnije disbanded, leaving the RV i PVO with an all-jet frontline. The following year, the F-86D 'Sabre Dog' all-weather interceptor was introduced into service with 117 and 184 Puk at Pleso, replacing the Sabre and RF-84G respectively in those units. Thanks to improving relations with the Khrushchev regime in the USSR, the RV i PVO also acquired the MiG-21F-13 [Fishbed] in 1962. The aircraft were allocated initially to 204 Puk based at Batajnica. A further reorganisation in 1964, called Drvar-2, streamlined the RV i PVO back into a two-*Korpusima* command structure: 1, 3 and 7 VaK-da were merged to form 1 Va K, while controlled the flying

A Yugoslav-British collaboration, the Soko J-21 Jastreb (Hawk), which replaced the Republic F-84G Thunderjet as a light ground-attack aircraft from 1968, was powered by a Rolls Royce Viper turbojet, fitted with a Martin-Baker ejection seat and avionics of British manufacture. It was developed from the Soko G-2A Galeb (Seagull) training aircraft. (Maranovic)

units in the east of the country, while 5 and 9 VaK-da merged into 5 VaK, which controlled those in the west. The number of combat units had reduced to eight: four *Pukovnije* with the F-84G, two with the F-86D, one with the F-86E and one with the MiG-21. In addition, 103 Puk at Tuzla continued in the reconnaissance role with the IT-33. During the late 1960s, the Yugoslavian aircraft company SOKO, formerly Ikarus, working in collaboration with British manufacturers, produced the J-21 *Jastreb* (hawk) as a replacement for the obsolete F-84G and the upgraded MiG-21PFM was also supplied by the USSR. For a short while the RV i PVO had an interestingly mixed inventory of western and eastern types, but the Sabre and F-86D were phased out of service in the early 1970s. Following the example of the Swiss, the Yugoslavians tunnelled aircraft shelters and command bunkers into the sides of mountains at the air bases at Bihać, Pristina, Titograd and Mostar. These facilities were completed in the early 1970s. By the middle of the decade the RV i PVO comprised four *Pukovnije* operating variants of the MiG-21, plus two *Avijacijske Brigade* (aviation brigades), (enlarged regiments) and two *Pukovnije* all operating the Jastreb

SOKO continued with collaborative work, this time with the Romanian company Avioane Craiova to produce the J-22 *Orao* (Eagle). This aircraft, which was also built in Romania under the designation IAR-93 *Vultur* (Vulture), was built to replace the Jastreb in the RV i PVO and it entered service in 1984. The MiG-21bis also became available, replacing the obsolescent MiG-21F. Another reorganization of the RV i PVO command structure was carried out in 1986, when the two VaK were re-aligned to become three *Korpusima* RV i PVO (air force and air defence corps). Once again, these new formations were geographically based, with 1 Ko RV i PVO covering the centre of the country, 3 Ko RV i PVO the south-east and 5 Ko RV i PVO the north-west. Each Ko RV i PVO comprised one *Puk* and two *Eskadrite* operating the MiG-21, one *Avijacijska Brigada* and two *Eskadrile* operating the Jastreb or Orao and a reconnaissance *Eskadrila*.

In the late 1950s, the RViPVO acquired the supersonic MiG-21F-13. The type was operated by 83.*Puk* based at Pristina and 204.*Puk*, based at Batajnica. This aircraft is carrying a PTB-800 (800litre) fuel drop tank on the centreline and Vympel R-35 [Atoll] AAMs on the wing pylons. (Topfoto)

ALBANIA

"We want peace, while imperialism does not want peace and is preparing for a third world war." Enver Hoxha, 1960

An original signatory of the Warsaw Pact, Albania became increasingly estranged from the USSR in the late-1950s as the policies of the Khrushchev administration diverged from the hard-line Stalinist doctrine of the Albanian leadership. Relations between the two countries finally broke down in 1961 when the USSR withdrew its military and economic support for Albania, which became non-aligned. At the time of the diplomatic split, the *Forca Ajrore e Republikës së Shqipërisë* (FAj – Republic of Albania Air Force), which in turn was part of the *Komandës së Mbrojtjes Kundërajrore* (MKA – air defence command), included two *Regjimente të Gjuajtës* (fighter regiments) equipped with Soviet-made aircraft: R 1875 AvG based at Kuçovë with two MiG-15 [NATO – Fagot] *Skuadrilje* (Sku – squadron) and R 7594 AvG with one MiG-17F [NATO – Fresco C] *Skuadril*, one MiG-19PM [NATO – Farmer D] *Skuadril* and a single Il-28 [NATO – Beagle] based at Rinas near Tirana.

China, which was also experiencing a doctrinal shift from the USSR, was quick to fill the void left by the Soviets in Albania and in 1964 the Chinese offered to exchange the twelve Albanian MiG-19PM airframes for 80 of the Shenyang J-6 [J – *Jiānjíjī*, fighter] Chinese-built version of the MiG-19S. These aircraft were used to form another *Skuadril* at Rinas and to expand the strength of the other units. Over time, the Soviet-built MiG-17 was also replaced in FAj service by its Chinese equivalent, the Shenyang J-5. Coincident with the departure of the Soviet military assistance, the FAj expanded its role from pure air defence to include ground-attack missions; its regiments therefore became *Regjimente të Gjuajtës-Bombardues* (fighter-bomber regiments).

Neighbouring Yugoslavia was perceived to be the main threat to Albania and there were incursions into Albanian airspace by Yugoslav aircraft. On 21 July 1967, an armed Yugoslav F-84F strayed into Albania and was intercepted by three J-6s which had been launched from Rinas; the Yugoslavian aircraft was forced to land at Rinas. As with most such incidents, it was established that the airspace violation had been caused accidentally by a navigational error, rather than hostile intent. Nevertheless, the J-6 was considered to be obsolescent as an air defence fighter and in 1969 China supplied the FAj with 12 Chengdu J-7A fighters, the Chinese version of the MiG-21-F13. The new fighters were initially based at Rinas, but a

A Shenyang J-6, a Chinese-built version of the MiG-19, of the Forca Ajrore e Republikës së Shqipërisë (FAj) at Kuçovë airbase. The original Soviet-supplied equipment was replaced by the Chinese after Albania split from the Warsaw Pact. (Schleiffert)

new airbase was under construction in the north of the country, near the mountain village of Zadrima.

The new airfield, known as Gjäder air base, was opened in early 1974. The main airstrip was built in a mountain valley, but taxiways led from the runway to either end of a tunnel excavated under the mountain; this 600m construction could shelter up to 50 aircraft. R 5646 AvGB was established at Gjäder in 1976 with a *Skuadril* of J-7A (which had been transferred from Rinas) and two *Skuadrilje* of J-6 (one of which had been transferred from Kuçovë). By the mid-1970s, the front-line combat strength of the FAj still comprised some 80 J-6 aircraft plus a squadron-strength each of J-5 and J-7A. These were deployed in three Regjimente: two *Skuadrilje* operating a mix of J-5 and J-6 were based at Kuçovë, two J-6 *Skuadrilje* were based at Rinas while two more F-6 *Skuadrilje* and the J-7A *Skuadril* flew from Gjäder. The Il-28 at Rinas had been replaced by a Harbin-Hong H-5, the Chinese version of the same aircraft type. Two more H-5s were to have been delivered, but after the breakdown in diplomatic relations between China and Albania in 1976, he delivery was cancelled.

Tensions over the border with Yugoslavia continued into the 1980s and in one incident during 1982 an Albanian J-7A flown by *Kapiten* (captain) L.R. Sadikaj strayed into Yugoslavian airspace, where he was intercepted by two Yugoslavian MiG-21s. Sadikaj was forced to land at Kosovo, with one Yugoslav aircraft on each wing, but as soon as the Yugoslavians had deployed their brake-chutes on the runway, he applied full power and took off again, managing to return safely to Albania at high speed. Although the FAj was relatively well-equipped, its pilots enjoyed very little flying practice: they typically experienced as little as 10–20 hours per year. At the close of the Cold War, Albania remained a police state which was largely isolated from the outside world.

A Shenyang J-6C outside a hardened shelter at Rinas airbase. The J-6 was the mainstay of the FAj during the 1970s and 1980s and was operated by units at all three of the main operating bases: Rinas, Kuçovë and Gjadër. (Schleiffert)

ALBANIA 271

Above:
A Chengdu F-7A (Chinese-built MiG-21F) at Rinas. The FAj had 12 of these aircraft, which were moved from Rinas to Gjadër in 1976, where they were operated by R 5646 AvGB. (Schleiffert)

Left:
A Shenyang J-5 (Chinese-built MiG-17) at Kuçovë airbase. From the late 1960s, the J-5 replaced the original Soviet-built MiG-17 in the FAj inventory. J-6s from the other Skuadril are parked in the background. (Schleiffert)

SPAIN

"The defence of internal peace and order constitutes the sacred mission of a nation's armed forces." Generalissimo Franco, 1939

In contrast to Albania, which had started off as a member of an alliance but left it to become non-aligned, Spain started the Cold War as a non-aligned country and went on later to join NATO. Spain had officially been neutral during World War II, despite having sympathy for the Axis cause, and having dispatched the *División Azul* (Blue Division), to fight against the USSR on the Eastern Front. Because of its connections with Nazi Germany, Spain was ostracized by the victorious Allies in the immediate post-war years, so the country remained non-aligned. However, a rapprochement with the USA in the early 1950s gave Spain access to US arms. Under the terms of the Help Agreement for Mutual Defense, the Economic Assistance Agreement and the Defensive Agreement, all three of which were signed in 1953, the USA undertook to provide military aid, including provision of F-86F fighters, in exchange for use of the airbases at Morón, Torrejón, Zaragoza and Rota [Cadiz]. These airfields were to be used by the USAF as forward operating bases for Operation *Reflex*, the dispersal of the SAC B-47 strike force.

The Ejército del Aire (EdA – air force), had also seen action on the Eastern Front during World War II and at the beginning of the Cold War it was a large organization, with almost 1,000 aircraft in its inventory. The basic operational unit of the EdA was the *Grupo de Fuerza Aérea* (GdFFAA – air force group), each of which contained two *Escuadrones* (Esc – squadrons). However, pure numbers can be misleading: in fact, the EdA had only around 600 serviceable aircraft and of these over two-thirds were transport or training aircraft. The actual combat strength of the EdA comprised just 32 fighters and 83 bombers of assorted, mostly obsolete, types. The fighters included Fiat CR-32 and Polikarpov I-15bis biplanes as well as six Messerschmidt Bf-109 and a further 14 Hispano Suiza HA-1112 locally-built versions of the Bf-109G (which were also known by the service designation C.4J). The majority of the bombers were of the B.2 type, being either the Heinkel He111 or the Spanish-built version of it, the CASA C.2111 '*Pedro*' (Peter). A small number of Savoia-Marchetti SM.79 and Junkers Ju88, which equipped GdFFAA 12 at Granada and 13 at Los Llanos (Albecete) respectively, also remained in service until the mid-1950s.

A modernization programme for the EdA was initiated in 1952 and from 1955, the GdFFAA structure was progressively replaced by *Alas* (wings), and independent Escuadrones. The *Ala*, most of which

A flight of four Hispano Aviación HA-1112-M1-_ from 7 Ala, based at El Copero, near Seville. Designated the C.4K and known as the *Buchón* (Pouter - Pigeon), the type was based on the Messerschmidt Bf-109G airframe and powered by a British-built Rolls Royce Merlin 500-45 engine. The Buchón was armed with four 20mm Hispano-Suiza HS-404/408 cannons, but they created turbulence when fired requiring wing fences to be fitted. A rack was mounted under each wing to carry 8cm Oerlikon/Pilatus air-to-ground rockets. (EdA)

Right:
From 1955, a total of 270 North American F-86F Sabres – designated C.5 – were delivered to the EdA. This particular aircraft was used for tactical training by Escuadron 732 at the Escuela de Reactores (jet training school) at Talavera de la Reina. (EdA)

Below:
Like the Buchón, the CASA 2.111 – known as 'Pedro' – was based on a German-designed airframe, the Heinkel 111. The type was also powered by Rolls Royce Merlin engines. (Jarret)

comprised a single squadron, was based in the USAF model of an autonomous unit containing all the resources requited for independent air operations. The *grupos* at Granada, Agoncillo, and Rabasa (Alicante) were disbanded as front-line units, while the remainder of GdFFAA were re-structured into *Alas* or *Escuadrones*. The *Mando de la Defensa Aérea* (air defence command), was established in 1956, taking command of the F-86F units which comprised *Ala de Caza* 1 (AdC 1 – 1st Fighter Wing), at Manises (Valencia) and AdC 2 at Zaragoza, as well as *Escuadron de Caza* (EdC – fighter squadron), 41 based at San Son Juan (Mallorca), EdC 51 at Reus (Tarragona) and EdC 61 at Getafe (Madrid).

The EdA ground attack assets were grouped under the aegis of the *Mando de la Aviación Táctica* (tactical aviation command), and included *Ala de Bombero Liego* (Light Bomber Wing) 21 based at Tablada, *Ala* 26 based at Albecate and *Ala* 27 based at Malaga. All of these units flew the B.21, a Merlin-engined development of the CASA 2.111. These aircraft were joined in service by another Merlin modification to a World War II German design, the Hispano-Suiza HA-1112-M1L (designated in service as the C.4K), a variant of the Bf-109G. The C.4K *Buchon* (Pouter pigeon) light attack aircraft became the most numerous type in the EdA inventory and equipped *Alas de Caza-Bombero*, (fighter-bomber wings), 7 and 47 at El Copero and Tablada, two airfields close to Seville; it also equipped Escuadrilla 464, part of *Ala Mista* (mixed wing) 46 at Gando (Canary Islands)   Both the B.21 and the C.4K saw action during the 'Ifni' War in North Africa and remained in service until the mid-1960s.

Despite its non-aligned status, Spain hosted USAF combat units which were based permanently in the country, as well as the visiting SAC aircraft. The F-86D-equipped 497th FIS deployed to Torrejón in 1958 in order to provide air defence cover for the B-47 forward operating bases. Two years later, the unit was re-equipped with the F-102. Although the 497th FIS returned to the USA in 1964, it was replaced at Torrejón two years later by the three F-100D squadrons of the 401st TFW.

Various organizational reshuffles took place within the EdA during the late 1960s, the last of which took place in 1969: Alas were re-numbered, then briefly disestablished, leaving independent escuadrons,

The prototype of the Spanish designed and built Hispano Aviación HA-200 Saeta (arrow), which was developed into the single-seat HA-220 Super Saeta light ground-attack aircraft. Designated C.10, the aircraft served with Ala 46 at Gando in the Canary Islands. In 1974, the C.10 was deployed in action against rebels in the Western Sahara. (Jarret)

Lockheed F-104G Starfighters (designation C.8) of Esc 161, part of Ala 16, which was formed in 1965 with 21 aircraft, and based at Torrejón de Ardoz, near Madrid. In 1967, the unit was renumbered as, perhaps appropriately, Esc 104 and performed the air-defence role until 1972. Remarkably the EdA suffered no accidents during its time operating the F-104G. After EdA service, the Starfighters were sold to Greece. (EdA)

then reformed once more. However, by the end of the decade the front-line units were equipped with, or in the process of re-equipping with, modern combat aircraft. The US supplied 21 F-104G Starfighters (EdA designation C.8), which entered service with 161 Sqn (later renumbered, appropriately, to become 104) of *Ala* 16 at Torrejón in 1965. At Morón, *Ala* 21 traded the F-86F for the F-5 (EdA designation C.9) and swapped its air-to-air role for that of ground attack, while at Manises, *Ala* 11 exchanged the F-86F for the Dassault Mirage IIIEE (EdA designation C.11) with which it retained its air-defence role. After the withdrawal of the C.4K in the mid-1960s, the need for a light attack aircraft within *Ala* 46 at Gando was met by the Hispano-Suiza HA-220 *Súper Saeta* (Super Arrow – designated the C.10C), a development of the HA-200 training aircraft.

The operational capability of *Ala* 12 at Torrejón was further upgraded in 1971 with the arrival of the F-4C Phantom (EdA designation C.12) for Esc 121 and Esc 122. These units operated closely with the resident USAFE 401st TFW which also re-equipped with the F-4C in the same timescale. Four KC-97 tanker aircraft were also procured by the EdA in 1972 to support the F-4 and these were based at Albacete until 1976.

The last F-86F unit, *Ala* 12 at Zaragoza, was disbanded in 1973, but the following year *Ala* 14 was established at Albacete with the Dassault Mirage F-1CE (EdA designation C.14A). The death of General Franco in 1975 precipitated a change of regime and in the following years, negotiations started for Spain to join NATO. Spain formally joined the alliance in 1982, although following the French model, its armed forces were not included in the NATO integrated command structure.

Left:
Between 1971 and 1972, the EdA received 36 ex-USAF McDonnell Douglas F-4C Phantoms, becoming the only non-US operator of that variant. Designated C.12, the F-4C was operated by *Ala* 12 at Torrejón de Ardoz until the end of the 'Cold War'. (EdA)

Below:
The re-equipment of the EdA in the early 1970s included procurement of 24 Dassault Mirage IIIEE, which were designated C.11. (EdA)

AFTERWORD

"We must concede that after the end of the Cold War, new leaders failed to create a modern security architecture, especially in Europe"
Mikhail Gorbachev, 2019

Thirty years on from the end of the Cold War, Tupolev Tu-95/142 [Bear] aircraft, those icons of the period, once more patrol the skies over the Norwegian and North Seas testing the defences and shadowing NATO naval forces. From forward deployments in Latvia and Romania, NATO interceptors frequently meet with Russian aircraft over the Baltic and Black Seas. After a period of introspection, Russia is resurgent, but harbouring a deep sense of injustice with regard to developments in Europe since the fall of the Berlin Wall.

The end of the Cold War gave all countries in Europe and North America the opportunity to step back from the crippling burden of defence expenditure. On both sides of the 'Iron Curtain' military units were disbanded with almost indecent haste against a backdrop of the disintegration of the Warsaw Pact and the prospect of lasting peace. The USSR in particular had been almost bankrupted by the cost of maintaining and equipping large military forces and its fighting services swiftly fell into disarray and disrepair. While Western economies suffered a short recession in the early 1990s, the USSR experienced a deep economic crisis. During the 1990s, Russian GDP fell by 50 percent and inflation was running at some 300 percent. In 1991, First Secretary Mikhail Gorbachev survived an attempted a coup in Moscow, but the episode set the scene for the dissolution of the USSR later that year. The Confederation of Independent States was formed in the same year, with Russia led by President Boris Yeltsin as the largest and most powerful member. The following year, Russia, Armenia, Kazakhstan, Kyrgyzstan, Tajikistan and Uzbekistan signed the Tashkent Treaty, forming the *Organizatsiya Dogovora o Kollektivnoy Bezopasnosti* (ODKB – Collective Security Treaty Organization): Three more countries, Azerbaijan, Belarus, and Georgia joined them at the end of 1992. Thus, Russia believed, as the nation struggled through economic and political challenges, that security was guaranteed. Russians also believed that there had been an understanding between the USA and its European allies that Eastern Europe would become a non-aligned 'buffer area' between Russia and the west.

Unfortunately for Russia, the populations of those countries wished to embrace the capitalist model of the west and to guarantee their own independence from Russian interference. Both NATO and the European Union also saw benefit in an expansion eastward and, despite grave reservations raised in the US Senate in 1997, Poland, Hungary and the Czech Republic joined NATO in 1999. In the same year, Azerbaijan, Georgia and Uzbekistan all left the ODKB. Russia was dismayed: as the new Russian President Vladimir Putin commented in 2001, 'NATO was built to counteract the Soviet Union in its day and time. At this point there is no threat coming from the Soviet Union, because there is no Soviet Union anymore. And where there was the Soviet Union once, there is now a number of countries, among them the new and democratic Russia.' A further expansion of NATO in 2004 included Bulgaria, Estonia, Latvia, Lithuania and Romania; without a shot being fired NATO had advanced across the 'buffer area' of central Europe and up to the very borders of Russia. In Moscow there was a sense of dismay and treachery. Even the non-aligned bloc had moved under the western European aegis: Sweden, Finland, Austria and much of the former Yugoslavia became members of the European Union, while Albania joined NATO in 2009. In 2019, exactly 30 years after the fall of the Berlin Wall, Ukraine, once a bastion of the USSR, was recognized as an aspiring member of NATO. To the Russians this seemed to be a direct threat to their security.

Three decades on, the optimism has been replaced by mutual suspicion and distrust. Both NATO and Russian air forces have modernized since the end of the Cold War, but air actions over the Balkans, the Caucasus, the Middle East and Afghanistan have switched their focus from large-scale war in central Europe to expeditionary warfare and counter-insurgency operations. The air forces of NATO and Russia may have lost the ability to fight a sustained campaign in continental Europe, but they will doubtless continue to be an important tool in the projection of political power, just as they were in the days of the Cold War.

AIR ORDER OF BATTLE: 1955
TACTICAL FIXED-WING COMBAT AIRCRAFT

Note: Combat units moved, were re-equipped and/or renumbered frequently throughout the Cold War. This Order of Battle reflects the deployments of each of the air forces in Europe at various stages during each listed year.

NATO
AAFNE

Norway	Kongelige Norsk Luftforsvaret		
	Gardemoen	330, 336 Skv	F-84G
	Sola	331, 332, 334 Skv	F-84G
	Ørland	338 Skv	F-84G
	Rygge	717 Skv	RF-84G
Denmark	Kongelige Dansk Flyvevåbnet	Flyverkommando	
	Karup	Esk 725, 726, 727	F-84G
	Skrydstrup	Esk 728, 729, 730	F-84G
	Aalborg	Esk723	Meteor
	Aalborg	Esk723, 724	Meteor

AAFCE
2 ATAF

Netherlands	Koninklijke Luchtmacht	Commando Tactische Luchtstrijdkrachten, (CTL)		
	Volkel	311, 312, 313 Sqn		F-84G
	Eindhoven	314, 315, 316 Sqn		F-84G
	Volkel	306 Sqn		RF-84G
Belgium	Belgische Luchtmacht/Force Aérienne Belge			
	Florennes	1, 2, 3 Sqns		F-84G
	Kleine-Brogel	23, 27, 31 Sqns		F-84G
	Bierset	22, 26, 30 Sqns		F-84G
	Beauvechain	349, 350 Sqns		Meteor NF11
UK	Royal Air Force	2nd Tactical Air Force (2TAF)		
	2 Group			
	Laarbruch	34 Wg	31, 69 Sqn	Canberra PR3/7
			79, 541 Sqn	Meteor FR9/10
	Fassberg	121 Wg	14, 98, 118 Sqn	Venom
	Jever	122 Wg	4, 93 Sqn	Sabre
	Wuntsdorf	123 Wg	5, 11, 266 Sqn	Venom
	Oldenburg	124 Wg	20, 26 Sqn	Sabre
	Ahlhorn	125 Wg	96, 256 Sqn	Meteor NF11

AIR ORDERS OF BATTLE

83 Group

Brüggen	135 Wg	67, 71, 112, 130 Sqn	Sabre
Geilenkirchen	138 Wg	2 Sqn	Meteor FR9
		3, 234 Sqn	Sabre
Celle	139 Wg	16, 94, 145 Sqn	Venom
Wahn	148 Wg	68, 87 Sqn	Meteor NF11
Gutersloh	551 Wg	102, 103, 104, 149 Sqn	Canberra

4 ATAF

USA — United States Air Force — United States Air Force in Europe (USAFE)

Bitburg	36th FIW	23rd, 53rd FIS	F-86
Soesterburg		32nd FIS	F-86
Hahn	50th FIW	10th, 81st, 417th FIS	F-86
Landstuhl	86th FIW	525th, 526th & 527th FIS	F-86
Spangdahlem	10th TRW	1st TRS	RB-57
		32, 38th TRS	RF-84F
Sembach	66th TRW	30th TRS	RB-57
		302nd, 303rd TRS	RF-84F
Chambley-Bussières	21st FIW	92nd, 416th, 531st FIS	F-86
Chaumont	48th FIW	492nd, 493rd, 494th FIS	F-86
Étain-Rouvres	388th FIW	561st, 562nd, 563rd FIS	F-86
Laon-Couvron	38th BW	71st, 405th, 822nd BS	B-57
Manston	406th FIW	512th, 513th, 514st FIS	F-86
Wethersfield	20th FBW	55th, 77th FBS	F-84F
Woodbridge		79th FBS	F-84F
Bentwaters	81st FBW	91st, 92nd FBS	F-84F
Shepherd's Grove		78th FBS	F-84F
Sculthorpe	47th BW	84th, 85th, 422d BS	B-45
Alconbury		86th BS	B-45

Canada — Royal Canadian Air Force — 1 Air Division Europe

Marville	1 Wing	410, 439, 441 Sqn	Sabre
Grostenquin	2 Wing	416, 421, 430 Sqn	Sabre
Zweibrucken	3 Wing	413, 427, 434 Sqn	Sabre
Baden-Solingen	4 Wing	414, 422, 444 Sqn	Sabre

France — Armée de l'Air Française

1ier Commandement Aérien Tactique (CATac)

St Dizier	1ier EC	ECs 1/1 'Corse' 2/1 'Morvan' 3/1 'Argonne'	F-84G
Dijon-Longvic	2ème EC	ECs 1/2 'Cigognes' 2/2 'Côte d'Or' 3/2 'Alsace'	Ouragan
Reims	3ème EC	ECs 1/3 'Navarre', 2/3 'Champagne', 3/3 'Ardennes'	F-84G
Bremgarten	4ème EC	EC 1/4 'Dauphine', 2/4 'La Fayette', 3/4 'Flandre'	Ouragan
Lahr–Hugsweier	9ème EC	EC 1/9 'Limousin', 2/9 'Auvergne'	F-84E/G
Luxeuil-St Sauveur	11ème EC	EC 1/11 'Roussillon', 2/11 'Vosges', 3/11 'Jura'	F-84G
Cognac	33ème ER	GR 1/33 'Belfort', ERT 2/33 'Savoie', 3/33 'Moselle'	F-84G

Défense Aèrienne du Territoire (DAT)

Orange-Caritat	5ème EC	EC 1/5 'Vendée', 2/5 'Île de France', 3/5 'Comtat Venaissin'	Mistral
Creil	10ème EC	EC 1/10 'Paris'	Vampire
Cambrai-Epinoy	12ème EC	EC 1/12 'Cambrésis', 2/12 'Picardie', 3/12 'Cornouaille'	Ouragan
Tours	30ème ECN	ECN 1/30 'Loire', 2/30 'Carmargue', 3/30 'Lorraine'	Meteor NF11

AFSOUTH

Portugal	Força Aérea Portuguesa			
	Tancos		Esq 10	F-47
	Ota		Esq 20, 21	F-84G

5 ATAF

Italy	Aeronautica Militare			
	56 Tactical Air Force			
	Villafranca	3° St	28°, 132° Gr	RF-84
		5ª AB	101°, 102°, 103° Gr	F-84G
	Ghedi	6ª AB	154°, 155°, 156° Gr	F-84G
	Istrana	51ª AB	20°, 21°, 22° Gr	F-84G
	Vicenza	2° St	8°, 13° Gr	Vampire
	Capodochino	4° St	9°, 10° Gr	Vampire

6 ATAF

Greece	Ellinikí Vasilikí Aeroporía			
	Larissa	110 PM	337, 338, 339 Moira	F-84G
	Néa Aghios	111 PM	335, 336, 340 Moira	F-84G
	Elefsis	112 PM	341, 343 Moira	F-86E

Turkey	Türk Hava Kuvvetleri			
	1 Hava Kuvveti			
	Eskişehir	1^{nci} HU	111, 112, 113 Filo	F-84G
			141 Filo	F-86E
	Bandirma	6^{nci} HU	161, 162, 163 Filo	F-84G
	Balikesir	9^{ncu} HU	191, 192, 193 Filo	F-84G
	3 Hava Kuvveti			
	Merzifon	5^{ncu} HU	142 & 143 Filo	F-86E
	Diyabarkir	8^{nci} HU	181, 182 & 183 Filo	F-84G

WARSAW PACT

NORTH-WESTERN & WEST TVDs

Czechoslovakia	Československé Letectvo			
	1.Stíhací Letecký Divise			
	České Budějovice	1, 9, 19.SLPl		S102/103
	Mladá	17.SLPl		S102/103
		47.PLP		MiG-15R
	2.Stíhací Letecký Divise			

Bratislava	2.SLPl	S-102/103
Čáslav	6.SLPl	S-102/103
Košice	7.SLPl	MiG-17
3.Stíhací Letecký Divise		
Dobřany	5, 16.SLPl	S102/103
Praha	8.SLP	S102/103
5.Stíhací Letecký Divise		
Žatec	11, 15.SLPl	S102/103
22.Stíhací Letecký Divise		
Brno	3.SLPl	S102/103
Pardubice	4, 18.SLPl	S102/103
46.Bombardovací Letecká Divize		
Hradčany	24.BoLPl	C-3 Siebel
	29.BoLPl	B-228
Přerov	25.BoLPl	B-228
34.Bitevni Letecka Divize		
Brno	28.BiLPl	B-33
Piešťany	30.BiLPl	B-33
Trenčín	32.BiLPl	B-33
--		
Plzeň	45.Letecky Delostrelecky Pluk	MiG-15R

Poland — Wojska Lotnicze

5. Dywizja Lotnictwa Myśliwskiego		
Warsaw	1.PLM	MiG-15/15bis/Lim-1/2
Leźnica Wielka	13.PLM	MiG-15/15bis/Lim-1/2
Łask	31.PLM	MiG-15/15bis/Lim-1/2
6. Dywizja Lotnictwa Myśliwskiego		
Wroclaw-Strachowice	3.PLM	MiG-15/15bis/Lim-1/2
7. Dywizja Lotnictwa Myśliwskiego		
Czyżyny	2.PLM	MiG-15/15bis/Lim-1/2
Mierzęcice	39.PLM	MiG-15/15bis/Lim-1/2
9. Dywizja Lotnictwa Myśliwskiego		
Orneta	29.PLM	MiG-15/15bis/Lim-1/2
Malbork	41 PLM	MiG-15/15bis/Lim-1/2
10. Dywizja Lotnictwa Myśliwskiego		
Debrzno	11.PLM	MiG-15/15bis/Lim-1/2
Pruszcz Gdański	25.PLM	MiG-15/15bis/Lim-1/2
Słupsk	28.PLM	MiG-15/15bis/Lim-1/2
11. Dywizja Lotnictwa Myśliwskiego		
Zegrze-Pomorski	26.PLM	MiG-15/15bis/Lim-1/2
Świdwin	40.PLM	MiG-15/15bis/Lim-1/2
8. Dywizja Lotnictwa Szturmowego		
Bydgoszcz	4, 5, 48.PLSz	Il-10 /B-33
16. Dywizja Lotnictwa Szturmowego		
Pila	6, 51.PLSz	Il-10 /B-33
Mirosławiec	53.PLSz	Il-10 /B-33
15. Dywizja Lotnictwa Bombowego		
Modlin	7, 33, 35.PLB	Il-28
Sochaczew Bielice	21.PLR	Il-28R
Gdynia-Babie Doły	34.PLM	Lim-1/2

USSR	Voyenno-Vozdushnye Sily		

37ya Vozdushnaya Armiya
149ya IAD
    Szprotawa — 3 IAP — MiG-15
    Zhagan — 42 GvIAP — MiG-15
    Szprotawa — 18 IAP — MiG-17
239ya IAD
    Chojna — 582 IAP — MiG-15
    Kluczewo — 159 GvIAP, 871 IAP — MiG-17
183ya BAD
    Brzheg — 131, 1101, 1107 BAP — Il-28
172ya ShAD
    Olawa — 189 GvShAP — Il-10
    Szprotawa — 669 GvShAP — Il-10
    Krzywa — 756 GvShAP — Il-10

24ya Vozdushnaya Armiya
71y Istrebitel'nyy Aviatsionnyy Korpus
16ya GvIAD
    Damgarten — 19 IAP — MiG-15bis
                      773 IAP — MiG-15
    Parchim — 20 IAP — MiG-15 & 17F/PF
123ya IBAD
    Rechlin-Laerz — 417, 743 IAP — MiG-17
    Wittstock — 965 IAP — MiG-17
125ya IAD
    Finow — 33 IAP — MiG-15 & 17F
               730 IAP — MiG-17F/PF
    Neurippen — 787 IAP — MiG-17F/PF
61ya Gvardeyskiy Istrebitel'nyy Aviatsionnyy Korpus
126ya IAD
    Zerbst — 35 IAP — MiG-17F/PF
    Jüterbog — 116 Gv IAP, 833 IAP — MiG-17
6ya GvIAD
    Köthen — 73 IAP — MiG-17F/PF
    Brandis — 31 IAP — MiG-17F/PF
    Merseburg — 85 IAP — MiG-17F/PF
105ya IAD
    Grossenheim — 559 IAP — MiG-17F
                     497 IAP — MiG-17
    Altenburg — 296 IAP — MiG-17
75ya Shturmovoy Aviatsionnyy Korpus
200ya GvShAD
    Brandenburg-Briest — 830 GvShAP — Il-10
    Brandenburg-Neuendorf — 823 GvShAP — Il-10
    Stendal — 710 GvShAP — Il-10
114ya GvShAD
    Falkenburg — 664 GvShAP - — MiG-15
    Finsterwalde — 635, 725 ShAP — MiG-15
132ya BAD
    Werneuchen — 63, 668 BAP — Il-28
    Brand — 277 BAP — Il-28

    Welzow — 11 ORAP — Il-28R
    Altenburg — 294 ORAP — MiG-15R
    Stendal — 931 ORAP — Il-28R

SOUTHERN REGION/SOUTH-WESTERN TVD

USSR — Voyenno-Vozdushnye Sily

177ya BAD			
	Debrecen	67, 880 GvBAP	Il-28
	Kunmadaras	727 GvBAP	Il-28
11ya GvIAD			
	Szentkirályszabadja	1 GvIAP	MiG-17
	Tököl	5 GvIAP	MiG-17
	Papa	106 GvIAP	MiG-17

Hungary — Magyar Légierő

25.Vadászrepülő-Hadosztály			
	Sármellék	24.VadE	Sas
	Taszár	35, 50.VadE	Sas
66. Vadászrepülő-Hadosztály			
	Kalocsa	31.VadE	Sas
	Kiskunlacháza	47.VadE	Sas
	Kecskemét	62.VadE	Sas
28.Csatarepülő-Hadosztály			
	Tapolca	23.CsE	Párduc
	Székesfehérvár	30.CsE	Párduc
	Börgönd	59.CsE	Párduc
--			
	Kiskunlacháza	37.ÖFE	Il-28

Romania — Forțele Aeriene Române

Divizia 23 Aviație Vânătoare cu Reacție			
	Siliștea Gumești	R125AvVR	MiG-15
	Mihail Kogălniceanu	R172AvVR	S-102
	Bucharest-Otopeni	R206AvVR	MiG-15 & 17
Divizia 66 Aviație Vânătoare cu Reacție			
	Craiova	R158AvVR	MiG-17
		R227AvVR	MiG-15
	Caracal-Deveslu	R226AvVR	MiG-15
Divizia 97 Aviație Vânătoare cu Reacție			
	Caransebeș	R135AvVR	MiG-15
	Timișoara-Giarmata.	R294AvVR	MiG-15
Divizia 68 Aviatie Asalt			
	Brașov	R167AvAs	Il-10
	Sibiu	R251AvAs	Il-10
	Turda	R263AvAs	Il-10
--			
	Bucharest-Otopeni	R239AvBom	Tu-2 & Il-28
	Titu-Boteni	R282AvBom	Tu-2 & Il-28

Bulgaria — Balgarski Voenno Vŭzdushni Sili

1 Iztrebitelen Aviatsionen Diviziya			
	Tolbukhin	22, 25 IAP	MiG-15&17
	Bezmer	27 IAP	MiG-15&17
4 Iztrebitelen Aviatsionen Diviziya			
	Sofia-Kumaritsa	11, 43 IAP	MiG-15&17
	Gabrovnitsa	18 IAP	MiG-15&17

		10 Iztrebitelen Aviatsionen Diviziya		
		Ravntez	15 IAP	MiG-15 & 17
		Graf Ignatievo	19 IAP	MiG-15 & 17
		Bezmer	21 IAP	MiG-15 & 17
		5 Shturmova Aviatsionen Diviziya		
		Plovdiv	23 ShAP	Il-10
		Krumovo	17, 20 ShAP	Il-10
		2 Bombardirovŭchen Aviatsionen Diviziya		
		Stara Zagora	34 BAP	Tu-2 & Pe-2
		3 Bombardirovŭchen Aviatsionen Diviziya		
		Balchik	28, 42, 46 BAP	Tu-2 & Pe-2
		--		
		Gorna Oryahovitsa	26 RAP	Tu-2 & Il-28
Albania	Forcës Ajrore			
		Kuçovë	R 23AvG	MiG-15

AIR ORDER OF BATTLE: 1965 — TACTICAL FIXED-WING COMBAT AIRCRAFT

Note: Combat units moved, were re-equipped and/or renumbered frequently throughout the Cold War. This Order of Battle reflects the deployments of each of the air forces in Europe at various stages during each listed year.

NATO

AAFNE

Norway	Kongelige Norsk Luftforsvaret			
		Gardemoen	337 & 339 Skvs	F-86K
		Bodø	331 Skv	F-104G
			334 Skv	F-86F
		Ørland	338 Skv	F-86F
		Rygge	332 Skv	F-86F
			336 Skv	F-5
			717 Skv	RF-84F
Denmark	Kongelige Dansk Flyvevåbnet	Flyvertaktiske Kommando		
		Aalborg	Esks 723 & 726	F-104G
		Karup	Esks 725 & 730	F-100D
			Esk 729	RF-84F
		Skrydstrup	Esk 724	Hunter F51
			Esk 728	F-86D

AAFCE
2 ATAF

Netherlands	Koninklijke Luchtmacht	Commando Tactische Luchtstrijdkrachten, (CTL)		
	Volkel		311 Sqn	F-104G
			312 Sqn	F-84F
	Eindhoven		314 & 315 Sqns	F-84F
	Leeuwarden		322 & 323 Sqns	F-104G
			324 & 325 Sqns	Hunter
	Soesterburg		326 & 327 Sqns	Hunter
	Twenthe		306 Sqn	RF-104
Belgium	Belgische Luchtmacht/Force Aérienne Belge			
	Beauvechain	1 Wg	349 & 350 Sqns	F-104G
	Florennes	2 Wg	1 & 2 Sqns	F-84F
	Bierset	3 Wg	42 Sqn	RF-84F
	Kleine-Brogel	10 Wg	23, & 31 Sqns	F-104G
BRD	Luftwaffe			
	Büchel	JaBoG 33		F-104G
	Hopsten	JaBoG 36		F-104G
	Lechfeld	JaBoG 32		F-104G
	Memmingen	JaBoG 34		F-104G
	Nörvenich	JaBoG 31		F-104G
	Husum	JaBoG 35		G-91
	Pferdsfeld	JaBoG 42		F-86
	Oldenburg	JaBoG 43		F-86
	Leipheim	LeKG 44		G-91
	Neuburg	JG 74		F-104G
	Wittmundhaven	JG 71		F-104G
	Ingolstadt	AG 51		RF-104G
	Leck	AG 52		RF-104G
UK	Royal Air Force	RAF Germany (RAFG)		
	Brüggen		80 Sqn	Canberra PR7
			213 Sqn	Canberra B(I)6
	Geilenkirchen		3 Sqn	Canberra B(I)8
			11 Sqn	Javelin FAW9
	Gutersloh		19 Sqn	Lightning F2
			2 & 4 Sqn	Hunter FR10
	Laarbruch		5 Sqn	Javelin FAW9
			16 Sqn	Canberra B(I)8
			31 Sqn	Canberra PR7
	Wildenrath		14 Sqn	Canberra B(I)8
			17 Sqn	Canberra PR7

4 ATAF

USA — United States Air Force — United States Air Force in Europe (USAFE)

17th Air Force
Base	Wing	Squadrons	Aircraft
Bitburg	36th TFW	22nd, 23rd, 53rd TFS	F-105D
	86th AD	525th FIS	F-102
Spangdahlem	49th TFW	7th, 8th, 9th TFS	F-105D
Hahn	50th TFW	10th, 81st, 417th FIS	F-100D
	86th AD	496th FIS	F-102
Landstuhl	86th AD	526th FIS	F-102
Soesterburg	86th AD	32nd FIS	F-102
Chambley-Bussières	25th TRW	19th & 42nd TRS	RB-66
Toul-Rosières	26th TRW	22nd & 32nd TRS	RF-101
Laon-Couvron	66th TRW	17th & 18th TRS	RF-101C

3rd Air Force
Base	Wing	Squadrons	Aircraft
Alconbury	10th TRW	1st & 30th TRS	RF-4C
Lakenheath	48th TFW	492nd, 493rd, 494th TFS	F-100D
Bentwaters	81st TFW	91st, 92nd TFS	F-101C
Woodbridge	81st TFW	78th TFS	F-101C
	20th TFW	79th TFS	F-100D
Wethersfield	20th TFW	55th & 77th TFS	F-100D

Canada — Royal Canadian Air Force — 1 Air Division Europe

Base	Wing	Squadrons	Aircraft
Marville	1 Wing	439 & 441 Sqns	CF-104
Zweibrucken	3 Wing	427, 430 & 434 Sqns	CF-104
Baden-Solingen	4 Wing	421, 422 & 444 Sqns	CF-104

France — Armée de l'Air Française

Commandement de la Force Aérienne Tactique/1re Région Aérienne (FATac/1re RA)
Base	EC	Escadrons	Aircraft
St Dizier	1ier EC	ECs 1/1 'Corse' 2/1 'Morvan'	F-84F
Dijon-Longvic	2ème EC	ECs 1/2 'Cigognes' 2/2 'Côte d'Or' 3/2 'Alsace'	Mirage III
Lahr	3ème EC	ECs 1/3 'Navarre', 2/3 'Champagne'	F-100
Luxeuil-St Sauveur	4ème EC	ECs 1/4 'Dauphine', 2/4 'La Fayette'	F-84F
	33ème EC	EC 1/33 'Belfort'	RF-84F
Bremgarten	11ème EC	ECs 1/11 'Roussillon', 2/11 'Vosges'	F-100
Colmar	13ème EC	ECs 1/13 'Artois', 2/13 'Alpes'	Mirage III
Strasbourg	33ème EC	ECs 2/33 'Savoie', EC 3/33 'Moselle'	Mirage IIIR

Commandement des Forces de Défense Aérienne (CAFDA)
Base	EC	Escadrons	Aircraft
Orange-Caritat	5ème EC	ECs 1/5 'Vendée', 2/5 'Île de France'	Super Mystère
Ochey	7ème EC	ECs 1/7 'Provence', 3/7 Languedoc'	Mystère IVA
Creil	10ème EC	ECs 1/10 'Valois', 2/10 'Seine'	Super Mystère
Cambrai-Epinoy	12ème EC	ECs 1/12 'Cambrésis', 2/12 'Cornouaille'	Super Mystère
Reims	30ème ECTT	ECTTs 2/30 'Normandie-Niémen', 3/30 'Lorraine'	Vautour

AFSOUTH

Portugal — Força Aérea Portuguesa

1.ª Região Aérea
Base	Group	Squadron	Aircraft
Monte Real	GO 501	Esq 51	F-86F

AIR ORDERS OF BATTLE

5 ATAF

Italy — Aeronautica Militare

Base	Stormo	Gruppi	Aircraft
Treviso	2° St	14° and 103° Gr	G-91R
Villafranca	3° St	28° and 132° Gr	F-104G
Grosseto	4° St	9°, 21° and 20° Gr	F-104G
Rimini	5ª St	102° Gr	F-104G
		23° Gr	F-86K
Ghedi	6° St	154° Gr	F-104G
		156° Gr	F-84F
Gioia Del Colle	36° St	12° Gr	F-104G
Istrana	51° St	22° and 155° Gr	F-104G

6 ATAF

Greece — Ellinikí Vasilikí Aeroporía

Base	PM	Moira	Aircraft
Larissa	110 PM	348 Moira	RF-84F
Néa Anghialos	111 PM	337 Moira	F-5
		341 and 343 Moira	F-86D
Tanagra	114 PM	335 and 336 Moira	F-104G
Souda	115 PM	338 and 340 Moira	F-84F
Andravida	117 PM	339 Moira	F-84F

Turkey — Türk Hava Kuvvetleri

1ⁿᶜⁱ Hava Kuvveti

Base	AJÜ	Filo	Aircraft
Eskişehir	1ⁿᶜⁱ AJÜ	111 Filo	F-100C/D
		112 Filo	F-84Q
		114 Kesif Filo	RF-84F
Murted	4ⁿᶜⁱ AJÜ	141 and 144 Filo	F-104G
Bandirma	6ⁿᶜⁱ AJÜ	161 Filo	F-84G
		163 Filo	F-84Q
Balikesir	9ⁿᶜᵘ AJÜ	191 and 192 Filo	F-84Q

3ⁿᶜᵘ Hava Kuvveti

Base	AJÜ	Filo	Aircraft
Merzifon	5ⁿᶜᵘ AJÜ	142 and 143 Filo	F-86E
Malatya Erhaç	7ⁿᶜⁱ AJÜ 1	113 Filo	F-100C/D
		182 Kesif Filo	RF-84F
Diyabarkir	8ⁿᶜⁱ AJÜ	181 and 183 Filo	F-84F
		184 Kesif Filo	RF-84F

WARSAW PACT

NORTH-WESTERN & WESTERN TVDS

DDR — Luftstreitkräfte/Luftverteidigung der Nationalen Volksarmee (LSK/LV)

1. Luftverteidigungsdivision

Base	Unit	Aircraft
Cottbus	JG-1	MiG-21
Drewitz	JG-7	MiG-21

Marxwalde	JG-8	MiG-21
Preschen	JG-3	MiG-21

3. Luftverteidigungsdivision

Neubrandenburg	JG-2	MiG-21
Peenemünde	JG-9	MiG-21

Czechoslovakia — Československé Letectvo — Velitelství Protivzdušné Obrany Státu

7. Armáda Protivzdušné Obrany Státu
  2. Sbor Protivzdušné Obrany Státu

Piešťany	7.SLPl	MiG-17 F/PF
Ostrava-Mošnov	8.SLPl	MiG 19S/P, MiG-21 F

  3. Sbor Protivzdušné Obrany Státu

České Budějovice	1.SLPl,	MiG-21 F/PF/PFM
Pardubice	4.SLPl	MiG-19PM, MiG-21 F
Žatec	11.SLPl	MiG-21 F/PF

10. Letecká Armáda

Perov	10. protiradiotechnický letecký oddíl	Il-28
Dobřany	45. dělostřelecký průzkumný letecký pluk	MiG-15R
Mladá.	47. průzkumný letecký pluk	MiG-15R, Il-28R

  1. Stíhací Letecký Divise

Dobřany	5.SLPl	MiG-19S/PM
Bechyně	9.SLPl	MiG-21 F

  2. Stíhací Bombardovací Letecká Divize

Přerov	6.SBoLPl	MiG-15
Oslavou	20.SBoLPl	Su-7BM

  34. Stíhací Bombardovací Letecká Divize

Hradčany	2.SBoLPl	MiG-15
Pardubice	18.SBoLPl	MiG-15
Čáslav	28.SBoLPl	Su-7BM/BKL
Hradec Králové	30.SBoLPl	MiG-15bisSB

Poland — Wojska Obrony Powietrznej Kraju

1 Korpus Obrony Powietrznej Kraju

Mińsk Mazowiecki	1. PLM-OPK	MiG-21 F/PF
Czyżyny	2. PLM-OPK	MiG-21 F/PF
Leźnica Wielka	13. PLM-OPK	MiG-21 F/PF
Mierzęcice	39. PLM-OPK	MiG-19P/PM

2 Korpus Obrony Powietrznej Kraju

Debrzno	11. PLM-OPK	MiG-21 & LiM-5
Pruszcz Gdański	25. PLM-OPK	LiM-5P
Zegrze-Pomorski	26. PLM-OPK	MiG-21 PF
Słupsk	28. PLM-OPK	MiG-19P/PM
Gdynia-Babie Doły	34. PLM	MiG-21 F/PF

3 Korpus Obrony Powietrznej Kraju

Wroclaw-Strachowice	3. PLM-OPK	LiM-5
Babimost	45.PLM-OPK	MiG-15
Krzesiny	62.PLM-OPK	MiG-21 F/PF

Wojska Lotnicze — Dowództwa Lotnictwa Operacyjnego

  5. Dywizja Lotnictwa Myśliwskiego

Świdwin	4. PLM	MiG-21 F/PF
	40. PLM	MiG-21 F/PF

  8. Dywizja Lotnictwa Myśliwskiego-Szturmowego

Bydgoszcz	5. PLM-Sz	Su-7BM
Inowrocław	48. PLM-Sz	LiM-5M

9. Dywizja Lotnictwa Myśliwskiego
- Orneta — 29. PLM — LiM-5
- Malbork — 41. PLM — LiM-5P

16. Dywizja Lotnictwa Myśliwskiego-Szturmowego
- Pila — 6 & 51. PLM-Sz — LiM-6bis/M
- Mirosławiec — 53. PLM-Sz — LiM-6bis/M

--
- Powidz — 7. PLRO — Il-28E
- Modlin — 33. PLRO — Il-28E
- Sochaczew Bielice — 21 & 32. PLRT — Lim-6bisR
- Simirowice — 30. PLMSz MW — Lim-6bis
- 15 ESLR MW — Il-28

USSR — Voyenno-Vozdushnye Sily

37ya Vozdushnaya Armiya
149ya IBAD
- Krzywa — 3 IBAP — Su-7B
- Zhagan — 42 GvIAP — MiG-17F/PF
- Szprotawa — 18 IAP — MiG-17

239ya IAD
- Chojna — 582 IAP — MiG-21 PF/PFM
- Kluczewo — 159 GvIAP — MiG-21 PF/PFM
- Kolobrzheg — 871 IAP — MiG-21 PFM

--
- Brzheg — 164 OGvRAP — Yak-27R
- 215 OGvRAP — MiG-21 R

24ya Vozdushnaya Armiya
61y Gvardeyskiy Istrebitel'nyy Aviatsionnyy Korpus
6ya GvIAD
- Altenburg — 296 IAP — MiG-21 PF
- Falkenburg — 31 IAP — MiG-21 PF
- Merseburg — 85 IAP — MiG-21 PF

105ya IBAD
- Finsterwalde — 559 IAP — Su-7B/BM
- Grossenheim — 497 IAP — Su-7B
- Jüterbog — 116 Gv IBAP — MiG-17

126ya IAD
- Zerbst — 35 IAP — MiG-21 F/PF
- Jüterbog — 833 IAP — MiG-21 PF/PFM
- Köthen — 73Gv IAP — MiG-21 PF

71y Istrebitel'nyy Aviatsionnyy Korpus
16ya GvIAD
- Wittstock — 33 IAP — MiG-21 PF/PFM
- Damgarten — 773 IAP — MiG-21 PF/PFM
- Templin — 787 IAP — MiG-21 PF/PFM

125ya IBAD
- Lärz — 19 GvIBAP — Su-7B
- Templin — 20 GvIBAP — Su-7B
- Neurippen — 730 IAP — MiG-17F/PF

132ya BAD
- Werneuchen — 63 BAP — Il-28
- Brand — 277 and 668 BAP — Il-28

--
- Welzow — 11 ORAP — Il-28R
- Altenburg — 294 ORAP — MiG-15R
- Stendal — 931 ORAP — Il-28R

SOUTHERN REGION/SOUTH-WESTERN TVD

USSR — Voyenno-Vozdushnye Sily

11ʸᵃ GvIAD
Sármellék	5 IAP	MiG-21PF
Kiskunlacháza	14 IAP	MiG-21PF
Tököl	515 GvIAP	MiG-21PF
Kunmadaras	1 GvIBAP	Su-7B, Mig-21R
	315 GvRAP	MiG-15R

Independent
Debrecen	727 GvBAP	Il-28
	97 GvRAP	Il-28R

Hungary — Magyar Légierő

Taszár	31.Vre.E	MiG-21F/PF, MiG-17PF
Papa	47.Vre.E	MiG-21F/PF
Kecskemét	59.Vre.E	MiG-21F, MiG-17PM, MiG-15bis

Romania — Fortele Aeriene ale Republicii Socialiste Romane

Divizia 16 Aviație Vânătoare Tactica
Ianca	R49AvVB	S-102
Mihail Kogălniceanu	R57AvVt	MiG-21F
Borcea-Fetesti	R86AvVt	MiG-19
	Esc38AvCc	Il-28

Divizia 34 Aviație Vânătoare Tactica
Craiova	R67AvB	MiG-17PF/S-102
Caracal-Deveslu	R91AvVt	MiG-19
Timișoara-Giarmata.	R93AvVt	MiG-21F

Bulgaria — Protivovazdushna Otbrana I Vonnovazsushni Sili (PVOiVVS)

1 PVO-Korpus
Dobroslavti	18 IAP	1 IAE	MiG-19
	18 IAP	3 IAE	MiG-17
Gabrovnitsa	18 IAP	2 IAE	MiG-21PF

2 PVO-Korpus
Ravnetz	15 IAP	1 IAE	MiG-21PFM
Balchik	15 IAP	2 IAE	MiG-17F
	15 IAP	3 IAE	MiG-17PF

10 Smesen Aviatsionen Korpus
Graf Ignatievo	19 IAP	1 IAE	MiG-19PF
	19 IAP	2 IAE	MiG-21F
	19 IAP	3 IAE	MiG-19S
Uzundzhovo	21 IAP		MiG-19S
Bezmer	22 IBAP		MiG-15&17
Cheshnegirovo	25 IBAP		MiG-15&17
Tolbukhin	26 RAP		Il-28& MiG-15bisR

AIR ORDER OF BATTLE: 1975 TACTICAL FIXED-WING COMBAT AIRCRAFT

Note: Combat units moved, were re-equipped and/or renumbered frequently throughout the Cold War. This Order of Battle reflects the deployments of each of the air forces in Europe at various stages during each listed year.

NATO

AAFNE

Norway	Kongelige Norsk Luftforsvaret			
	Bodø		331 & 334 Skvs	F-104G/CF-104
	Ørland		338 Skv	F-5A
	Rygge		332 & 336 Skvs	F-5A
			717 Skv	RF-5A
	Sola		718 Skv	RF-5A
Denmark	Kongelige Dansk Flyvevåbnet	Flyvertaktiske Kommando		
	Aalborg		Esks 723 & 726	F-104G
	Karup		Esk 725	Draken F-35
			Esk 729	Draken RF-35
	Skrydstrup		Esk 727 & 730	F-100D

AAFCE
2 ATAF

Netherlands	Koninklijke Luchtmacht	Commando Tactische Luchtstrijdkrachten, (CTL)		
	Volkel		311 & 312 Sqns	F-104G
	Eindhoven		314 Sqn	NF-5A
	Leeuwarden		322 & 323 Sqns	F-104G
	Twenthe		313 & 315 Sqns	NF-5A
			306 Sqn	RF-104G
	Gilze-Rijen		316 Sqn	NF-5A
Belgium	Belgische Luchtmacht/Force Aérienne Belge			
	Beauvechain	1 Wg	349 & 350 Sqns	F-104G
	Florennes	2 Wg	2 Sqn	Mirage V
			42 Sqn	Mirage V BR
	Bierset	3 Wg	1 & 8 Sqns	Mirage V
	Kleine-Brogel	10 Wg	23 & 31 Sqns	F-104G
BRD	Luftwaffe			
	Nörvenich	JaBoG 31		F-104G
	Lechfeld	JaBoG 32		F-104G
	Büchel	JaBoG 33		F-104G
	Memmingen	JaBoG 34		F-104G

	Pferdsfeld	JaBoG 35		F-4F
	Hopsten	JaBoG 36		F-4F
	Neuburg	JG 74		F-4F
	Wittmundhaven	JG 71		F-4F
	Ingolstadt	AG 51		RF-4E
	Leck	AG 52		RF-4E
	Husum	LeKG 41		G-91
	Oldenburg	LeKG 43		G-91
	Leipheim	LeKG 44		G-91

UK	Royal Air Force	RAF Germany (RAFG)		
	Brüggen		14, 17 & 31 Sqns	Phantom FGR2
	Gutersloh		19 & 92 Sqns	Lightning F2A
	Laarbruch		2 Sqn	Phantom FGR2
			15 & 16 Sqns	Buccaneer S2
	Wildenrath		3, 4 & 20 Sqns	Harrier GR3

4 ATAF

USA	United States Air Force	United States Air Force in Europe (USAFE)		
	17th Air Force			
	Bitburg	36th TFW	22nd, 53rd & 525th TFS	F-4D
	Spangdahlem	52nd TFW	23rd TFS	F-4D
			81st TFS	EF-4C
	Hahn	50th TFW	10th, 496th FIS	F-4E
	Ramstein	86th TFW	526th TFS	F-4E
	Soesterburg		32nd FIS	F-4E
	Zweibrucken	26th TRW	17th & 38th TRS	RF-4C
	3rd Air Force			
	Alconbury	10th TRW	1st, 30th & 32nd TRS	RF-4C
	Lakenheath	48th TFW	492nd, 493rd, 494th TFS	F-4D
	Bentwaters	81st TFW	91st, 92nd TFS	F-4D
	Woodbridge	81st TFW	78th TFS	F-4D
	Upper Heyford	20th TFW	55th, 77th & 79th TFS	F-111E

Canada	Canadian Armed Forces	1 Canadian Air Group (1 CAG)		
	Baden-Solingen	4 Wing	421, 439 & 441 Sqns	CF-104

France	Armée de l'Air Française			
	Commandement de la Force Aérienne Tactique/1re Région Aérienne (FATac/1re RA)			
	Dijon-Longvic	2ème EC	ECs 1/2 'Cigognes' 2/2 'Côte d'Or' 3/2 'Alsace'	Mirage IIIE
	Nancy-Ochet	3ème EC	ECs 1/3 'Navarre', 2/3 'Champagne', 3/3 'Ardennes'	Mirage IIIE
	Luxeuil-St Sauveur	4ème EC	ECs 1/4 'Dauphine', 2/4 'La Fayette'	Mirage IIIE
	St Dizier	7ème EC	ECs 1/7 'Provence', 2/7 'Argonne', 3/7 Languedoc	Jaguar A
	Toul	11ème EC	ECs 1/11 'Roussillon', 2/11 'Vosges', 3/11 'Corse'	Jaguar A
	Colmar	13ème EC	ECs 1/13 'Artois', 2/13 'Alpes'	Mirage IIIE
			EC 3/13 'Auvergne'	Mirage 5F
	Strasbourg	33ème EC	ECs 1/33 'Belfort, 2/33 'Savoie', EC 3/33 'Moselle'	Mirage IIIR

Commandement des Forces de Défense Aérienne (CAFDA)

Orange-Caritat	5ème EC	ECs 1/5 'Vendée', 2/5 'Île de France'	Mirage F1C
Creil	10ème EC	ECs 1/10 'Valois', 2/10 'Seine'	Mirage IIIC
Cambrai-Epinoy	12ème EC	ECs 1/12 'Cambrésis', 2/12 'Cornouaille'	Super Mystère
Reims	30ème EC	ECs 2/30 'Normandie-Niémen', 3/30 'Lorraine'	Mirage F1C

AFSOUTH

Portugal — Força Aérea Portuguesa

1.ª Região Aérea

Monte Real	BA 5	Esq 51	F-86F
Montijo	BA 6	Esq 62	G-91

USA — United States Air Force — United States Air Force in Europe (USAFE)

16th Air Force

Torrejon	401st TFW	612nd, 613rd & 614th TFS	F-4C

5 ATAF

Italy — Aeronautica Militare

Treviso	2° St	14° & 103° Gr	G-91R
Villafranca	3° St	28° & 132° Gr	F-104G
Grosseto	4° St	9° Gr	F-104S
		20° Gr	F-104G
Rimini	5a St	23° & 102° Gr	F-104S
Ghedi	6° St	154° Gr	F-104G
Cervia	8° St	101° Gr	G-91Y
Grazzanise	9° St	10° Gr	F-104S
Brindisi	32° St	13° Gr	G-91Y
Gioia Del Colle	36° St	12° & 156° Gr	F-104S
Istrana	51° St	22° & 155° Gr	F-104S
Cameri	53° St	21° Gr	F-104S

6 ATAF

Greece — Ellinikí Polemikí Aeroporía

Larissa	110 PM	348 Moira	RF-84F
Néa Anghialos	111 PM	337 & 341 Moira	F-5A
Thessaloniki	113 PM	343 Moira	F-5A
Tanagra	114 PM	335 Moira	F-104G
		342 Moira	F-102A
Souda	115 PM	340 Moira	A-7H
		345 Moira	F-84F
Araxos	116 PM	336 Moira	F-104G
Andravida	117 PM	338 & 339 Moira	F-4E

Turkey	Türk Hava Kuvvetleri			
	1ⁿᶜⁱ Hava Kuvveti			
	Eskişehir	1ⁿᶜⁱ AJÜ	111 & 112 Filo	F-100C/D
			113 Kesif Filo	RF-84F
	Konya	3ⁿᶜⁱ AJÜ	131 & 132 Filo	F-100C/D
	Murted	4ⁿᶜⁱ AJÜ	141 Filo	F-104G
			142 Filo	F-102A
	Bandirma	6ⁿᶜⁱ AJÜ	161 & 162 Filo	F-5A/RF-5A
	Balikesir	9ⁿᶜᵘ AJÜ	191 Filo	F-104G
			192 Filo	F-5A/RF-5A
	2ⁿᶜᵘ Hava Kuvveti			
	Merzifon	5ⁿᶜᵘ AJÜ	151 & 152 Filo	F-5A
	Malatya Erhaç	7ⁿᶜⁱ AJÜ	171 & 172 Filo	F-100C/D
	Diyabarkir	8ⁿᶜⁱ AJÜ	181 Filo	F-84Q
			182 Filo	F-102A
			184 Kesif Filo	RF-84F

WARSAW PACT

NORTH-WESTERN & WESTERN TVDs

DDR	Luftstreitkräfte/Luftverteidigung der Nationalen Volksarmee (LSK/LV)		
	1. Luftverteidigungsdivision		
	Cottbus	JG-1	MiG-21 SPS/K
	Drewitz	JG-7	MiG-21 SPS/K
		JBG-31	MiG-17F
	Marxwalde	JG-8	MiG-21 SPS/K
	Preschen	JG-3	MiG-21 SPS/K
	3. Luftverteidigungsdivision		
	Neubrandenburg	JG-2	MiG-21 SPS/K
	Peenemünde	JG-9	MiG-21 SPS/K

Czechoslovakia	Československé Letectvo	Velitelství Protivzdušné Obrany Státu	
	7. Armáda Protivzdušné Obrany Státu		
	2. Divize Protivzdušné Obrany Státu		
	Ostrava-Mošnov	8. SLPl	MiG-21 PF/PFM
	3. Divize Protivzdušné Obrany Státu		
	České Budějovice	1. SLPl,	MiG-21 MF
	Žatec	11. SLPl	MiG-21 PF/PFM
	10. Letecká Armáda		
	Pardubice	47. průzkumný letecký pluk	MiG-21R, L-29R
	1. Stíhací Letecký Divise		
	Pardubice	4. SLPl	MiG-21 MF/MA
	Dobřany	5. SLPl	MiG-21 MF/MA
	Bechyně	9. SLPl	MiG-21 PFM
	34. Stíhací Bombardovací Letecká Divize		
	Přerov	6. SBoLPl	MiG-21 MF
	Oslavou	20. SBoLPl	Su-7BM/BKL
	Čáslav	28. SBoLPl	Su-7BM/BKL
	Hradec Králové	30. SBoLPl	MiG-15bisSB

AIR ORDERS OF BATTLE

Poland	Wojska Obrony Powietrznej Kraju		
	1 Korpus Obrony Powietrznej Kraju		
	Mińsk Mazowiecki	1.PLM-OPK	MiG-21PF/PFM
	Łask	10.PLM-OPK	MiG-21PF/PFM
	Mierzęcice	39.PLM-OPK	MiG-21PF/PFM
	2 Korpus Obrony Powietrznej Kraju		
	Zegrze-Pomorski	26.PLM-OPK	MiG-21MF
	Słupsk	28.PLM-OPK	MiG-21MF
	Gdynia-Babie Doły	34.PLM MW	MiG-21MF
	3 Korpus Obrony Powietrznej Kraju		
	Wroclaw-Strachowice	11.PLM-OPK	MiG-21PFM
	Krzesiny	62.PLM-OPK	MiG-21PFM
	Wojska Lotnicze	Dowództwa Lotnictwa Operacyjnego	
	2 Brandenburską Dywizję Lotnictwa Szturmowo-Rozpoznawczego		
	Piła	6.PLM-Sz	LiM-6bis/M
	Babimost	45.PLM-Sz	LiM-6bis/M
	Powidz	21.PLRTiA	LiM-6bisR
	3 Brandenburska Dywizja Lotnictwa Szturmowo-Rozpoznawczego		
	Mirosławiec	8.PLM-Sz	LiM-6bis/M
	Świdwin	40.PLM-Sz	LiM-6bis/M
	Sochaczew Bielice	32.PLRT	MiG-21R
	4 Pomorską Dywizję Lotnictwa Myśliwskiego		
	Goleniów	2.PLM	MiG-21F/PF
	Debrzno	9.PLM	MiG-21M
	Malbork	41.PLM	MiG-21M
	--		
	Bydgoszcz	3.PLM-B	Su-7BM
	Powidz	7.PLB-R	Su-20
		15.SELR MW	LiM-2/Il-28
USSR	**Voyenno-Vozdushnye Sily**		
	Central'naya Gruppa Voysk		
	131 Smeshannaya Aviatsionnaya Diviziya		
	Sliach	114 IAP	MiG-21PF
		100 OSAE	MiG-21R
	Hradčany	192 IAP	MiG-21PF
	4ya Vozdushnaya Armiya		
	149^{ya} IBAD		
	Krzywa	3 IBAP	Su-7BM
	Zhagan	42 GvIBAP	MiG-21PFM
	Szprotawa	18 IBAP	Su-17M
	239^{ya} IAD		
	Chojna	582 IAP	MiG-21SMT
	Kluczewo	159 GvIAP	MiG-21SM
	Kołobrzeg	871 IAP	MiG-23MLA
	--		
	Brzheg	164 OGvRAP	Yak-28R/PP
		215 OGvRAP	MiG-21R
	16ya Vozdushnaya Armiya		
	61^y Gvardeyskiy Istrebitel'nyy Aviatsionnyy Korpus		
	6^{ya} GvIAD		
	Altenburg	296 IAP	MiG-21SMT
	Falkenburg	31 IAP	MiG-23M
	Merseburg	85 IAP	MiG-21SMT
	105^{ya} IBAD		
	Finsterwalde	559 IBAP	Su-7B/BM

Grossenheim	497 IBAP	Su-7BKL
Jüterbog	116 GvIBAP	Su-7B
126ʸᵃ IAD		
Zerbst	35 IAP	MiG-23ML
Jüterbog	833 IAP	MiG-21bis
Köthen	73Gv IAP	MiG-23M
71ʸ Istrebitel'nyy Aviatsionnyy Korpus		
16ʸᵃ GvIAD		
Wittstock	33 IAP	MiG-21PFM
Damgarten	773 IAP	MiG-21PFM/SM
Finow	787 IAP	MiG-21PFM/SM
125ʸᵃ IBAD		
Lärz	19 GvIBAP	Su-7B
Templin	20 GvIBAP	Su-7/Su-17M
Neurippen	730 IBAP	Su-7B
Welzow	11 ORAP	Yak28R/PP
--		
Allstedt	294 ORAP	MiG-15R
Werneuchen	931 ORAP	Yak-28R

SOUTHERN REGION/SOUTH-WESTERN TVD

USSR — Voyenno-Vozdushnye Sily

36ʸᵃ Vozdushnaya Armiya

11ʸᵃ GvIAD		
Sármellék	5 IAP	MiG-21SM/SMT
Kiskunlacháza	14 IAP	MiG-23M
Tököl	515 GvIAP	MiG-21SM/SMT
--		
Kunmadaras	1 GvIBAP	Su-7B/BM
	315 GvRAP	MiG-21R
Debrecen	727 GvBAP	Yak-28
	97 GvRAP	Yak-28R

Hungary — Magyar Légierő

Taszár	31.Vre.E	MiG-21PF/MF
Pápa	47.Vre.E	MiG-21bis
Kecskemét	59.Vre.E	MiG-21PF/MF
Szolnok	101.Ö.Fre.Szd	L-29

Romania — Fortele Aeriene ale Republicii Socialiste România

Divizia 16 Aviaţie Vânătoare Tactica

Ianca	R49AvVtB	S-102
Mihail Kogălniceanu	R57AvVt	MiG-21RFM/RFMM
Borcea-Fetesti	R86AvVt	MiG-21F/RFM/RFMM
	Esc38AvCc	Harbin Hong-5

Divizia 34 Aviaţie Vânătoare Tactica

Craiova	R67AvB	MiG-17PF/S-102
Caracal-Deveslu	R91AvVt	MiG-21F/RFM/RFMM
Timişoara-Giarmata.	R93AvVt	MiG-21RFM/RFMM
	Esc31AvCc	MiG-21C

Bulgaria	Protivovazdushna Otbrana I Vonnovazsushni Sili (PVOiVVS)			
1 PVO-Korpus				
	Dobroslavti	18 IAP	1 IAE	MiG-21 MF
		18 IAP	3 IAE	MiG-17
	Gabrovnitsa	18 IAP	2 IAE	MiG-21 PF
2 PVO-Korpus				
	Ravnetz	15 IAP	1 IAE	MiG-21 PFM
	Balchik	15 IAP	2 IAE	MiG-17F
		15 IAP	3 IAE	MiG-17PF
10 Smesen Aviatsionen Korpus				
	Graf Ignatievo	19 IAP	1 IAE	MiG-21 PF
		19 IAP	2 IAE	MiG-21 M
	Uzundzhovo	21 IAP		MiG-17F/PF
	Bezmer	22 IBAP		MiG-17
	Cheshnegirovo	25 IBAP		MiG-17
	Tolbukhin	26 RAP		MiG-15R/21R, Il-28R

AIR ORDER OF BATTLE: 1985
TACTICAL FIXED-WING COMBAT AIRCRAFT

Note: Combat units moved, were re-equipped and/or renumbered frequently throughout the Cold War. This Order of Battle reflects the deployments of each of the air forces in Europe at various stages during each listed year.

NATO

AAFNE

Norway	Kongelige Norsk Luftforsvaret		
	Bodø	331 & 334 Skvs	F-16A
	Ørland	338 Skv	F-5A
	Rygge	332 Skv	F-16A
		336 Skv	F-5A
Denmark	Kongelige Dansk Flyvevåbnet	Flyvertaktiske Kommando	
	Aalborg	Esk 723	F-16A
		Esk 726	F-104G
	Karup	Esk 725	Draken F-35
		Esk 729	Draken RF-35
	Skrydstrup	Esk 727 & 730	F-16A

AAFCE
2 ATAF

Netherlands	Koninklijke Luchtmacht	Commando Tactische Luchtstrijdkrachten, (CTL)		
	Volkel		306, 311 & 312 Sqns	F-16A
	Eindhoven		314 Sqn	NF-5A
	Leeuwarden		322 & 323 Sqns	F-16A
	Twenthe		313 & 315 Sqns	NF-5A
	Gilze-Rijen		316 Sqn	NF-5A
Belgium	Belgische Luchtmacht/Force Aérienne Belge			
	Beauvechain	1 Wg	349 & 350 Sqns	F-16A
	Florennes	2 Wg	2 Sqn	Mirage V
			42 Sqn	Mirage V BR
	Bierset	3 Wg	1 & 8 Sqns	Mirage V
	Kleine-Brogel	10 Wg	23 & 31 Sqns	F-16A
BRD	Luftwaffe			
	Nörvenich	JaBoG 31		Tornado IDS
	Lechfeld	JaBoG 32		Tornado IDS
	Büchel	JaBoG 33		Tornado IDS
	Memmingen	JaBoG 34		F-104G
	Pferdsfeld	JaBoG 35		F-4F
	Hopsten	JaBoG 36		F-4F
	Neuburg	JG 74		F-4F
	Wittmundhaven	JG 71		F-4F
	Ingolstadt	AG 51		RF-4E
	Leck	AG 52		RF-4E
	Husum	JaBoG 41		Alphajet
	Oldenburg	JaBoG 43		Alphajet
UK	Royal Air Force	RAF Germany (RAFG)		
	Brüggen		14, 17 & 31 Sqns	Tornado GR1
	Gutersloh		3 & 4 Sqns	Harrier GR3
	Laarbruch		2 Sqn	Jaguar GR1
			15, 16 & 20 Sqns	Tornado GR1
	Wildenrath		19 & 92 Sqns	Phantom FGR2

4 ATAF

USA	United States Air Force	United States Air Force in Europe (USAFE)		
	17th Air Force			
	Bitburg	36th TFW	22nd, 53rd & 525th TFS	F-15C
	Spangdahlem	52nd TFW	23rd, 81st & 480th TFS	F-4G/E
	Hahn	50th TFW	10th, 313rd & 496th TFS	F-16A
	Ramstein	86th TFW	512nd & 526th TFS	F-16A
	Soesterburg		32nd TFS	F-15C

AIR ORDERS OF BATTLE

	Zweibrucken	26th TRW	38th TRS	RF-4C
	3rd Air Force			
	Alconbury	10th TRW	1st TRS	RF-4C
	Lakenheath	48th TFW	492nd, 493rd, 494th TFS	F-11F
	Bentwaters	81st TFW	92nd, 510th & 511th TFS	A-10
	Woodbridge	81st TFW	78th, 91st & 509th TFS	A-10
	Upper Heyford	20th TFW	55th, 77th & 79th TFS	F-111E
			42nd ECS	EF-111A

Canada

Canadian Armed Forces — 1 Canadian Air Group (1 CAG)

Baden-Solingen	4 Wing	409 & 439 Sqns	CF-188
		441 Sqn	CF-104

France

Armée de l'Air Française

Commandement de la Force Aérienne Tactique/1re Région Aérienne (FATac/1re RA)

Dijon-Longvic	2ème EC	ECs 2/2 'Côte d'Or'	Mirage IIIR
Nancy-Ochet	3ème EC	ECs 1/3 'Navarre', 2/3 'Champagne', 3/3 'Ardennes'	Mirage IIIE
Luxeuil-St Sauveur	4ème EC	ECs 1/4 'Dauphine', 2/4 'La Fayette'	Mirage IIIE
St Dizier	7ème EC	ECs 1/7 'Provence', 2/7 'Argonne', 3/7 Languedoc'	Jaguar A
Istrès		EC 4/7 'Limousin'	Jaguar A
Toul	11ème EC	ECs 1/11 'Roussillon', 2/11 'Vosges', 3/11 'Corse'	Jaguar A
Bourdeaux-Mérignac		EC 4/11 'Jura'	Jaguar A
Colmar	13ème EC	ECs 1/13 'Artois'	Mirage IIIE
		ECs 2/13 'Alpes' 3/13 'Auvergne'	Mirage 5F
Strasbourg	33ème EC	ECs 1/33 'Belfort, 2/33 'Savoie', EC 3/33'Moselle'	Mirage IIIR

Commandement des Forces de Défense Aérienne (CAFDA)

Dijon-Longvic	2ème EC	ECs 1/2 'Cigognes' 3/2 'Alsace'	Mirage 2000C
Orange-Caritat	5ème EC	ECs 1/5 'Vendée', 2/5 'Île de France', 3/5 'Comtat Venaissin'	Mirage F1C
Cambrai-Epinoy	12ème EC	ECs 1/12 'Cambrésis', 2/12 'Picardie', 3/12 'Cornouaille'	Mirage F1C
Reims	30ème EC	ECs 1/30 'Valois'; 2/30 'Normandie' - Niémen; 3/30 'Valais'	Mirage F1C

AFSOUTH

Portugal

Força Aérea Portuguesa

Comando Operacional da Força Aérea (COFA)

Monte Real	BA 5	Esq 302 & 304	A-7P
Montijo	BA 6	Esq 301	G-91
Lajes	BA 4	Esq 303	G-91

Spain

Ejército del Aire

Mando Aéreo de Combate (MACOM)

Manises	Ala 11	Esc 111, 112	C.11 [Mirage IIIE]
Torrejon	Ala 12	Esc 121, 122	C.12 [F-4C]
Albacete	Ala 14	Esc 141, 142	C.14A [Mirage F.1CE]

Mando Aéreo Táctico (MATAC)

Moron	Ala 21	Esc 211	C.9 [SF-5A]
		Esc 212	CR.9 [SRF-5A]

Mando Aéreo de Canarias (MACAN)

Gando, Canary Islands	Ala 46	Esc 462	C.14B [Mirage F.1EE]

USA	United States Air Force	United States Air Force in Europe (USAFE)		
	16th Air Force			
	Torrejon	401st TFW	612nd, 613rd & 614th TFS	F-16A

5ATAF

Italy	Aeronautica Militare			
	Treviso	2° St	14° & 103° Gr	G-91R
	Villafranca	3° St	28° & 132° Gr	F-104G
	Grosseto	4° St	9° Gr	F-104S
			20° Gr	F-104G
	Rimini	5ª St	23° & 102° Gr	F-104S
	Ghedi	6° St	154° & 155° Gr	Tornado IDS
	Cervia	8° St	101° Gr	G-91Y
	Grazzanise	9° St	10° Gr	F-104S
	Brindisi	32° St	13° Gr	G-91Y
	Gioia Del Colle	36° St	12° Gr	F-104S
			156° Gr	Tornado IDS
	Istrana	51° St	22° Gr	F-104S
	Cameri	53° St	21° Gr	F-104S

6ATAF

Greece	Ellinikí Polemikí Aeroporía			
	Larissa	110 PM	347 Moira	A-7H
			348 Moira	RF-4E
	Néa Anghialos	111 PM	341 & 343 Moira	F-5A
			349 Moira	RF-5A
	Tanagra	114 PM	334 & 342 Moira	Mirage F1CG
	Souda	115 PM	340 & 345 Moira	A-7H
	Araxos	116 PM	335 & 336 Moira	F-104G
	Andravida	117 PM	337, 338 & 339 Moira	F-4E

Turkey	Türk Hava Kuvvetleri			
	1^{nci} Hava Kuvveti			
	Eskişehir	1^{nci} AJÜ 1	11 & 112 Filo	F-4E
			113 Kesif Filo	RF-4E
	Konya	3^{nci} AJÜ	131 & 132 Filo	F-4E
	Murted	4^{nci} AJÜ	141 & 142 Filo	F-104G
	Bandirma	6^{nci} AJÜ	161 & 162 Filo	F-104G
	Balikesir	9^{ncu} AJÜ	191 & 192 Filo	F-104S
			193 Filo	F-104G
	2^{ncu} Hava Kuvveti			
	Merzifon	5^{ncu} AJÜ	151 & 152 Filo	F-5A
	Malatya Erhaç	7^{nci} AJÜ	171, 172 & 173 Filo	F-4E
	Diyabarkir	8^{nci} AJÜ	181 & 182 Filo	F-100D
			184 Kesif Filo	RF-5A

WARSAW PACT

NORTH-WESTERN TVD AND WESTERN TVDs

DDR — Luftstreitkräfte/Luftverteidigung der Nationalen Volksarmee (LSK/LV)

1. Luftverteidigungsdivision
- Holzdorf — JG-1 — MiG-21M
- Drewitz — JG-7 — MiG-21M
- Marxwalde — JG-8 — MiG-21bis
- Preschen — JG-3 — MiG-21MF

3. Luftverteidigungsdivision
- Neubrandenburg — JG-2 — MiG-21M
- Peenemünde — JG-9 — MiG-23ML

Führungsorgan Front- und Militärtransportfliegerkräfte (FO FMTFK)
- Drewitz — JBG-37 — MiG-23BN, MiG-17F
- Laage — JBG-77 — Su-22M4
- — MFG-28 — Su-22M4
- Preschen — TAFS-47 — MiG-21F13

Czechoslovakia — Československé Letectvo — Velitelství Protivzdušné Obrany Státu

7. Armáda Protivzdušné Obrany Státu

2. Divize Protivzdušné Obrany Státu
- Brno — 8.SLPl — MiG-21PF/PFM

3. Divize Protivzdušné Obrany Státu
- České Budějovice — 1.SLPl, — MiG-23MF/ML
- Žatec — 11.SLPl — MiG-21MF/MiG-23MF

10. Letecká Armáda
- Hradec Králové — 47. PzLP — MiG-21R, L-29R, Su-22M4

1. Stíhací Letecký Divise
- Pardubice — 4.SLPl — MiG-21MF/MA
- Dobřany — 5.SLPl — MiG-21MF/MA
- Bechyně — 9.SBoLPl — MiG-21PFM/MF/MA

34. Stíhací Bombardovací Letecká Divize
- Přerov — 6.SBoLPl — MiG-21MF
- Náměšť nad Oslavou — 20.SBoLPl — Su-7BM/BKl
- Čáslav — 28.SBoLPl — MiG-23BD
- Pardubice — 30.SBoLPl — Su-25K

Poland — Wojska Obrony Powietrznej Kraju

1 Korpus Obrony Powietrznej Kraju
- Mińsk Mazowiecki — 1.PLM-OPK — MiG-21PF/PFM
- Łask — 10.PLM-OPK — MiG-21PF/PFM
- Mierzęcice — 39.PLM-OPK — MiG-21PF/PFM

2 Korpus Obrony Powietrznej Kraju
- Zegrze-Pomorski — 26.PLM-OPK — MiG-21bis
- Słupsk — 28.PLM-OPK — MiG-21MF
- Gdynia-Babie Doły — 34.PLM MW — MiG-21bis

3 Korpus Obrony Powietrznej Kraju
- Wroclaw-Strachowice — 11.PLM-OPK — MiG-21M/MF
- Krzesiny — 62.PLM-OPK — MiG-21PFM

	Wojska Lotnicze	Dowództwa Lotnictwa Operacyjnego	
	2 Brandenburską Dywizję Lotnictwa Szturmowo-Rozpoznawczego		
	Piła	6.PLM-B	Su-22M4
	Babimost	45.PLM-Sz	LiM-6bis/M
	Powidz	21.PLBR	LiM-6bisR
	3 Brandenburska Dywizja Lotnictwa Szturmowo-Rozpoznawczego		
	Bydgoszcz	3.PLM-B	Su-7BM/BKL
	Mirosławiec	8.PLM-Sz	LiM-6bis/M
	Świdwin	40.PLM-B	Su-22M4
	Sochaczew Bielice	32.PLRT	MiG-21R
	4 Pomorską Dywizję Lotnictwa Myśliwskiego		
	Goleniów	2.PLM	MiG-21PF/PFM
	Debrzno	9.PLM	MiG-21M/MF
	Malbork	41.PLM	MiG-21M/MF
	--		
	Powidz	7.PLB-B	Su-20
		15.SELR MW	LiM-2A

USSR	Voyenno-Vozdushnye Sily	

Central'naya Gruppa Voysk
131 Smeshannaya Aviatsionnaya Diviziya

Milovice	114 IAP	MiG-23M
Mimon-Gradchany	236 IAP	MiG-23BM
Sliach	100 OSAE	Su-17M3R

4ya Vozdushnaya Armiya VGK ON
132 BAD

Chernyakhovsk	4 GvBAP	Su-24
	63 BAP	Su-24M
Tukums	668 BAP	Su-24M

149ya BAD

Krzywa	3 BAP	Su-24
Zhagan	42 GvBAP	Su-24M
Szprotawa	89 BAP	Su-24

239ya IAD

Chojna	582 IAP	MiG-21bis
Kluczewo	159 GvIAP	MiG-21bis
Kołobrzeg	871 IAP	MiG-23MLA
--		
Brzheg	164 OGvRAP	MiG-25BM, Su24MR
	151 OAPREB	Yak-28PP

VVS Gruppa Sovetskikh Voysk v Germanii
71y Istrebitel'nyy Aviatsionnyy Korpus
6ya GvIAD

Altenburg	296 IAP	MiG-27/21SMT
Falkenburg	31 IAP	MiG-23M
Merseburg	85 IAP	MiG-23M

16ya GvIAD

Wittstock	33 IAP	MiG-23MLA
Damgarten	773 IAP	MiG-23ML
Finow	787 IAP	MiG-25PD, MiG-23M

105ya IBAD

Finsterwalde	559 APIB	MiG-27K
Grossenheim	497 APIB	Su-24
Brand	116 GvAPIB	Su-24

125ya IBAD

Lärz	19 GvAPIB	MiG-27K

	Templin	20 GvAPIB	Su-17M3
	Neurippen	730 APIB	Su-17M4
126ʸᵃ IAD			
	Zerbst	35 IAP	MiG-23M
	Jüterbog	833 IAP	MiG-23MLA
	Köthen	73Gv IAP	MiG-23MLA
	--		
	Welzow	11 ORAP	Yak28R/PP
	Allstedt	294 ORAP	Su-17M3R
	Werneuchen	931 ORAP	Yak-28R, MiG-25R
	Brandis	357 OShAP	Su-25

SOUTHERN REGION/SOUTH-WESTERN TVD

USSR — Voyenno-Vozdushnye Sily

VVS Yuzhnyy Gruppa Voysk

11ʸᵃ GvIAD			
	Sármellék	5 IAP	MiG-23M
	Kiskunlacháza	14 IAP	MiG-23ML
	Tököl	515 GvIAP	MiG-21bis
	--		
	Kunmadaras	1 GvAPIB	Su-17M2
		328 GvRAP	Yak-28R, Su-17M4R
	Debrecen	727 GvBAP	Su-24M

Hungary — Magyar Légierő

Taszár	31.Vre.E	MiG-21bis
	101.Ö.Fre.Szd	Su-22M3
Pápa	47.Vre.E	MiG-23MF, MiG-21bis
Kecskemét	59.Vre.E	MiG-21MF

Romania — Fortele Aeriene ale Republicii Socialiste România

Statul Major al Fortelor Aeriene

Mihail Kogălniceanu	R57AvVt	MiG-23MF
Borcea-Fetesti	R86AvVt	MiG-21F/RFM/RFMM
Caracal-Deveslu	R91AvVt	MiG-21F/RFM/RFMM
Timișoara-Giarmata	R93AvVt	MiG-23MF/MiG-21

Divizia 59 Aviație

Campia Turzii	R71AvVt	MiG-21F/RFM/RFMM
Timișoara-Giarmata	Esc31AvCc	MiG-21C

Divizia 70 Aviație

Ianca	R49AvVtB	IAR-93/MiG-15
Craiova	R67AvVtB	IAR-93/MiG-15
Borcea-Fetesti	Esc38AvCc	Harbin Hong-5

Bulgaria — Protivovazdushna Otbrana I Vonnovazsushni Sili (PVOiVVS)

1 PVO-Korpus

Dobroslavti	18 IAP	1 IAE	MiG-23MF/MLA
Gabrovnitsa	18 IAP	2 IAE	MiG-21PF

2 PVO-Korpus
Ravnetz	15 IAP	1 IAE	MiG-21PFM
Balchik	15 IAP	2 IAE	MiG-21MF

10 Smesen Aviatsionen Korpus
Graf Ignatievo	19 IAP	MiG-21bis
Uzundzhovo	21 IAP	MiG-21M/MF
Bezmer	22 IBAP	Su-25K
Cheshnegirovo	25 IBAP	MiG-23BN
Tolbukhin	26 RAP	MiG-25RBT, MiG-21R, MiG-17F

NATO Reporting Names for Soviet Aircraft

Backfire (Tu-22M); Badger (Tu-16); Bat (Tu-2); Beagle (Il-28); Bear (Tu-95); Bear F/J (Tu-142); Beast (Il-10); Bison A (M-4); Bison B/C (Mya 3M); Blackjack (Tu-160); Blinder (Tu-22); Bob (Il-4); Brewer (Yak-28); Buck (Pe-2); Bull (Tu-4); Fagot (MiG-15); Fang (La-11); Fargo (MiG-9); Farmer (MiG-19); Feather (Yak-15); Fencer (Su-24); Fiddler (Tu-128P); Firebar (Yak-28P); Fishbed (MiG-21); Fishpot (Su-9); Fitter A (Su-7); Fitter B (Su-17); Flagon (Su-15); Flanker (Su-27); Flashlight (Yak-25); Flogger D/J (MiG-27); Flogger A (MiG-23); Flora (Yak-23); Foxbat (MiG-25); Foxhound (MiG-31); Fresco (MiG-17); Frogfoot (Su-25); Fulcrum (MiG-27); Mail (Be-12); Mainstay (Il/Be-A50); Mandrake (Yak-25RV); May (Il-38); Midas (Il-78M); Moss (Tu-126)

NON-ALIGNED AIR FORCES

AIR ORDER OF BATTLE: TACTICAL FIXED-WING COMBAT AIRCRAFT IN NON-ALIGNED AIR FORCES

Note: Combat units moved, were re-equipped and/or renumbered frequently throughout the Cold War. This Order of Battle reflects the deployments of each of the air forces in Europe at various stages during each listed year.

1. Sweden — Svenska Flygvapnet

Location	Unit	1950	1955	1960	1965	1970	1975	1980	1985
Västerås/Hässlö	F1	J 30	J 33	J 32B	J 32B	J 35F	J 35F	J 35F	disbanded
Linköping/Malmen	F3	J 28	J 29	J 29	J 35D	J 35D	disbanded	---	---
Östersund/Frösön	F4	J 26	J 28B	J 29	J 29F	J 35D	J 35D	J 35D	AJ 37
Karlsborg	F6	A 21A	A 29B	A 32A	A 32A	A 32A	A 32A	AJ 37	AJS 37
Såtenäs	F7	B 18	A 29B	A 32A	A 32A	A 32A	AJ 37	AJ 37	AJS 37
Stockholm/Barkarby	F8	J 28B	J 29B	J 34	disbanded	---	---	---	---
Göteborg/Säve	F9	J 28B/J 21A	J 29	J 29F	J 34	disbanded	---	---	---
Ängelholm/Barkåkra	F10	J 21R	J 29	J 29F	J 34/J 35D	J 35F	J 35F	J 35F	J 35F
Nyköping/Skavsta	F11	S 31	S 29C	S 32C	S 32C/S 35E	S 32C/S 35E	S 32C/S 35E	disbanded	---
Kalmar/Törneby	F12	J 21A	J 29A	J 32B	J 32B	J 35F	J 35F	disbanded	---
Norrköping/Bråvalla	F13	J 28A	J 29A	J 35A	J 35F/D	J 35F	J 35F	SH/SF/JA 37	SH/SF/JA 37
Halmstad/Mickledala	F14	B 18B	A 28B	A 32A	A 32A	disbanded	---	---	---
Söderhamn/Östansjö	F15	J 21A	J 28B	A 32A	A 32A	A 32A	AJ 37	AJ 37	AJS 37
Uppsala/Ärna	F16	J 26	J 29	J 29	J 35A	J 35A	J 35A	J 35F	J 35F
Ronneby/Kallinge	F17	T 18B	T 18B	A 32A	A 32A	A 32A	J 35F	J35 F/SH/SF 37	SH/SF/JA 37
Stockholm/Tullinge	F18	J 28B	J 28B	J 34	J 35B	J 35B	disbanded	---	---
Luleå/Kallax	F21	S 18A/ S 26	S 29C	S 29C	J 32B	S 35E/J 35D	S 35E/J 35D	J35 D/SH/SF 37	SH/SF/JA 37

2. Finland — Ilmavoimat

Location	Unit	1950	1955	1960	1965	1970	1975	1980	1985
		Le.R 4	1.Lsto	Hämeen Lennosto (HämLsto)			Lapin Lennosto (LapLstc)		
Luonetjärvi	HLe.Lv 41	Bf109G	disbanded						
	HävLtue	--	Vihuri	re-named HävLv 21					
	TieLtue	--	Blenheim	disbanded					
	HävLv 21	--	--	Gnat	re-named HävLLV 11				
	HävLLv 11	--	--	--	Gnat	Gnat	to Rovaneimi		
	TieLlv	--	--	--	--	--	MiG-21F	MiG-21F	MiG-21F
Rovaneimi	HävLLv 11	--	--	--	--	--	Draken	Draken	Draken
		Le.R 1	2.Lsto	Satakunnan Lennosto (SatLsto)					
Pori	HLe.Lv 11	Bf109G	re-named HävLv 11						
	HLe.Lv 13	Bf109G	re-named HävLv 13						
	HävLv 11	--	Vampire	Magister	re-named HävLLV 21				
	HävLv 13	--	Vampire	disbanded					
	HävLLv 21	--	--	--	Magister	Magister	Magister	Hawk	to Pirkkala
Pirkkala	HävLLv 21	--	--	--	--	--	--	--	Draken
		Le.R 3	3.Lsto	Karjalan Lennosto (KarLsto)					
Uti	HLe.Lv 31	Bf109G	re-named HävLv 31						
	HLe.Lv 33	Bf109G	re-named HävLv 33						
	HävLv 31	--	Vihuri	to Rissala					
	HävLv 33	--	Vihuri	disbanded					
Rissala	HävLv 31	--	--	re-named HävLLV 31					
	HävLLv 31	--	--	Magister	MiG-21F	MiG-21F	MiG-21F	MiG-21bis	MiG-21bis

3. Austria — Österreichische Luftstreitkräfte

Location	Unit	1950	1955	1960	1965	1970	1975	1980	1985
					JaBoGeschw 1		Fliegerregiment 3		
Linz-Hörsching	1 Sta	—	—	—	J-29	S-105Ö	S-105Ö	S-105Ö	S-105Ö
	2 Sta	—	—	—	J-29	To Graz/Nittner			
	3 Sta	—	—	—	—	S-105Ö	S-105Ö	S-105Ö	S-105Ö
							Fliegerregiment 2		
Graz-Thalerhof	2 Sta					S-105Ö	S-105Ö	S-105Ö	S-105Ö

4. Switzerland — Schweizer Flugwaffe

Location	Unit	1950	1955	1960	1965	1970	1975	1980	1985
Raron*	FlSt 1	--	--	Hunter	Hunter	Hunter	Hunter	Hunter	to Turtmann
	FlSt 5	--	Vampire	Hunter	Hunter	Hunter	Hunter	Hunter	Hunter
	FlSt 9	Vampire	Vampire	Vampire	Vampire	Venom	Venom	Venom	disbanded
	FlSt 17	C-3607	to Buochs	--	--	--	--	--	--
	FlSt 21	--	--	--	--	--	--	--	Hunter
Ulrichen	FlSt 2	Vampire	Venom	Venom	Venom	Venom	Venom	Venom	Hunter
	FlSt 22	--	--	Hunter	disbanded?	--	--	--	--
Sior	FlSt 6	--	Vampire	Venom	Venom	Venom	Venom	Hunter	F-5
	FlSt 24	--	--	--	--	--	--	Hunter	Hunter
Turtmann*	FlSt 1	--	--	--	--	--	--	--	F-5
	FlSt 4	--	--	--	--	--	Hunter	Hunter	Hunter
	FlSt 17	--	--	--	--	Mirage IIIS	Mirage IIIS	to Payerne	--
	FlSt 21	--	--	--	--	Hunter	Hunter	Hunter	to Raron

Location	Unit								
Payerne	FlSt 17	--	--	--	--	--	--	Mirage IIIS	Mirage IIIS
	FlSt 18	F-51	F-51	Venom	Venom	Venom	Hunter	F-5	F-5
	FlSt 24	--	--	--	--	--	--	Hunter	Hunter
St Stephan*	FlSt 4	--	Venom	Venom	Venom	Venom	to Turtmann	--	--
	FlSt 15	D-3800	Venom	Venom	Venom	Venom	Venom	Hunter	Hunter
Interlaken	FlSt 7	Vampire	Vampire	Vampire	Venom	Venom	to Meiringen	--	Hunter
	FlSt 12	--	Vampire	Vampire	Vampire	Vampire	Zielflugstaffel		
Meiringen*	FlSt 7	--	--	--	--	--	Hunter	Hunter	to Interlaken
	FlSt 8	Vampire	Vampire	Hunter	Hunter	Hunter	Hunter	F-5	F-5
	FlSt 11	--	--	Hunter	Hunter	Hunter	to Alpnach	--	--
	FlSt 13	--	--	--	--	--	--	--	F-5
Ambri*	FlSt 3	C-3603	Venom	Venom	Venom	Venom	Venom	Hunter	Hunter
	FlSt 13	D-3800	Venom	Venom	Venom	Venom	Venom	Venom	to Meiringen
Alpnach	FlSt 11	Vampire	Vampire	to Meiringen	--	--	Hunter	F-5	F-5
	FlSt 19	F-51	F-51	Venom	Venom	Venom	Hunter	F-5	F-5
Buochs*	FlSt 10	D-3801	Venom FB1R	Venom FB1R	Venom FB1R	Mirage IIIRS	Mirage IIIRS	Mirage IIIRS	Mirage IIIRS
	FlSt 16	C-3603	Venom	Venom	Venom	Mirage IIIS	Mirage IIIS	Mirage IIIS	Mirage IIIS
	FlSt 17	--	Venom	Venom	Venom	to Turtmann	--	--	--
	FlSt 21	F-51	F-51	Hunter	Hunter	to Turtmann	--	--	--
Mollis	FlSt 20	F-51	F-51	Venom	Venom	Venom	Venom	Hunter	Hunter
Dübendorf	FlSt 1	--	Vampire	to Raron	--	--	--	--	--
Saanen	FlSt 14	--	Venom	Venom	Venom	disbanded	--	--	--

5. Yugoslavia — Ratno Vazduhoplovstvo i Protivvazdušna Odbrana (RV i PVO)

Location	Unit	1950	1955	1960	1965	1970	1975	1980	1985
Niš	81.Puk	Il-2	F-47D	F-47D	disbanded				
	107.Puk	Il-2	to Leskovac						
	150.Puk	--	F-47D	disbanded					
Skopsi Petrovac	94.Puk	Yak-9	F-84G	F-86E	disbanded				
	116.Puk	Yak-3	S-49C	disbanded					
	98.ABr/247.LBAE	--	--	--	--	--	Jastreb	Jastreb	Jastreb
	198.Puk	Yak-3	F-84G	F-84G	F-86E	disbanded			
Velika Gorica	88.Puk	Pe-2	Mosquito	to Batajnica					
Batajnica	117.Puk	--	F-84G	F-86E	to Pleso				
	204.Puk	--	F-84G	F-86E	MiG-21F	MiG-21	MiG-21PFM/MF	MiG-21PFM/MF	MiG-21MF
	88.Puk	--	--	F-84G	F-84G	disbanded			
	98.ABr/123.LAE	--	--	--	--	F-86D	to 83.LAP		
Tuzla	103.Puk	--	--	RT-33A	IT-33A	IT-33A	Jastreb	Jastreb	Jastreb
	98.ABr/350.IAE	--	--	--	--	RT-33A	Jastreb	Jastreb	Jastreb
Ladeveci	98.ABr/235.LBAE	--	--	--	--	Jastreb/Galeb	Jastreb/Galeb	Jastreb	Jastreb
Pristina	83.Puk	--	--	--	--	MiG-21F	MiG-21F	MiG-21PFM/MF	MiG-21/bis
Pula	83.Puk	Yak-3	to Zemunica						
	40.Puk	--	S-49C	disbanded					
Zemunica	97.Puk	Pe-2	Mosquito FB6	to Mostar					
	117.Puk	S-49A	to Batajnica						
	172.Puk	Bf109G	F-84G	F-84G	F-84G	to Titograd			
	204.Puk	S-49A	to Batajnica						
	83.Puk	--	F-84G	F-86E	disbanded				
Pleso	109.Puk	Pe-2	Mosquito FB6	F-84G	to Cerklje				
	184.Puk	--	Mosquito NF38	RF-84G	F-86D	disbanded			
	117. Puk	--	--	--	F-86D	to Bihač			
Cerklje	111.Puk	Il-2	F-47D	F-47D	disbanded				
	96.Puk	Il-2	F-47D	disbanded					

Location	Unit	1950	1955	1960	1965	1970	1975	1980	1985
	82.ABr	--	--	--	F-84G	Jastreb/F-84G	Jastreb	Jastreb	Jastreb/Orao
	109.Puk	--	--	--	F-84G	disbanded			
Bihać	352.IAE	--	--	--	--	MiG-21R	MiG-21R	MiG-21R	MiG-21R
	117.Puk	--	--	--	--	MiG-21F	MiG-21PFM	MiG-21bis	MiG-21bis
Leskovac	107.Puk	--	S-49A	F-47D	helicopter				
Mostar	97.Puk/Abr	--	--	Ikarus-214	various	F-86E/ RF-84G	Jastreb	Jastreb	Orao
Pancevo	103.Puk	various	Mosquito NF38	to Tuzla					
Titograd	172.Puk	--	--	--	--	Jastreb	Jastreb	Jastreb	Jastreb

6. Albania — Forca Ajrore e Republikës së Shqipërisë (FAj)

Location	Unit	1950	1955	1960	1965	1970	1975	1980	1985
Kuçovë	R 1875 AvGB	WP	WP	WP	MiG-15	J-5, J-6	J-5, J-6	J-5, J-6	J-5/J-6
Rinas	R 7594 AvGB	--	--	--	MiG-17F, J-6	J-6	J-6	J-6	J-6
Gjadër	R 5646 AvGB	--	--	--	--	--	J-6, J-7A	J-6, J-7A	J-6, J-7A

7. Spain — Ejército del Aire (EdA))

Location	Unit	1950	1955	1960	1965	1970	1975	1980	1985
				Mando de Defensa Aérea					
Manises	AdC 1	--	C.5	C.5	became Ala 11				
	Ala 11	--	--	--	C.5	C.11	C.11	C.11	NATO
Zaragoza	14 GdFFAA	B.2H	became AdC 2						
	AdC 2	--	C.5	C.5	became Ala 12				
	Ala 12	--	--	--	C.5	C.5	disbanded		
Mallorca	3 GdFFAA	B.2H	became EdC 41						
	EdC 41	--	C.5	disbanded					
Reus	23 GdFFAA	I-15bis	became EdC 51						
	EdC 51	--	C.5	to Moron as AdC 5					
Morón	AdC 5	--	--	C.5	became Ala 15				
	Ala 15	--	--	--	C.5	became Ala 21			
	Ala 21	--	--	--	--	C.9 CR.9	C.9 CR.9	C.9 CR.9	NATO
	Ala 27	--	B.2H	to Malaga					
Getafe	31 GdFFAA	B.2H	became EdC 61						
	EdC 61	--	C.5	to Torrejon as AdC 6					
Torrejón	AdC 6	--	C.5	C.5	became Ala 16				
	Ala 16	--	--	--	C.5	became Ala 12			
	Ala 12	--	--	--	--	C.8, C.12	C.12	C.12	NATO
				Mando de la Aviación Táctica					
Malaga	Ala 27	--	--	B.21	B.21	disbanded			
Tablada	11 GdFFAA	B.2H	became Ala 21						
	Ala 21	--	B.2H	B.21	B.21	disbanded			
	Ala 47	--	--	C.4K	C.4K	disbanded			
El Copero	Ala 7	--	--	C.4K	C.4K	disbanded			
Villanubla	33 GdFFAA	I-15bis	T-33	became Ala 43 - re-roled training					
Albacete	13 GdFFAA	Ju-88	became Ala 26						
	Ala 26	--	B.2H	became Ala 37					
	Ala 37	--	--	B.21	re-roled transport				
	Ala 14	--	--	--	--	--	C.14A	C.14A	NATO
Gando	Ala Mista 36	--	B.2H, T6	became Ala 46					
	Ala 46	--	--	C.4K, B.21	C.4K, B.21	C.10	C.10	C.9	NATO

Equipped with a sideways looking radar for tactical reconnaissance, the Lockheed TR-1A was a development of the U-2. The 17th Reconnaissance Wing operated the type from RAF Alconbury, Cambridgeshire, England. (USAFM)

INDEX

Afghanistan, invasion of 1979	174, 179, 185, 188, 199, 201, 206, 209, 223
Alaska	21, 24, 40, 47, 69, 85, 98, 102, 105, 124, 130, 137, 181, 183, 211, 215
Albanian Air Force (Forca Ajrore)	61, 77, 101, 268-71
AMX International A-11 Ghibli	226, 230
Andropov, Yuri	179
Arkhangelsk	40, 48, 78, 96, 121, 139, 187, 207
Armstrong Whitworth Meteor NF	50, 51, 56, 57
Austrian Air Force (Österreichische Luftstreitkräfte)	12, 18, 19, 55, 252-57, 307
Avia S-199	37
Avioane Craiova IAR-93 Vultur	200, 267
Avro Blue Steel	88, 91, 118
Avro CF-100 Canuck	47, 48, 49, 70, 105, 106
Avro Lincoln	26, 40, 50, 55
Avro Shackleton	93, 107, 133, 143, 147, 218
Avro Vulcan	64, 88, 91, 93, 118, 125, 135, 150, 167, 170, 180, 190
Bagotville	47, 106, 183, 211, 213
Ballistic Missile Early Warning System (BMEWS)	72, 103, 137
Baltic Express	154, 241
Belgian Air Force (Belgische Luchtmacht)	30, 31, 49, 50, 66, 88, 107, 123, 136, 154, 165, 190, 212, 220, 280, 287, 293, 300
Bell P-63 Kingcobra	15, 18, 19
Beriev Be-6	108
Berlin Crisis, 1961	81-86
Berlin Wall	9, 81, 86, 229, 278
Boeing B-29 Superfortress	15, 20, 23, 24, 39, 46
Boeing B-47 & RB-47 Stratojet	10, 39, 40-42, 46, 72, 74, 78, 80-81, 91, 102, 124, 273
Boeing B-50 Superfortress	17, 21, 24, 46
Boeing B-52 Stratofortress	40, 46, 70, 72, 80, 91, 103, 122, 123, 126, 131, 154, 156-7, 180, 181, 184, 202, 227
Boeing E-3 Sentry	155, 165, 185, 189, 193, 197, 218,
Boeing KC-97 Stratofreighter	23, 42, 72, 276
Boeing KC-135 Stratotanker	70-71, 72, 93, 153, 154, 181, 182, 278-79
Boeing Vertol AH-1G Cobra	174
BOMARC CIM-10	69, 105, 131
Brezhnev, Leonid	129, 175, 179
Bristol Bloodhound	65, 120, 237, 133
British Aerospace Hawk	8, 251, 263, 307
Bulgarian Air Force (PVO i VVS)	12, 32, 37, 56, 102, 153-4, 171, 201, 229
Canadair CP-107 Argus	93, 107
Canadian Air Force (RCAF/CAF)	14, 26, 47, 48, 52, 69, 93, 102, 103, 105, 106, 107, 114, 124, 135, 143, 154, 173, 183, 187, 190, 211,
Canadian Air Force (RCAF/CAF)	212-13, 231
Carter, Jimmy E	179
CATac (French Tactical Air Command)	52
CGV (Soviet Group of Central Forces)	19, 118
Chengdu J-7A	269, 270, 309
Chernenko, Konstantin	179
Chrysler PGM-19 Jupiter	89, 94
Comox	47, 106, 183
Convair B-36 Peacemaker	15, 24, 40, 46, 72
Convair B-58 Hustler	93, 94-5, 103, 131, 132
Convair F-102 Delta Dagger	70, 76, 85, 91, 98, 105, 107, 131, 143, 150, 152, 170, 196, 277, 288, 295, 296
Convair F-106 Delta Dart	70, 77, 84-5, 91, 105, 124, 131, 161, 183, 203
Cuban missile crisis, 1962	86-94
Curtiss SB2C Helldiver	61
Cyprus, invasion of 1974	150-52
Czechoslovakia, invasion of, 1968	115
Czechoslovakian Air Force (Československé Letectvo)	13, 37, 53-4, 102, 115, 138, 154, 164, 171, 200, 203, 226, 282-3, 290, 296, 303
Danish Air Force (Kongelige Dansk Flyvevåbnet)	30, 31, 49, 66, 106, 107, 124, 143, 154, 190, 211, 280, 286, 293, 299
Dassault MD452 Mystère	61, 65, 114, 120, 288
Dassault Mirage III	120, 137, 193, 195, 196, 212, 218, 260, 263, 276, 288, 294-5, 300, 301, 307, 308, 309
Dassault Mirage IV	116-7, 120, 218, 228-9
Dassault Mirage V	124, 136, 293, 300
Dassault Mirage F-1	14, 137, 195, 196, 218, 276, 295, 301, 309
Dassault Mirage 2000	193, 195, 218, 220, 226, 301
Dassault Ouragan	52, 53, 61, 281
Dassault Super Mystère	120, 126, 195, 288, 295
de Havilland Mosquito	30, 35, 37, 49, 50, 235, 265, 266, 306, 308-9
de Havilland Vampire	14, 26, 30, 31, 34, 35, 51, 52, 53, 61, 235, 239, 246, 247, 248, 253, 254, 259, 260, 281, 282, 307-8
de Havilland Venom	51-52, 57, 63, 236, 260, 263, 280-1, 307-8
Distant Early Warning Line (DEW)	69, 103, 105, 181, 207, 211
Douglas B-26 & RB-26 Invader	23, 26, 27
Douglas C-124 Globemaster	84, 90
Douglas SM-75 Thor	65, 88, 93, 120
East German Air Force (LSK/LV)	66, 137, 196-7, 198-9, 200, 223, 289-90, 296, 303
Eisenhower, Dwight D	63, 78
EKW C-3603	259, 261, 308
EKW D-3800	259, 260, 308
English Electric Canberra	39, 40, 50-1, 55, 63, 64, 88, 92, 96, 118, 134, 170, 280-1, 287
English Electric Lightning	81, 107, 120, 125, 143, 144-6, 154, 165, 170, 192, 217, 287, 294
Exercise Blue Moon	164
Exercise Central Enterprise	164
Exercise Checkmate	81
Exercise Cirrus	42
Exercise Coronet	42
Exercise Datex	164, 219
Exercise Desert Rock	46
Exercise Elder Joust/Elder Forest	164
Exercise Granit	161
Exercise Karpaty	141

Exercise Lato-67	126		127, 147, 151, 167, 170, 190, 217, 219, 226, 282, 289, 295, 302
Exercise Ombrelle	42		
Exercise Red Flag	158, 219, 221-22		
Exercise Shchit	161, 164		
Exercise Soyuz	161, 179	Jaruzelski, Wojciech	179
Exercise Sumava	115		
Exercise Zapad	161	Keflavik	47, 107, 143, 165, 202, 211
Exercise Zenit-70	154	Kennedy John F	9, 81, 91
Fairchild A-10 Thunderbolt	155, 160, 165, 193, 202, 214-5, 216, 301	Khrushchev, Nikita	62, 77 81, 94, 267, 269
		King Salmon	98, 105, 131, 183
FIAT G-91	147, 151, 195, 226, 294, 301	Korean War	23, 37 39
Finnish Air Force (Ilmavoimat)	244-51, 307		
Folland Gnat	247, 248, 247, 307	Lavochkin La-5	37
Fouga Magister	248, 250, 254, 255, 309	Lavochkin La-11	18
French Air Force (Armée de l'Aire)	14, 31, 34, 52, 63, 65, 81, 114, 115, 117, 118, 120, 139, 167, 175, 193, 104, 219, 229, 281, 288, 294-5, 301	Ling-Temco-Vought A-7 Corsair	170, 195, 196, 203, 226, 295, 301, 302
		Lockheed EC-121 Warning Star	69, 143, 155
French Strategic Air Command (CFAS)	117, 120, 218, 229	Lockheed F-80 Shooting Star	14, 23, 24, 26, 28-9
		Lockheed F-94 Starfire	24, 42, 44-5, 47
General Dynamics F-16 Fighting Falcon	155, 158-9, 165, 190, 193, 196, 202, 211, 212, 213, 226, 299, 300, 302	Lockheed F-104 & CF-104 Starfighter	70, 90 103, 106, 112-3, 114, 124, 127, 136, 140, 143, 147, 150, 152, 154, 165-7, 170-71, 180, 189, 190, 192-3, 196, 212, 213, 226, 276, 287-89, 293-5, 298-302, 309
General Dynamics F-111	124, 135, 171, 181, 192, 193, 202, 203, 216, 223, 294, 301		
General Dynamics FB-111	131, 181, 202		
Gloster Javelin	65, 81, 106, 107, 120, 287	Lockheed F-117 Nighthawk	203, 231
Gloster Meteor	14, 28-9, 30, 31, 39, 50, 51, 53, 56, 57, 65, 280, 281	Lockheed P-2 Neptune	107
		Lockheed P-3 Orion	107, 139, 143, 187, 211
Goose Bay	124, 167, 219	Lockheed SR-71 Blackbird	152, 154, 197, 223, 241, 244
Gorbachev, Mikhail	179, 201, 278	Lockheed U-2	72, 74, 78-9, 91, 93
Greek Air Force (EVA/EPA)	61, 66, 106, 124, 150, 152, 170, 196, 226, 282, 289, 295, 302	Martin B-57B	50, 96, 283
		McDonell F-4 Phantom	91, 105, 114, 122-3, 124, 131, 133, 135, 137, 143, 150, 152, 154, 155, 158-9, 165, 170, 173, 182, 189, 190, 192, 193, 196, 202, 203, 217, 218, 226, 278-9, 290, 296-7, 302-4
GSVG (Group of Soviet Forces in Germany)	14, 19, 197, 223		
Handley Page Victor	64, 65, 88, 91, 93, 118, 135, 138, 143, 144, 147, 218		
Hawker Hunter	51, 59, 64, 81, 89, 107, 236, 238, 240, 260, 261, 263, 286, 287, 307-8	McDonnell-Douglas F-15 Eagle	155, 165, 182, 188, 193, 202-3, 211, 213, 223, 224-5, 300
		McDonnell Douglas F-18 & CF-18E Hornet	183, 186-7, 189-90, 210, 212-213, 226, 301
Hawker Hurricane	14, 31	McDonnell F-101 & CF-101 Voodoo	70, 71, 93, 102, 104-5, 106, 114, 124, 148-9, 133, 190, 288
Hawker Siddeley Buccaneer	133, 135, 145, 190, 294		
Hawker Siddeley Harrier	128, 134-5, 136, 143, 190, 294, 300	McDonnell Douglas KC-10	181, 182
		Messerschmidt Bf-109	37, 246, 265
Hawker Siddeley Nimrod	135, 143, 146, 170, 218	Messerschmidt Me-262	37
Hispano Suiza HA-1112	273, 275, 309	Mikoyan Gurevich MiG-9	14, 25
Hispano-Suiza HA-220 Súper Saeta	275, 276, 309	Mikoyan Gurevich MiG-15	14, 15, 16, 28, 19, 26, 32, 37, 39, 40, 47-8, 53, 54, 55, 56, 61, 66, 67, 68, 101, 236, 269, 282-6, 290-2, 296, 298-9, 305, 309
Hungarian Air Force (Magyar Légiero)	32, 55, 56, 62, 63, 66-7, 102, 152-3, 154, 171, 200, 227, 285, 292, 298, 305		
Hungary, invasion of, 1956	62-3, 74	Mikoyan Gurevich MiG-17	39, 40, 41, 48, 54, 55, 56, 62, 63, 66, 67, 68, 98, 101, 115, 137, 139, 140, 153 154, 161, 229, 272, 273, 283-5, 290-2, 296, 298-9, 303, 306, 309
Ikarus S-49	265, 266, 308-9		
Ilyushin Il-10	18, 32, 48, 53, 54, 55, 56, 68, 285-8		
Ilyushin Il-28	48, 51, 53, 54-5, 56, 63, 89, 91, 200, 269, 270, 283-6, 290-2, 297	Mikoyan Gurevich MiG-19	66, 78, 80, 109-11, 154, 269, 292
		Mikoyan Gurevich MiG-21	75, 89, 98, 100-1, 115, 118, 122, 124, 137, 138, 140, 142, 152, 153, 154, 155, 160, 171, 188, 189, 197, 200, 201, 223, 226, 227, 237, 244, 248,
Ilyushin Il-78M	204, 205, 109		
Ilyushin-Beriev A-50	205, 213		
Inner German Border (IGB)	12, 40, 108,		
Italian Air Force (AMI)	14, 31, 61, 66, 71, 89, 97, 106, 112,		

	249, 250, 251, 267, 267, 270, 269, 289-92, 296-299, 303-6, 307-308
Mikoyan Gurevich MiG-23	121, 138, 141, 153, 160, 171, 173, 187, 188, 189, 197, 198-9, 200, 201, 206, 223, 226, 227, 229, 251, 297-298, 303-6
Mikoyan Gurevich MiG-25	132, 134, 155, 160, 165-7, 188, 201, 207, 223, 241, 304-6
Mikoyan MiG-27	171, 197, 205, 210, 223, 227, 304
Mikoyan MiG-29	200, 205, 206, 223, 226, 227, 229, 249
Mikoyan MiG-31	178, 179, 184, 187, 205, 206
Mil Mi-8	174
Mil Mi-24D	174-5
Mutual Defence Assistance Programme (MDAP)	42, 49, 88
Myasishchev M-4/3M	66, 67, 68, 97, 120, 121, 131, 132-3, 186, 203, 204
NATO 2 ATAF	49, 51, 64, 192, 280-1, 287, 295-4, 300
NATO 4 ATAF	49, 52, 135, 136, 155, 281, 288, 294-5, 300-1
Netherlands Air Force (KLu)	30, 49, 50, 66, 106, 107, 113, 124, 136, 154, 165, 190, 212, 219, 280, 287, 293, 300
Nike-Ajax	69
Nixon, Richard M	129
NORAD	69, 70, 98, 105, 124, 148, 154, 161, 181, 183, 211
North American B-45 & RB-45 Tornado	23, 36, 39, 47, 50
North American F-51 Mustang	19, 23, 24, 26, 31, 235, 237, 259, 310
North American F-82 Twin Mustang	17, 20, 24
North American F-86 & Canadair CL-13 Sabre	15, 24, 26, 33, 36-7, 50, 52, 54, 61, 62, 70, 84, 97, 124, 147, 195, 266, 267, 275, 276, 278, 283, 284, 288-9, 290, 291, 297, 310-11
North American F-86D/K Sabre Dog	46, 47, 65, 106, 115, 288, 291, 308
North American F-100 Super Sabre	47, 74-5, 81, 93, 106, 110-11, 114, 120, 123, 124, 139, 150, 152, 154, 196, 226, 275, 286, 288-9, 293, 296, 302
North Warning System (NWS)	211
Northrop F-5 & Canadair CF-116 Freedom Fighter	124, 127, 136, 140, 143, 150, 152, 158, 162-3, 165, 196, 211, 212, 226, 262, 263, 276, 286, 289, 293, 295-6, 299-302, 307-9
Northrop F-89 Scorpion	43, 47, 70
Norwegian Air Force (Kongelige Norsk Luftforsvaret)	16, 30, 49, 66, 124, 127, 140, 165-7, 187, 190, 211, 280, 286, 293, 299
Novaya Zemlya	84, 96, 121, 135, 139, 206
Oil crisis, 1973	132
Operation Anadyr	89
Operation Chrome Dome	72, 81, 93, 122
Operation Common Cause	91
Operation Grand Slam	78
Operation Jiu Jitsu	39, 40
Operation Power Flite	72
Operation Quick Fox	89
Operation Reflex	46, 124, 275
Operation Stair Step	84
Operation White Shoes	105, 124
Panavia Tornado	188, 189, 190, 213, 216-7, 218, 219, 221-22, 223, 226, 300, 302
Petlayakov Pe-2	13, 19, 32, 38, 48-9, 56, 265, 286, 308
Pine Tree Line	47, 69
Polish Air Force (Wojska Lotnicze)	13, 54, 62, 63, 66, 101, 124, 138, 154, 226, 230, 283, 290-91, 299, 305-6
Portuguese Air Force (FAP)	14, 31, 61, 147, 170, 195, 282, 288, 295, 301
Project Homerun	74
PZL-Mielec Lim-1/2	54, 283
PZL-Mielec Lim-5	39, 62, 292-3
PZL-Mielec Lim-6	62, 101, 138, 197, 226, 291, 297, 304
PZL-Mielec TS-11 Iskra	226, 230
Quick Reaction Alert (QRA)	9, 50, 78, 93, 108, 131, 143, 144, 165, 183, 202, 236, 241, 243, 251
Raytheon HAWK	161, 237
Reagan, Ronald W	179, 180, 201, 202
Republic F-47 Thunderbolt	17, 23, 24, 26, 31, 61, 265, 266, 267, 282, 308-9
Republic F-84 Thunderjet	14, 22-3, 24, 26, 27, 32, 40, 42, 49, 50, 52, 61, 62, 66, 106, 124, 265, 266, 267, 269, 280-2, 309
Republic F-84F Thunderstreak	38, 46, 47, 50, 66, 81, 84, 88, 106, 120, 124, 127, 136, 150, 170, 196, 281, 287, 295-6
Republic RF-84F Thunderflash	38, 46, 61, 66, 71, 74, 150-51, 286-7, 288-89, 295-6
Republic F-105 Thunderchief	72-3, 75, 81, 82-4, 106, 123, 124, 155, 288
Rockwell B-1	180-1, 202, 204-5,
Romanian Air Force (FAR)	32, 56, 102, 153, 171, 200-1, 227, 269, 285, 292, 298, 305
Royal Air Force (RAF)	14, 26, 28, 30, 34, 39, 40, 49, 50, 51-52, 55, 58-9, 63, 64-5, 81, 88, 91, 92-3, 107, 120, 125, 134-5, 136, 142, 144-6, 154, 165, 167, 168-9, 176-7, 189, 190, 192, 203, 213, 217-9, 221-22, 231, 280-81, 287, 294, 300
Royal Auxiliary Air Force (RAuxAF)	17, 30
S-125 Neva SAM	96
S-200 Vega SAM	197, 213
S-25 SAM	68
S-75 SAM	68, 78, 89, 96, 135, 266
SAAB 1050	253, 254, 256, 307
SAAB 21	235, 239, 306
SAAB 29 Tunnen	235, 240, 253, 255, 307-8
SAAB 32 Lansen	236, 238, 241, 306
SAAB 35 Draken	124, 212, 236, 237, 238, 242, 249, 251, 256-7, 293, 299, 306-7
SAAB 37 Viggen	234, 238, 241, 242-3, 306
SACEUR	12, 88, 106
SAGE	69, 70, 105
SEPECAT Jaguar	137, 165, 168-9, 176-7, 190, 194, 218, 294, 300-1
Shenyang J-5	101, 268, 271, 309
Shenyang J-6	101, 268, 269, 270, 309
Siebel S-204D	37, 283
SNCASE SE-532 Mistral	34, 53, 281
SNCASO SO4050 Vautour	65, 118-9, 120, 288
SOKO Galeb	266, 308
SOKO J-21 Jastreb	267, 266, 308-9
SOKO J-22 Orao	267, 308

Soviet Air Defence (PVO)	16, 40, 48, 68, 69, 75, 78, 94, 120, 121, 131-32, 159, 160, 186
Soviet Strategic Aviation (DA)	16, 18, 23, 48, 66, 86, 96-8, 114-21, 126, 131, 159, 183, 184, 186, 203, 204, 206, 210
Soviet Tactical Aviation (FA)	16, 18, 48, 98, 101, 129, 139, 160, 161, 171, 174, 187, 188, 197, 205, 206
Spanish Air Force (EdA)	194, 195, 196, 226, 272-7
Stalin, Josef	62, 101, 265
Suez crisis, 1956	63
Sukhoi Su-7	75, 98, 101, 124, 126, 138, 140, 142, 154, 161, 200, 226, 290-2, 296-298, 303-6
Sukhoi Su-9	75, 78, 80, 94-5, 96, 122
Sukhoi Su-15	81, 122, 131, 143, 160, 187, 188, 205, 207
Sukhoi Su-17/22	138, 161, 189, 196, 197, 202, 206, 223, 226, 227, 297, 298, 303-4,
Sukhoi Su-24	161, 171, 184, 200, 201, 206, 223, 227, 304-5
Sukhoi Su-25	185, 189, 203, 205, 206, 223, 229, 303, 305
Sukhoi Su-27	183, 187, 205, 206, 223
Supermarine Spitfire	16, 17, 18, 30, 31, 36, 49, 61, 238
Supermarine Swift	51, 58-9, 87
Swedish Air Force (Svenska Flygvapnet)	232-41, 304
Swiss Air Force (Schweizer Flugwaffe)	258-63, 307-8
Thule	47, 72, 74, 91, 103, 122, 137
Truman, Harry S	42
Tupolev Tu-4	15, 18, 39, 46, 48, 66
Tupolev Tu-16	48, 67, 97, 98, 99, 105, 121, 131, 133, 159, 184, 189, 204, 211
Tupolev Tu-22	81, 97, 98, 99, 115, 121, 131, 159, 184, 204
Tupolev Tu-22M	159, 166, 184, 204, 206, 208-9
Tupolev Tu-95 & Tu-142	67, 68, 84, 96, 98, 105, 108, 124, 126, 131, 139, 140, 184, 186, 203, 204, 210, 278
Tupolev Tu-126	120, 205
Tupolev Tu-128	81, 86, 121, 139, 187
Tupolev Tu-160	203, 204, 206, 207, 212
Turkish Air Force (THK)	61-62, 66, 89, 94, 106, 113, 124, 150-52, 170, 196, 226, 282, 289, 296, 302
U-2 crisis 1960	78
US Air Defense Command (ADC)	21, 24, 26, 43, 47, 48, 68, 69, 70, 77, 90, 91, 124, 154, 155
US Air Defense, Tactical Air Command (ADTAC)	155, 181, 183
US Air National Guard (ANG)	17, 19, 21, 23, 24, 26, 27, 32, 42, 77, 84, 90, 124, 148, 161, 183, 202
US Continental Air Defense Command (CONAD)	68, 69, 91, 124, 131, 154
US Strategic Air Command (SAC)	11, 21, 23, 42, 46, 47, 70, 72, 91, 93, 94, 102, 103, 122, 125, 126, 131, 154, 180-1, 202, 273, 275
US Strategic Air Command (SAC)	
US Tactical Air Command (TAC)	21, 26, 47, 74, 123, 124, 154, 155, 202, 217
Valmet Vihuri	246-7, 248, 307
Vickers Valiant	51, 63, 64, 65, 88, 93, 106, 118
Vietnam War	83, 96, 108, 110, 123-4, 134, 154, 158, 163
Vozdukh	95, 121
Warsaw Pact	9, 51, 53, 56, 62, 72, 77, 93, 94, 101, 114, 126, 134, 138, 152-3, 155, 161, 171, 173, 174, 179, 190, 193, 196, 200, 213, 223, 226, 229, 231, 236, 241, 269, 278, 282-6, 289-92, 296-298, 300-6
West German Air Force (Luftwaffe)	53, 66, 81, 136, 143, 154, 164, 167, 171, 190, 213, 219, 224, 287, 293, 300
Wild Weasel	123, 135, 158, 190-1, 193, 203
Yakovlev Yak-9	18, 32, 37
Yakovlev Yak-15	14, 25
Yakovlev Yak-17	18, 25
Yakovlev Yak-23	14, 19, 32, 37
Yakovlev Yak-25	48, 50, 78
Yakovlev Yak-27	115, 293
Yakovlev Yak-28	81, 96, 121, 135, 139, 140, 159, 160, 187, 188, 223, 227, 297-298, 304-5
Yugoslavian Air Force (RV i PVO)	264-9, 308-9
Zerbst	108-9, 111, 139, 284, 291, 298, 305

An RAF Hawker Siddeley (BAe) Nimrod MR2 submarine hunter on a winter patrol off the Norwegian coast near Bodø. (Brewell)

GLOSSARY

AAC	Alaskan Air Command (US)
AAFN/CE	Allied Air Forces Northern/ Central Europe (NATO)
AAM	Air-to-Air Missile
AAR	Air-to-Air Refuelling
ADC	Air Defense Command (US)
ADIZ	Air Defence Identification Zone (NATO)
ADTAC	Air Defense, Tactical Air Command (US) mid-1980s aerodromy podskoka (Soviet) bounce airfields in the Arctic
AEW&C	Airborne Early Warning and Command
AFB	Air Force Base (US),
AJÜ	Ana Jet Üssü - (Turkish) Main Jet Base
AK/AD/AP	Aviatsiya Korpus / Aviatsionnyy Diviziya / Polk - (Soviet) Aviation Corps/ Aviation Division/ Regiment
A/GLCM	Air-/Ground-Launched Cruise Missile
ANG	Air National Guard (US)
ARM	Anti-Radiation Missile
AV-MF	Aviatsiya Voyenno-Morskogo Flota - (Soviet) Naval Aviation
AWACS	Airborne Warning and Control System
BAFO	British Air Forces of Occupation
BAOR	British Army of the Rhine
BDR	Bundesrepublik Deutschland - Federal Republic of (West) Germany
BMEWS	Ballistic Missile Early Warning System (USA, Canada, Denmark, UK)
CAFDA	Commandement des Forces de Défense Aérienne - (French) Air Defence Command
CATAac	Commandement Aérien Tactique - (French) Tactical Air Command (1950s)
CAF	Canadian Armed Forces (post 1968)
CAS	Close Air Support
CFAS	Commandement des Forces Aeriennes Strategique - (French) Strategic Air Command
ConAC	Continental Air Command (US) 1950s
CONAD	Continental Air Command (US) from 1957
DA	Dal'naya Aviatsiya - (Soviet) long-range (strategic) aviation
DAT	Défense Aèrienne du Territoire - (French) Territorial Air Defence 1950s
DDR	Deutsche Demokratische Republik - (East) German Democratic Republic
DEFCOMUS	Defence Condition (5 is the normal peacetime state of readiness)
DEW	Distant Early Warning Line (US & Canada)
DOL	Drogowe Odcinki Lotniskowe - (Polish) highway strip operations
DRLO	Dal'nego Radiolokatsionnogo Obnaruzheniya - (Soviet) Long-Range Radar Surveillance
E/W/CADF	Eastern/ Western/ Central Air Defense Force (US)
EC/CTT/B	Escadre de Chasse/ Chasse de Tout Temps/ Bombardment - (French) Fighter / All-weather Fighter / Bomber Wing
ECM	Electronic Counter-Measures
Esk	Eskadrille - (Danish) Squadron
Esq	Esquadra - (Portuguese) Squadron
FI/FB/TF/TR/SR/BW	Fighter Interceptor/ Tactical Fighter/ Tactical Reconnaissance/ Strategic Reconnaissance/ Bombardment Wing (USAF)
FAC	Forward Air Controller
FATac	Commandement de la Force Aérienne Tactique - (French) Tactical Air Command
FG	Fliegergeschwader - (East German) Air Wing
Filo	(Turkish) Squadron
Elint	Electronic Intelligence
FA	Frontonaya Aviatsiya - (Soviet) frontal (tactical) aviation
GCI	Ground Control Intercept
GIUK	Gap Greenland-Iceland-UK Gap
GKVZ/YuZN	Glavnoye Komandovaniye Voysk Zapadnogo/ Yugo-zapadnogo Napravleniya - (Soviet) Western/South Western Directorate High Command
Gr	Gruppo - (Italian) Squadron
GSVG	Gruppa Sovetskikh Voysk v Germanii - Group of Soviet Forces in Germany
Gv	Gvardeyskiy - (Soviet) Guards
HAS	Hardened Aircraft Shelters
HU/V	Hava Üssü/ Kuvveti - (Turkish) Air Base/ Force
I/B/R/Sh/TB/A	PIstrebitel'naya/ Bombardirovochnaya/ Razvedyvatel'nyy/ Shturmovoy/ Tyazhelaya Bombardirovochnaya Polk - (Soviet) Fighter/ Bomber/ Reconnaissance / Assault/ Heavy Bomber Aviation Regiment
IA-PVO	Istrebitel'naya Aviatsiya - (Soviet) Fighter Aviation of the PVO
IC/SL/I/MRBM	Inter-Continental/ Submarine Launched/Intermediate/ Medium Range Ballistic Missiles
IGB	Inner German Border (between BDR and DDR)
JaBo/AG	Jagdbomber / Aufklärung Geschwader - (West German) Fighter-Bomber/ Reconnaissance Wing
LABS	Low Altitude bombing System (NATO)
MACAN	Mando Aéreo de Canarias - (Spanish), Canaries Air Command
MACOM	Mando Aéreo de Combate - (Spanish), Combat Air Command
MATAC	Mando Aéreo Táctico - (Spanish), Tactical Air Command
MDAP	Mutual Defence Assistance Programme (US)
Moira	(Greek) Squadron
NATO	North Atlantic Treaty Organisation
NORAD	North American Air Defence Command (US & Canada)
NSWP	Non-Soviet Warsaw Pact
OGA	Operativnuyu Gruppu v Arktike - (Soviet) Operational Group in the Arctic
Operation Chrome Dome	(US) B-52 Airborne alert
Operation White Shoes	(US) F-106 detachment to Alaska Otdel'nyy Independent - (Soviet)
OTBAK	Otdel'nyy Tyazhelyy Bombardirovshchik Aviatsionnyy Korpus - (Soviet) Independent Heavy Bomber Corps

PLM/Sz/Bo Pułk	Lotnictwa Myśliwskiego/ Szturmowego/ Bombowego/ Rozpoznawczego - (Polish) Fighter/ Ground-Attack/ Bomber reconnaissance Regiment	SEAD	Suppression of Enemy Air Defences
		SIOP	Single Integrated Operation Plan (US)
		SSR	Soviet Socialist Republic
		St	Stormo - (Italian) Wing
PMPtéryga	Máchis - (Greek) Combat Wing	TAC	Tactical Air Command (US)
PVO-Strany	Proti-Vovozdushnaya Oborona Strany - Air Defence of the (Soviet) Country	TFR	Terrain Following Radar
		TFW	Tactical Fighter Wing
QRA	Quick Reaction Alert	TVD	Teatr Voennykh Deystviy - (Soviet) Theatres of Military Operation
RAuxAF	Royal Auxiliary Air Force (British)		
R AvG	Regjimentit të Aviacionit Gjuajtës - (Albanian) Fighter Aviation Regiment	USAFE	United States Air Forces Europe
		USFET	United States Forces European Theater (1950s)
RAvVt/R/As/Bom/Cc	Regimentul de Aviatie Vanatoare / Reactoare / Asalt / Bombardment / Cercetare - (Romanian) Fighter / Jet / Assault / Bomber / Reconnaissance Regiment	USSR	Union of Soviet Socialist Republics
		Vad/Vre/CsE	Vadasz / Vadászrepülő Csatarepüle Ezred - (Hungarian) Fighter (1950s) / Fighter (1960s-) / Assault Regiment
		VA	Vozdushnaya Armiya - (Soviet) Air Armies
RCAF	Royal Canadian Air Force	VPVO	Voyska-PVO (Soviet) Air Defence Force (from 1981)
RWR	Radar Warning Receiver		
S/Bi/PLPl	Stíhací / Bitveny / Průzkumný Letecký Pluk - (Czechoslakian), Fighter / Ground Attack / Reconnaissance Regiment	VO	Voyennyy Okrug - (Soviet) Military Districts
		VGK ON VA	Verkhovnoye Glavnokomandovaniye Operativnogo Naznacheniya - (Soviet) Operational High Command
S/CGV	Severnaya / Central'naya Gruppa Voysk - (Soviet) Northern/ Central Group of Forces	VGK SN VA	Verkhovnogo Glavnogckomandovaniya Strategicheskogo Naznacheniya - (Soviet) Strategic High Command
SACEUR	Supreme Allied Commander Europe (NATO)		
SAC	Strategic Air Command (US)		
SAGE	Semi-Autonomous Ground Environment (US & Canada)	Vozdukh-1	Soviet GCI system
		WP	Warsaw Pact
SAM	Surface-to-Air Missile	2/4 ATAF	2nd/4th Allied Tactical Air Force (NATO)

The pilot of a Mikoyan Gurevich MiG-23ML [NATO reporting name Flogger-G] of the Czechoslovakian Air Force climbs out of the cockpit at the end of a training flight. (Schleiffert)

ACKNOWLEDGEMENTS

"Ninety-nine knights of the air, riding super high-tech jet fighters: every one's a super-hero, everyone's a Captain Kirk, with orders to identify, to clarify and to classify." 99 Luftballons - Nena, 1983

My research for this book has necessarily incorporated the work of others and I wish to acknowledge, with gratitude, the following whose published expertise has been invaluable:

Joseph F. Baugher who has an excellent website http://www.joebaugher.com with details of US Military aircraft.
Michael Holm whose excellent website http://www.ww2.dk contains details of Soviet VVS units.
Karol Placha Hetman whose website https://www.polot.net/jednostki has details of Polish units.
Ole Nikolajsen whose brief histories of the Danish and Turkish air forces are published on-line.
Peter Veith whose website http://home.snafu.de/veith/lsk-lv-m.htm gives details of the Lsk/Lv
Hugo Freudinger for his Geschichte der Schweizer Luftwaffe (accessed via internet).
Jean Hauviller & Georges Solans for their Une Petite Histoire De La Défense Aérienne Française (accessed via internet).
Paul van der Linden for his Istoria Aviatiei Romane Impartirea Pe Baze a Aeronavelor (accessed via internet).
József Martinkó for his Requiem for An Aircraft Type Family: The MiG Era in Hungary (accessed via internet).
James T. Quinlivan for his Soviet Strategic Air Defense: A Long Past and An Uncertain Future (accessed via internet).

I'm very grateful to distinguished former fighter pilots Bob Broad, Steve Gyles, Arnulf Hartl, Rolf Noel, Jyrki Laukkanen and Lars-Eric Blad for allowing me to use their Cold War stories to liven up my text. Also, to Richard Cornwall in Pretoria for his helpful advice in regard to the political nuances of the Cold War. I thank Maureen DeFelice, Executive Director of the Daedalian Foundation and the Daedalus Flyer, for permission to use the account of the RB-47 sortie over Russia in 1954 by Colonel 'Hal' Austen.

I am extremely grateful to the following for providing the excellent photographs which illustrate the text:

Jyrki Laukkanen, Tony 'Pax' Paxton, Geoff Lee, Rob Schleiffert, Rick Brewell, Graham Pitchfork, Eric Bannwarth, and Sven-Erik Jönsson.

Also to those who gave access to collections: Phillip Jarrett, Mathiue Durand (Dassault Aviation), Michael Sanz (Flyghistoria – Swedish Aviation Historical Society) Sofia Svalbard (Swedish AF Museum, Linköping), Per Kustvik and Anne Wolgers at SAAB, Andreas Klein (AirDOC), Major Anders Utgard (Norwegian Aviation Museum, Bodo), Simone Duringer (Swiss AF Museum, Dübendorf), Manfred Litscher and Wolfgang Hainzl (Austrian AF), and Igor Maranovic (Belgrade Aviation Museum).

A special thanks to Krista Strider, Deputy Director/Curator and Brett Stolle Curator/Archivist at The National Museum of the US Air Force, Dayton, Ohio for allowing access to the museum's photographic collection.

Finally, many thanks indeed to my editor, the ever-indefatigable Jasper Spencer-Smith, who came up with the idea for this book and even agreed to find all the images. Thanks to Marcus Cowper for commissioning the project to publication and a big thank-you to the ever patient and very talented Isobel Fiske who designed the book.

The V-Bombers: An Avro Vulcan leads a formation of a Vickers Valiant (right) and a Handley Page Victor (left). All carried the British independent nuclear deterrent from the late 1950s and into the early 1960s. (Crown Copyright)

BIBLIOGRAPHY

Anon	*Historia de La Aviación Española*	Instituto de Historia y Cultura Aérea, 1988.
Bojan B. Dimitrijević	*Jugoslovensko Ratno Vazduhoplovstvo 1942-1992*	Institut za Savremenu Istoriju 2006
Gordon, Y. & Komisssarov, D.	*Soviet Air Defence Aviation 1945-1991*	Hikoki, 2012
Gordon, Y.	*Soviet Strategic Aviation in the Cold War*	Hikoki, 2009.
Kostenuk, S. & Griffin, J.	*RCAF Squadrons and Aircraft*	A.M. Hakkert Ltd, 1977.
Laukkanen, J.	*Tehtävä Taivaalla Suomen Ilmavoimat 100 Vuotta*	Koala-Kustannus 2017.
Paloque, G	*Les Escadres de l'Armée de l'Air*	Heimdal, 2017.

A Cold War 'warrior': A Blackburn (Hawker Siddeley) Buccaneer S2B of 15 Sqn which was based at RAF Laarbruch, Germany in the 1970s. (Brewell)